THE OFFICIAL 1985 BLACKBOOK PRICE GUIDE OF UNITED STATES PAPER MONEY

SEVENTEENTH EDITION

BY MARC HUDGEONS, N.L.G.

COVER PHOTOGRAPH: $5 SILVER CERTIFICATE LARGE SIZE — SERIES OF 1899. Blue seal, signatures of Elliott and White. $950.00.

© MCMLXXXIV The House of Collectibles, Inc.

All rights reserved. No part of this book may be reproduced or utilized in any form or by any means, electronic or mechanical, including photocopying, recording, or by any information storage and retrieval system, without permission in writing from the Publisher.

Published by: The House of Collectibles, Inc.
　　　　　　　Orlando Central Park
　　　　　　　1904 Premier Row
　　　　　　　Orlando, FL 32809
　　　　　　　Phone: (305) 857-9095

Printed in the United States of America

Library of Congress Catalog Card Number: 80-644107

ISBN: 0-87637-457-7

TABLE OF CONTENTS

Market Review	3	New Treasury Seal	17
How U.S. Currency Began	4	Grades and Conditions	18
Collecting Paper Money	4	One Dollar Notes	20
Buying Paper Money	5	Two Dollar Notes	42
Care of Your Collection	6	Five Dollar Notes	57
Selling Your Collection	7	Ten Dollar Notes	90
Investing	8	Twenty Dollar Notes	118
Glossary	8	Fifty Dollar Notes	139
Currency Terms	13	One Hundred Dollar Notes	157
The Federal Reserve Banks	14	Mules	172
32 Subject Sheet Layout	14	Fractional Currency	174
The U.S. Numbering System	15	Error or Freak Notes	185
Portraits and Back Designs	16	Confederate Money	207
Dating U.S. Currency	16		

OFFICIAL BOARD OF CONTRIBUTORS TO THE SEVENTEENTH EDITION

Mr. Robert Cornely
Mr. Aubrey Bebee
Col. Grover Criswell
Mr. Harry E. Jones
Rev. F. H. Hutchins
Mr. Harry J. Forman

Mr. Chuck O'Donnell
Mr. Gene Hessler
Mr. Herbert Krisack
Mr. Seymour Berry
Mr. Harry R. Clements
Mrs. Dorothy Andrews Kabis (Elston)

A special thanks to Mr. Harry E. Jones for his contributions to the Error Note section and for the cover photograph.

PUBLISHER'S NOTE

The Official Blackbook Price Guide of United States Paper Money is designed as a reference aid for collectors, dealers and the general public. Its purpose is to provide historical and collecting data, as well as current values. Prices are as accurate as possible at the time of going to press but no guarantee is made. We are not dealers; persons wishing to buy or sell paper money, or have it appraised, are advised to consult collector magazines or the telephone directory for addresses of dealers. We are not responsible for typographical errors.

MARKET REVIEW

The overall strength and depth of the paper money hobby has been evident in its ability to make dramatic recoveries from our recent economic recession. Generally speaking, values of paper money were not as seriously affected by the recession, as were the values of coins and postage stamps; and the recovery, now in progress more than one year, has succeeded in bringing MANY of the values BEYOND the levels they had previously reached.

Many persons have asked why paper money did so well during, and after, the recession, considering that the hobby is obviously not as large as coins or stamps. In a sense its size was a redeeming factor. In the hectic investment years of 1979, 1980 and 1981, stamps and coins attracted many investors who simply wanted "hard assets." This was likewise true of oil paintings, diamonds, and other glamor items. Not too many investors got into paper money, as they either (a) knew nothing about the hobby, or (b) felt that paper money was inconsequential for investment purposes. Thus the paper money market remained chiefly in the control of collectors, even during those chaotic years. Values did fluctuate more than normally, but on the whole there were no wild "ups" and "downs" as witnessed in some other collecting areas.

Today the collectors are very firmly in control, and some interesting conclusions can be drawn about the market movements in 1984. Certainly the most striking and significant is the fact that a MAJORITY of the higher priced specimens have INCREASED in value during the past year. This has been accomplished with very little investor cash coming into the market. It has occurred, also, despite the fact that some investor-held specimens were returning to the open market and creating greater than normal availability. You will note in the listings in this book that even some specimens in the $10,000 and higher brackets rose in value, which was not predicted by most market analysts a year ago. Value increases were recorded, too, on notes in numerous other categories, encompassing all ranges of price and types of notes. Freak and error currency did particularly well (a sure sign of strong hobbyist activity, as this material is hardly ever — probably never — bought by investors).

For collectors of Federal Reserve Notes, the big event of the year was a change in signatures from Buchanan-Regan to Ortega-Regan and the switch from Series 1981 to Series 1981A notes. Mr. Regan (no relation to the President — the name is even spelled differently) continues as Secretary of the Treasury — and Mrs. Ortega is the new Treasurer of the United States. As the Buchanan-Regan notes were in production for less than a full Presidential term, there has been some speculation on their possible scarcity, but they are certainly far less scarce than the famous "Barr" notes — which, so far, have gained only a modest premium value. Beginning collectors should take note of the fact that the DATE on notes is not changed until a new President takes office; any changes made in signatures (or other changes) are simply indicated by adding a letter, such as 1981A, 1981B, and so on.

HOW UNITED STATES CURRENCY BEGAN

The present series of paper currency had its origins in 1861 and thus is "just" 120 years old. Obviously, modern business could not operate without currency, but very likely its appearance would not even have occurred as early as 1861, without pressing need brought about by the Civil War. Coinage came to be in very short supply almost from the war's outset and both sides, North and South, resorted to printing notes. This was in a sense "emergency money" and at first was disorderly and disorganized. The Union undoubtedly anticipated a return to bullion money as soon as possible upon the war's conclusion. Resumption of regular striking of coins in the mid to late 1860's fell short of meeting the need for money, however, and paper currency continued in use. It in fact increased and has been increasing since. The earliest U.S. notes (1861) are so-called Demand Notes. In 1862 Legal Tender Notes appeared and, subsequently, a variety of others, some of which were in circulation simultaneously.

COLLECTING PAPER MONEY

Paper money can be a fascinating hobby. Though of more recent origins than coinage, U.S. paper money exists in enormous varieties and can be collected from many different approaches.

Potential specialties are numerous. The following is not by any means a complete list.

1. **Series collecting.** Here the collector focuses upon a certain series of notes, such as the $5 1863-75 National Bank Notes, and attempts to collect specimens showing each of the different signature combinations, points of issue, seal colors, or whatever varieties happen to exist in the series. This may sound restrictive but, as an examination of the listings in this book will show, most series comprise a great deal of varieties. Generally, the older the series, the more difficult or expensive will be its completion, while certain series include great rarities beyond the budget range of most of us. The cost can be brought down somewhat if one does not demand the finest condition but is content to own an example of the note in whatever condition he can reasonably afford. (It should be pointed out, though, that in re-selling paper money there is generally a greater loss — or smaller profit — on notes whose condition is less than Very Fine.)

2. **Set collecting.** Sets are groups of notes of different denominations, issued at the same time (or approximately the same time), which were in current circulation together.

3. **Place or origin collecting** — collecting notes by the city whose Federal Reserve Bank issued them.

4. **Signature collecting,** or collecting one specimen of every note bearing the signature of a certain Secretary of the Treasury.

5. **Confederate currency collecting,** the notes issued for use within the Confederate States of America during the Civil War.

6. **Portrait collecting,** by the individual or individuals depicted on the note. This is sometimes known as topical collecting.

7. **Freak and oddity collecting.**
8. **Fractional currency collecting.**

One's imagination, especially if placed into use in a coin-shop well stocked with paper money, will suggest further possibilities. All is fair; there are no strict rules on what makes a worthwhile collection, so long as the material included is not seriously defective or of questionable authenticity.

Don't expect to build a large collection rapidly. Paper money is not comparable to stamps, where a beginner can buy a packet of 1,000 different stamps and instantly have a sizable collection. Nor should the size of a collection be regarded as a mark of its desirability or worth. Many prize-winning collections contain fewer than a hundred pieces; some consist of only two or three dozen. Direction and quality count much more in this hobby than weight of numbers. He who seeks to own a large collection generally ends up with one whose only recommendation is its size. It may impress beginners but is not likely to be regarded highly by more experienced collectors.

BUYING PAPER MONEY

Browsing in coin shops is the usual way in which beginners get their start buying paper money. Just about every coin dealer — and many stamp dealers — stock paper money to one degree or another, from a single display album with elementary material to vaults filled with literally millions of dollars worth of specimens. Be observant of condition when shopping from dealers' stocks. There is really no excuse for unsatisfactory purchases from shops — the buyer has ample opportunity for inspection. Don't buy in a rush. Get to know the dealer and become familiar with his grading practices. Some dealers will grade a specimen higher than another dealer (but this may be offset by the fact that they charge a lower price).

Bargains. Is it possible to get bargains in buying paper money? To the extent that prices vary somewhat from dealer to dealer, yes. But if you're talking about finding a note worth $100 selling at $50, this is unlikely to happen. The dealers are well aware of market values and the slight price differences that do occur are merely the result of some dealers being overstocked on certain notes or, possibly, having made a very good "buy" from the public. What may appear to be a bargain will generally prove, on closer examination, to be a specimen in undesirable condition, such as a washed bill on which the color has faded.

Auction sales. Many coin auctions feature selections of paper money, and there are occasional sales (mostly of the postal-bid variety) devoted exclusively to it. There is much to be said for auction buying if you have some experience and expertise and know how to read an auction catalogue.

Shows and conventions. Paper money is offered for sale at every coin show and exposition. These present excellent opportunities to buy, as the dealers exhibiting at such shows are generally out-of-towners whose stock you would not otherwise have a chance to examine. As many sellers are likely to be offering the same type of material, you have the opportunity to make price and condition comparisons before buying.

CARE OF YOUR COLLECTION

Paper money is not at all difficult to care for, store and display attractively. It consumes little space and, unlike many other collectors' items, runs no risk of breakage. Nevertheless, it is important that the hobbyist give some attention to its maintenance, as a poorly kept collection soon turns to aimless clutter and provides little enjoyment.

There is not much question but that **albums** are the favorite storage method of nearly all paper money enthusiasts. In the days before specially made albums with vinyl pocket-pages, collectors used ordinary scrapbooks and mounted their specimens with philatelic hinges or photo-corners. This, of course, may still be done if one wishes, but such collections do not have the advantage of displaying both sides of the notes. Furthermore, the use of gummed hinges may be objected to on grounds that they leave marks upon removal, whereas specimens may be removed and reinserted into vinyl-page albums without causing the slightest blemish. We especially recommend the albums and "currency wallet" sold by Anco Coin & Stamp Supply, P. O. Box 782, Florence, Alabama 35630.

Faded color. There is no known restorative for faded color.

Holes. It is suggested that no effort be undertaken to repair holes, as this will almost certainly result in a further reduction in value.

Missing corners. Missing corners can seldom be restored in a manner that is totally satisfactory. The best that can be done is to secure some paper of approximately the same color and texture, trim a small piece to the proper size, and glue it in place as described above. If a portion of printed matter is missing, this can be hand-drawn in ink after restoration. Obviously, this kind of repair is not carried out to "fool" anybody, simply to give a damaged specimen a less objectionable appearance.

Repairs to paper money. Repair work on damaged or defaced paper money is carried out strictly for cosmetic purposes: to improve its physical appearance. Repairs, even if skillfully executed, **will not enhance the value of a specimen,** as it will still be classified as defective. And amateurish repair efforts can very possibly make matters worse.

Tears. Tears can be closed by brushing a very small quantity of clear-drying glue to both sides of the tear, placing the note between sheets of waxed kitchen paper and setting it under a weight to dry. A dictionary of moderate size serves this function well. Allow plenty of drying time and handle gently thereafter.

Wrinkles. Wrinkles, creases and the like can sometimes be improved by wetting the note (in plain water) and drying it between sheets of waxed paper beneath a reasonably heavy weight — five pounds or more. This should not be done with a modern or recent specimen if there is danger of loss of crispness.

Many ills to which paper money falls prey result from not being housed in a suitable album, or any album at all. Framing and mounting presents some risk as the item may then be exposed to long periods of direct sunlight, almost sure to cause fading or "bleaching" of its color.

SELLING YOUR COLLECTION

Selling to a dealer. All dealers in paper money buy from the public, but not all buy every collection offered to them. Some are specialists and are interested only in collections within their fields of specialization. Some will not purchase (or even examine) collections worth under $100, or $500, or whatever their line of demarcation happens to be. Obviously, a valuable collection containing many hard-to-get notes in VF or UNC condition is easier to interest a dealer in than a beginner-type collection. If a dealer is interested enough to make an offer, this is no guarantee that another dealer would not offer more. In the case of a collection worth $50,000, offers from several dealers might vary by as much as $5,000. This is not an indication that the dealer making the lowest offer is unscrupulous. Dealers will pay as much as the material is worth **to them**, and one dealer may be overstocked on items that another needs badly. Or one dealer may have customers for certain material that another doesn't. For this reason it makes good sense, if you choose to sell to a dealer, to obtain several offers before accepting any. But should you sell to a dealer at all? The chief advantage is quick payment and lack of risk. The price may not be as high as would be obtained at auction, however, depending on the property's nature and pure luck.

Selling by auction. Auction selling presents uncertainties but at the same time offers the possibility of gaining a much better return than could be had by selling to a dealer. It is no easy matter deciding which route to follow. If your collection is better than average, you may be better advised to sell by auction. This will involve a waiting period of, generally, four to six months between consigning the collection and receiving settlement; over the summer months it may be longer. However, some auctioneers will give a cash advance, usually about 25 percent of the sum they believe the material to be worth. In special circumstances a larger advance may be made, or the usual terms and conditions altered. I know of one auctioneer who paid $100,000 under a special contract, stipulating that the money was not to be returned regardless of the sale's outcome or even if no sale took place. But this was on a million-dollar collection. Auctioneers' commissions vary. The normal is 20 percent but some houses take 10 percent from the buyer and 10 percent from the seller. This would appear to work to the seller's advantage, but such a practice may discourage bidding and result in lower sale prices.

Selling to other collectors. Unless the owner is personally acquainted with a large circle of collectors, this will likely involve running ads in periodicals and "playing dealer," which runs into some expense. Unless you offer material at very favorable prices, you are not apt to be as successful with your ads as are the established dealers, who have a reputation and an established clientele.

INVESTING

1. Buy only specimens in V.F. or better condition.
2. Restrict yourself to major issues or varieties rather than items which may be valuable but are so highly specialized that some dealers hesitate to handle them.
3. Do not build a miscellaneous portfolio but concentrate on purchasing specific series or types.
4. Count on waiting at least three years and possibly longer before selling, unless the market experiences a tremendous upsurge. Otherwise the normal pace at which values increase will not allow for a reasonable profit on **most** notes (there are always some exceptions) in less time than this.
5. Beware of bargains. Buy from established dealers or, if sufficiently confident of your abilities, auction houses. If buying for speculation at auction, do not pay more than 70-80 percent of the current retail value.

GLOSSARY

BROKEN BANK NOTE

Literally, a broken bank note is a note issued by a "broken" bank — a bank that failed and whose obligations could therefore not be redeemed. It may be presumed, by those who recall passing of legislation establishing the Federal Deposit Insurance Corporation, that banks failed only in the financial panic of 1929. During the 19th century, bank failures were common, especially in western and southwestern states. These were generally small organizations set up in frontier towns, which suffered either from mismanagement or a sudden decline in the town's fortunes. Some collectors make a specialty of broken bank notes.

DEMAND NOTES

Demand Notes have the distinction of being the first official circulating paper currency of this country, issued in 1861. There are three denominations: five, 10 and 20 dollars, each bearing its own design on front and back. Demand Notes arose out of the coinage shortage brought about by the Civil War. A total of $60,000,000 in Demand Notes was authorized to be printed, amounting to several million individual specimens. Though this was an extraordinary number for the time, it was small compared to modern output and only a fraction of the total survived. These notes were signed not by any specially designated Treasury Department officers but a battery of employees, each of whom was given authority to sign and affix their names **by hand** in a slow assembly-line process, two signatures to each note. Originally the spaces left blank for signatures were marked "Register of the Treasury" and "Treasurer of the United States." As the persons actually signing occupied neither of these offices they were obliged to perpetually add "for the . . ." to their signatures. In an effort to relieve their tedium, fresh plates were prepared reading "For the Register of the Treasury" and "For the Treasurer of the United States," which required nothing but a signature. This created a rarity status for the earlier specimens, which are now very desirable collectors' items.

ENGRAVING

Engraving is the process by which designs are printed on U.S. paper money. Engraving involves the use of a metal plate, traditionally copper, into which the design is drawn or scraped with sharply bladed instruments. Ink is smeared over the surface and allowed to work into the grooves or lines comprising the design. The ink is then cleaned away from raised portions (intended to show blank in the printing). The engraving is pressed against a sheet of moistened paper and the ink left in these grooves transfers to the paper resulting in a printed image. When done by modern rotary press, it's a fast-moving process, not much like the engraving work of Albrecht Durer or other Renaissance artists 500 years ago.

FEDERAL RESERVE NOTES

Federal Reserve Notes, the type of notes in current circulation, were authorized by the Federal Reserve Act of December 23, 1913. Issued under control of the Federal Reserve Board, these notes are released through 12 Federal Reserve Banks in various parts of the country. Originally they were redeemable in gold at the United States Treasury or "lawful money" (coins) at a Federal Reserve Bank. In 1934 the option of redemption for gold was removed.

FEDERAL RESERVE BANK NOTES

Federal Reserve Bank Notes were issued briefly in 1915 and 1918. Like National Bank Notes they were secured by bonds or securities placed on deposit by each Federal Reserve Bank with the U.S. government. While issued and redeemable by the member banks of the Federal Reserve system, these notes are secured by — and are obligations of — the government.

FREAK AND ERROR NOTES

Bills which, by virtue of error or accident, are in some respect different from normal specimens. See the section on Freak and Error Notes.

GOLD CERTIFICATES

When gold coinage became a significant medium of exchanges the government decided to hold aside certain quantities of it and issue paper notes redeemable by the Treasury Department. The first Gold Certificates for public circulation were released in 1882. The series lasted until the era of Small Size Currency, ending in 1928. In 1933 all were ordered returned to the Treasury Department for redemption, including those in possession of collectors. A new law in 1964 permitted their ownership by collectors, though they can no longer be redeemed for gold.

LARGE-SIZE CURRENCY

Large-size currency is the term generally used to refer to U.S. notes issued up to 1929, which were somewhat larger in size than those printed subsequently. The increased size permitted more elaborate designing and impressive appearance, which seldom fails to endear Large-Size Currency

10 / GLOSSARY

to beginners. Some of the earlier examples (especially of the 1870's, 1880's and 1890's) are masterworks of art. Though economic considerations were mainly responsible for the switch to a reduced size, there is no doubting that today's notes are far more convenient to handle and carry. They are sometimes referred to as "bedsheet notes."

NATIONAL BANK NOTES

This is the largest group of notes available to the collector. They were issued from 1863 to 1929 and present collecting potential that can only be termed vast. More than 14,000 banks issued notes, in all parts of the country. While the approach to collecting them is usually regional, sets and series can also be built up, virtually without end. The National Banking Act was instituted in 1863, during the Civil War, to permit chartered banks to issue and circulate their own currency. Printing was done at the U.S. Government Printing Office and the designs were all alike, differing only in names of the banks, state seals, bank signatures and the bank's charter number. Each charter bank was limited to issuing currency up to 90 percent of the value of bonds that it kept on deposit with the government. Charters remained in force for 20 years and could be renewed for an additional 20 years. National Bank Notes circulated in the same fashion as conventional currency and, thanks to the bond-deposit system, gained public confidence. The financial panic of 1929, which brought ruin or near-ruin to many banks, put an end to National Bank Notes.

NATIONAL GOLD BANK NOTES

These notes were issued exclusively by California banks during the 1870's under the same terms as ordinary National Bank Notes, their values backed by bonds deposited with the government. Events surrounding their origins form a unique chapter in the history of American economy. Following the discoveries of substantial quantities of gold in California in the late 1840's, that metal soon became the chief medium of local exchange, largely because it was more readily available in that remote region than coinage. Later, when gold coins and tokens began to circulate heavily in California, banks became so swamped with them that they petitioned Washington for authority to issue Gold Notes that could be substituted for the actual coinage. On July 12, 1870, Congress voted favorably on this measure, giving the right to issue such notes to nine banks in California and one in Boston. The Boston bank, Kidder National Gold Bank, appears not to have exercised its right as no Gold Notes of this institution have been recorded. The California banks wasted no time in exercising their authority, the result being a series of notes ranging from five to five hundred dollars in denomination. All were printed on yellow-toned paper so as to be instantly identifiable. The banks issuing these notes were permitted to redeem them in gold coins.

REFUNDING CERTIFICATES

Refunding Certificates, a sort of hybrid between currency and bonds or securities, were issued under a Congressional Act of February 26, 1879. These were notes with a $10 face value which could be spent and exchanged in the fashion of ordinary money but drew interest at the rate of 4 percent per year. The purposes behind Refunding Certificates were several. They were chiefly designed to encourage saving and thereby curb inflation, which even at that time was becoming a problem. Also, they provided a safe means of saving for persons who distrusted banks (safe so long as the certificates were not lost or stolen), and, probably more important, were readily obtainable in areas of the country not well served by banks. In 1907 the interest was halted. Their redemption value today, with interest, is $21.30.

SERIAL NUMBER

The serial number is the control number placed on all U.S. paper bills, appearing below left-center and above right-center. No two bills in the same series bear repetitive serial numbers. The use of serial numbers is not only an aid in counting and sorting bills as printed but a deterrent to counterfeiting.

SIGNATURES

The inclusion of signatures of Treasury Department officials on our paper bills, a practice as old as our currency (1861), was begun as a mark of authorization and a foil to counterfeiters. The belief was that the handwriting would be more difficult to copy than an engraved design. Persons whose signatures appear on notes did not always occupy the same office. From 1862 to 1923, the two signers were the Treasurer and the Register (or Registrar as it appears in old writings) of the Treasury. Subsequently, the Treasurer and Secretary of the Treasury were represented. These signatures are of extreme collector importance as some notes are relatively common with certain combinations of signatures and rare with others. A "series" collection is not considered complete until one obtains every existing combination, even though the specimens may be in other respects identical.

SILVER CERTIFICATES

Silver Certificates were authorized in 1878. America's economy was booming at that time and the demand for silver coinage in day to day business transaction outdistanced its supply. Silver Certificates were not intended to replace coinage but to create a convenient medium of exchange, whereby the government held specific quantities of Silver Dollars (later bullion) and agreed to redeem the notes or certificates against them. In 1934 the Treasury Department ceased redemption of these notes in Silver Dollars and on June 24, 1968, redemption in all forms was ended. The notes are still, however, legal tender at their face value. When printing of Silver Certificates was discontinued, a flurry of speculation arose and many persons began hoarding them. This was done not only in hope of eventual redemption for bullion but the belief that such notes would become valuable to collectors. Though Silver Certificates are popular with hobbyists, they have not increased sufficiently in price to yield speculators any great profits — especially since many of the latter were uninformed and saved specimens in less than uncirculated condition.

12 / GLOSSARY

STAR NOTES

United States Notes, Silver Certificates and Gold Certificates sometimes have a star or asterisk in place of the letter in front of the serial number. Federal Reserve Notes and Federal Reserve Bank Notes have it at the end of the serial number. These notes are known as **"Star Notes"**.

When a note is mutilated or otherwise unfit for issue, it must be replaced. To replace it with a note of the same serial numbers would be impractical, and **"Star"** Notes are therefore substituted. Other than having their own special serial number and a star, these notes are the same as the others. On United States Notes and Silver Certificates, the star is substituted for the prefix letter; on Federal Reserve Notes for the suffix letter. All defective notes are accounted for and destroyed by burning them in an incinerator.

Large stars after the serial number on the 1869 series of United States notes, and 1890 and 1891 Treasury Notes, do not signify replacement notes as are known in later and present day **"Star Notes"**.

Serial numbers on early large size notes were preceded by a letter and were ended by various and curious characters or symbols. These characters are not known to have any significance, except to show that the number was terminated, and prevented any elimination or addition of digits. The suffix characters were replaced by alphabet letters on later issues of notes.

TREASURY OR COIN NOTES

Treasury Notes were authorized by Congress in 1890. Their official title was Coin Notes, as they could be redeemed for silver or gold coins. The series did not prove popular and was discontinued after the issue of 1891.

TREASURY SEAL

The Treasury Seal is the official emblem of the U.S. Treasury Department, which has appeared on all our currency since 1862. It is missing only from the early Demand Notes, issued in 1861, and some Fractional Currency. Two versions have been employed, distinguished readily by the fact that one (the original) bears a Latin inscription, while the current Treasury Seal is worded in English. The basic motif is the same, a badge displaying scales and a key. The original type, somewhat more decorative, was in use until 1968.

UNITED STATES NOTES

Also known as Legal Tender Notes, this substantial and ambitious series followed Demand Notes and constitute the second earliest variety of U.S. paper currency. There are five distinct issues, running from 1862 to 1923. Though United States Notes are all "large size" and their designs not very similar to those in present use, they show in their successive stages the evolutionary advance from this nation's first efforts at paper money to its currency of today. The first issue is dated March 10, 1862. Denominations are $1, $2, $5, $10, $20, $50, $100, $500, $1,000, $5,000 and $10,000. Individuals portrayed included not only Presidents but other government officials: Salmon P. Chase (Lincoln's Secretary of the Treasury), Daniel Webster, and Lewis and Clark. Some of the reverse designs are masterpieces of geometrical linework. A number of rarities are to be found among Legal Tender Notes, but in general the lower denominations can be collected without great expense.

WILDCAT NOTES

Wildcat notes are the notes that were issued by so-called "Wildcat Banks," in the era of State Bank Notes (before the Civil War). Numerous banks sprang up around the middle part of the 19th century, mostly in the west and southwest, operated by persons of questionable integrity. Some never had capital backing and were instituted purely as a front for confidence swindles. After issuing notes, the bank shut down, its directors disappeared, and owners of the notes were left with worthless paper. As news traveled slowly in those days, the same persons could move from town to town and work the scheme repeatedly. Notes issued by these banks, or any banks that became insolvent, are also called Broken Bank Notes. Apparently the origin of the term "wildcat" derives from public sentiment of the time, which held that owners of such banks had no greater trustworthiness than a wild animal. "Wildcat" may also refer to the rapid movement of bank officials from one locality to another.

CURRENCY TERMS

14 / 32 SUBJECT SHEET LAYOUT

THE FEDERAL RESERVE BANKS

The Federal Reserve system is divided into 12 Federal Reserve districts, in each of which is a Federal Reserve Bank. There are also 24 branches. Each district is designated by a number and the corresponding letter of the alphabet. The district numbers, the cities in which the 12 banks are located, and the letter symbols are:

1-A—Boston
2-B—New York
3-C—Philadelphia
4-D—Cleveland
5-E—Richmond
6-F—Atlanta
7-G—Chicago
8-H—St. Louis
9-I—Minneapolis
10-J—Kansas City
11-K—Dallas
12-L—San Francisco

32 SUBJECT SHEET LAYOUT

All United States currency is now printed with 32 subjects (notes) to a large sheet. The first printing is the green back. The second printing is the face of the note in black. This includes the portrait and border, the year or series, the check letter and quadrant number, two signatures and the face plate number. The sheet is then cut in half vertically for the third printing. This includes the black Federal Reserve seal, the four Federal Reserve district numbers, the green Treasury seal and two green serial numbers.

The 32 subject sheet is divided into four quarters called quadrants for numbering and other controls. Each quadrant has its own numbering sequence for the eight notes, with serial numbers advancing by 20,000 to the next note. The quadrant number and check letter in the upper left section indicates the first, second, third or fourth quadrant and the position of the note in the quadrant. In the lower right corner the position letter is shown again with a plate number. On the back of the note the same small number in the lower right is the back plate number.

THE U.S. NUMBERING SYSTEM/15

32 SUBJECT SHEET LAYOUT

FIRST QUADRANT / THIRD QUADRANT

A1 A00000001A	A100	E1 A00080001A	E100	A3 A00320001A	A100	E3 A00400001A	E100
B1 A00020001A	B100	F1 A00100001A	F100	B3 A00340001A	B100	F3 A00420001A	F100
C1 A00040001A	C100	G1 A00120001A	G100	C3 A00360001A	C100	G3 A00440001A	G100
D1 A00060001A	D100	H1 A00140001A	H100	D3 A00380001A	D100	H3 A004600001A	H100
A2 A00160001A	A100	E2 A00240001A	E100	A4 A00480001A	A100	E4 A00560001A	E100
B2 A00180001A	B100	F2 A00260001A	F100	B4 A00500001A	B100	F4 A00580001A	F100
C2 A00200001A	C100	G2 A00280001A	G100	C4 A0050001A	C100	G4 A00600001A	G100
D2 A00220001A	D100	H2 A00300001A	H100	D4 A00540001A	D100	H4 A00620001A	H100

SECOND QUADRANT / FOURTH QUADRANT

THE NUMBERING SYSTEM OF UNITED STATES PAPER CURRENCY

The system of numbering paper money must be adequate to accommodate a large volume of notes. For security and accountability purposes, no two notes of any one class, denomination and series may have the same serial number. The two serial numbers on each note have a full complement of eight digits and an alphabetical prefix and suffix letter. When necessary, ciphers are used at the left of the number to make a total of eight digits.

Whenever a numbering sequence is initiated for United States Notes or Silver Certificates, the first note is numbered A 00 000 001 A; the second A 00 000 002 A; the hundredth A 00 000 100 A; the thousandth A 00 001 000 A; and so on through A 99 999 999 A. The suffix letter A will remain the same until a total of 25 groups, or **"blocks"** of 99 999 999 notes are numbered, each group having a different prefix letter of the alphabet from A to Z. When the letter **"O"** is omitted, either as a prefix or as a suffix, because of its similarity to zero. The 100 000 000th note in each group will be a star note, since eight digits are the maximum in the mechanical operation of numbering machines.

At this point, the suffix letter changes to B for the next 25 groups of 99 999 999 notes, and proceeds in the same manner as the suffix letter A. A total of 62,500,000,000 notes could be numbered before a duplication of serial numbers would occur. However, it has never been required to number that many notes of any one class, denomination and series.

The Federal Reserve Notes printed for the 12 districts are numbered in the same progression as United States Notes and Silver Certificates, except that a specific alphabetical letter identifies a specific Federal

16 / PORTRAITS AND BACK DESIGNS

Reserve district. The letter identifying each district is used as a prefix letter at the beginning of the serial numbers on all Federal Reserve Notes and does not change. Only the suffix letter changes in the serial numbers on Federal Reserve Currency.

PORTRAITS AND BACK DESIGN ON SMALL SIZE NOTES

DENOMINATION	PORTRAIT	BACK DESIGN
$1.00	Washington	Great Seal of the United States
$2.00	Jefferson	Monticello
$5.00	Lincoln	Lincoln Memorial
$10.00	Hamilton	United States Treasury
$20.00	Jackson	The White House
$50.00	Grant	United States Capitol
$100.00	Franklin	Independence Hall
$500.00	McKinley	"FIVE HUNDRED"
$1000.00	Cleveland	"ONE THOUSAND"
$5000.00	Madison	"FIVE THOUSAND"
$10,000.00	Chase	"TEN THOUSAND"
$100,000.00	Wilson	"ONE HUNDRED THOUSAND"

DATING UNITED STATES CURRENCY

Unlike coins, the date is not changed each year on United States Currency. The date appearing on all notes, large or small size, is that of the year in which the design was first approved or issued. For instance, large size One Dollar United States Notes of the series 1880 were issued with the same date until the new series of 1917 was issued. There was no further date change until the series of 1923.

The same rules apply to small size notes. However, in this case a letter is added after the date to designate or indicate a minor change in the main design or probably a change in one or both of the signatures. For example: the One Dollar Silver Certificate of 1935 was changed to 1935-A because of a change in the size of the tiny plate numbers appearing in the lower right corners of the face and back of the note. It was changed again from 1935-A to 1935-B in 1945 when the signatures of Julian-Morganthau were changed to Julian-Vinson. Subsequent changes in signatures continued the 1935 series to the year 1963 when the signatures of Smith-Dillon terminated the issue with the series of 1935-H. Therefore, these notes were issued for 28 years bearing the date 1935.

NEW TREASURY SEAL / 17

NEW TREASURY SEAL

FORMER DESIGN

The former design had the Latin inscription: *"Thesaur. Amer. Septent. Sigil."*, which has several translations. It was the Seal of the North American Treasury.

NEW DESIGN

This new design drops the Latin and states *"The Department of The Treasury 1789"*. First used on the $100 Note of the Series of 1966, as shown below.

GRADES AND CONDITIONS OF PAPER MONEY

CONDITION

The physical condition of a note or bill plays an important role in determining its value. There are many notes that have no premium value (beyond face value) in ordinary condition but are valuable or moderately valuable when uncirculated. Even in the case of scarce early specimens, the price given for an "average" example is generally much less than that commanded by Fine or Very Fine condition.

Defects encountered in paper money include:

Creases, Folds, Wrinkles. Generally the characteristic that distinguishes uncirculated notes from those that almost — but not quite — qualify for such designation is a barely noticeable crease running approximately down the center vertically, resulting from the note being folded for insertion into a wallet or billfold. It may be possible, through manipulation or storage beneath a heavy weight, to remove evidence of the crease; but the knowledge that it once existed cannot be obliterated.

Discoloration. Discoloration is not as easy to recognize as most defects but it must be classed as one. A distinction should be made between notes printed from under-inked rollers and those which originally were normally colored but became "washed out." Sometimes washing is indeed the cause; a well-intentioned collector may bathe a note, attempting to clean it, with the result that its color is no longer strong. This should not happen if warm (rather than hot) water is used, without strong cleanser. Atmospheric conditions may play some part in discoloration.

Foxing. Fox spots may sometimes be observed on old notes, especially those of the pre-1890 era, just as on old paper in general. They seem more common to foreign currency than American, but their presence on our notes is certainly not rare. These are tiny brownish-red dots, caused by an infestation of lice that attack the paper fibres.

Holes. Holes are more likely to be encountered in early paper money than specimens of recent origin. In early years it was customary for federal reserve banks to use wire clips in making up bundles of notes for distribution to banking organizations, and these clips or staples often drove their way through the bills. Another common occurrence in grandfather's day was the practice of shop clerks and cashiers in general to impale notes upon holders consisting of nails mounted on stands.

Missing pieces. Missing pieces are a highly undesirable defect which, except in the case of rare specimens, renders the item valueless to collectors. Even if only a blank unprinted corner is torn away, this is called a missing-piece note and hardly anyone will give it a second glance.

Stains. Notes sometimes become stained with ink or other liquids. If the specimen is commonplace and easily obtainable in VF or Uncirculated condition, it will be worthless with any kind of stain. In a note of moderate value, its price will be hurt to a greater or lesser degree depending on the stain's intensity, size, nature, and the area it touches. A stain in an outer margin or at a corner is not so objectionable as one occurring at the center or across a signature or serial number. Ink stains, because of their strong

GRADES AND CONDITIONS / 19

color, are generally deemed the worst, but bad staining can also be caused by oil, crayon, "magic marker" and food substances. Pencil markings, which frequently are found on bank notes, will yield to ordinary erasing with a piece of soft "artgum" worked gently over the surface and brushed away with an artist's camel-hair brush. Most other stains cannot be so easily removed. With ink there is no hope, as any caustic sufficiently strong to remove the ink will also injure the printing and possibly eat through the paper as well. Oil stains can sometimes be lightened, though not removed, by sprinkling the note on both sides (even if the stain shows only on one) with talcum powder or other absorbent powder, placing it between sheets of waxed kitchen paper, and leaving it beneath a heavy weight for several days in a room where the humidity is not unduly high.

Tears. Tears in notes are very common defects, which may be minute or run nearly the whole length of the bill. As a rule the paper on which American currency is printed is fairly rugged and will not tear so readily as most ordinary paper, but given careless or hurried handling anything is possible. An old worn note is more apt to tear in handling than a new one. Repaired tears are more common in the world of paper money collecting than may be generally supposed. A clean tear — that is, one which does not involve loss of surface — can be patched up so as to become virtually unnoticed, unless examined against a light or through a strong glass. X-ray examination will reveal repairs when all else fails.

CONDITION STANDARDS

The following condition standards have been used throughout this book and, with slight variations depending upon individual interpretation, are current generally in the trade.

UNCIRCULATED — UNC. A specimen that for all appearances has not been handled or passed through general circulation; a crisp fresh note in "bank" condition. There may be minor blemishes, such as a finger smudge or pinhole, but if these are in any respect severe the condition merits description as "almost uncirculated." There is not much satisfaction to be taken in a note fresh and crisp that has gaping holes and fingerprints. Obviously, an 1870 "uncirculated" note should not be expected to match a 1970 in appearance or feel. Some respect must be had for age.

ALMOST UNCIRCULATED — A.U. In the case of modern or semi-modern notes, this is generally taken to mean a specimen that shows no evidence of having passed through general circulation but because of some detraction fails to measure up to a rating of "uncirculated." The problem may be finger smudges, counting crinkles, a light crease, a fold along one or more of the corners, or pinholes. But if more than one of these impairments were present, the item would surely not deserve a classification of "almost uncirculated."

EXTREMELY FINE — X.F. A note exhibiting little evidence of wear from handling, but not so perfect or near-perfect as to qualify for a rating of "uncirculated" or "almost uncirculated." On a used note issued before 1900 there may be clear evidence of circulation but no disfiguring marks.

20 / ONE DOLLAR NOTES

VERY FINE — V.F. A very fine note has experienced some circulation but escaped without "being mangled". It is still clean and crisp and its creases are not offensive.

FINE — F. Here the scale begins sliding down. It is obvious that, being the fifth in rank of condition grades, "fine" notes are quite a good deal removed from "uncirculated." They have been handed around pretty thoroughly and suffered the normal consequences, but still are without serious blemishes such as tears, missing corners, serious stains or holes.

VERY GOOD — V.G. A well-circulated note bearing evidence of much folding, creasing and wrinkling. It may possibly be lightly stained, smudged or pin punctured, but major defects — such as a torn-off corner — would drop it into an even lower category.

GOOD — G. Heavily circulated, worn stamps that are possibly stained or scribbled on, edges could be frayed or "dog-eared." There may be holes larger than pin punctures, but not on the central portion of design. This is the lowest grade of condition acceptable to a collector, and only when nothing better is available. Unless very rare, such specimens are considered space-fillers only.

A.B.P. — AVERAGE BUYING PRICES
The average buying prices given here are the approximate sums paid by retail dealers for specimens in good condition. As selling prices vary, so do buying prices, and in fact they usually vary a bit more.

RECORD KEEPING

For your convenience, we suggest you use the following record-keeping system to note condition of your paper money in the checklist box:

☒FAIR   ☒VERY GOOD   ☐VERY FINE   ☒ALMOST UNC.
☒GOOD   ☐FINE   ☒EXTREMELY FINE   ■UNCIRCULATED

ONE DOLLAR NOTES

ORDER OF ISSUE

	FIRST ISSUE	LAST ISSUE	PAGE
1. UNITED STATES NOTE	1862	1928	21
2. NATIONAL BANK NOTES	1863	1875	26
3. SILVER CERTIFICATES	1886	1957	27
4. TREASURY OR COIN NOTES	1890	1891	35
5. FEDERAL RESERVE BANK NOTES	1918 only		37
6. FEDERAL RESERVE NOTES	1963	current	39

ONE DOLLAR NOTES / 21

ONE DOLLAR NOTES (1862) UNITED STATES NOTES
(ALSO KNOWN AS LEGAL TENDER NOTES)

(Large Size) **NOTE NO. 1**

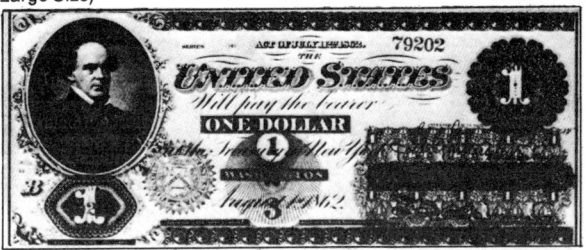

Face Design: Portrait of Salmon Portland Chase (1808-1873), Secretary of the Treasury under Lincoln, red Treasury Seal, signatures of Chittenden and Spinner, lower right.

Back Design: Large circle center with legal tender obligation.

SERIES SIGNATURES	SEAL	A.B.P.	GOOD	V. FINE	UNC.
1862 Chittenden-Spinner					
☐ Type I-National Bank Note, American Bank Note without Monogram	Red	40.00	65.00	150.00	775.00
☐ Type II-National Bank Note, American Bank Note with Monogram ABNCO	Red	25.00	47.00	115.00	450.00
☐ Type III-National Bank Note, National Bank Note without Monogram	Red	30.00	52.00	122.00	480.00
☐ Type IV-National Bank Note, National Bank Note with Monogram ABNCO	Red	30.00	52.00	122.00	480.00

22 / ONE DOLLAR NOTES

ONE DOLLAR NOTES (1869) UNITED STATES NOTES
(ALSO KNOWN AS LEGAL TENDER NOTES)

(Large Size) **NOTE NO. 2**

Face Design: Portrait of President Washington in the center, large red seal to the right. Scene of Columbus in sight of land, to left, also called "Rainbow Note" because of the many colors used in printing. Black ink for main design, red seal and serial numbers, green background for the serial number, green shading in upper half and blue tint in paper left of portrait to deter counterfeiting.

Back Design: Green, "ONE DOLLAR" and "ONE" over "1" center, letters U. S. interwoven to left. Legal tender obligation to right of center.

SERIES	SIGNATURES	SEAL	A.B.P.	GOOD	V. FINE	UNC.
☐ 1869	Allison-Spinner	Red	45.00	77.50	160.00	750.00

ONE DOLLAR NOTES (1874-1917) UNITED STATES NOTES
(ALSO KNOWN AS LEGAL TENDER NOTES)
(Large Size) **NOTE NO. 3**

Back Design: Large green "X" with United States of America in the center. Legal tender obligation and counterfeiting warning to right.
Face Design: No blue or green shading and tinting.

SERIES	SIGNATURES	SEAL	A.B.P.	GOOD	V. FINE	UNC.
☐1874	Allison-Spinner	Red Sm.	13.75	32.00	100.00	470.00
☐1875	Allison-New	Red Sm.	12.50	28.00	75.00	285.00
☐1875	Same Series A	Red Sm.	36.00	70.00	235.00	975.00
☐1875	Same Series B	Red Sm.	33.00	63.00	220.00	940.00
☐1875	Same Series C	Red Sm.	45.00	87.00	280.00	1065.00
☐1875	Same Series D	Red Sm.	55.00	95.00	330.00	1120.00
☐1875	Same Series E	Red Sm.	75.00	150.00	475.00	1625.00
☐1875	Allison-Wyman	Red Sm.	15.00	30.00	85.00	275.00
☐1878	Allison-Gilfillan	Red Sm.	15.00	30.00	90.00	415.00
☐1878	Allison-Gilfillan	Maroon Sm.	—	—	—	1725.00
☐1880	Scofield-Gilfillan	Brown Lg.	13.00	25.00	120.00	270.00
☐1880	Bruce-Gilfillan	Brown Lg.	14.00	28.00	115.00	245.00
☐1880	Bruce-Wyman	Brown Lg.	14.00	28.00	115.00	245.00
☐1880	Rosecrans-Huston	Red Lg.	33.00	70.00	225.00	615.00
☐1880	Rosecrans-Huston	Brown Lg.	38.00	70.00	225.00	700.00
☐1880	Rosecrans-Nebeker	Brown Lg.	35.00	70.00	220.00	680.00
☐1880	Rosecrans-Nebeker	Red Sm.	11.00	23.00	52.00	250.00
☐1880	Tillman-Morgan	Red Sm.	10.00	22.00	52.00	250.00
☐1917	Tehee-Burke	Red Sm.	9.00	15.00	32.00	145.00
☐1917	Elliott-Burke	Red Sm.	8.50	14.00	28.00	145.00
☐1917*	Burke-Elliott	Red Sm.	13.50	30.00	90.00	170.00
☐1917	Elliott-White	Red Sm.	8.00	14.00	34.00	140.00
☐1917	Speelman-White	Red Sm.	8.00	14.00	34.00	145.00

Sm.—Small Seal, Lg.—Large Seal
*This note with signatures of Burke and Elliott is an error issue. The regular procedure was to have the signature of the Register of the Treasury on the left, and that of the Treasurer to the right. The signatures were transposed in this instance.

24 / ONE DOLLAR NOTES

ONE DOLLAR NOTES (1923) UNITED STATES NOTES
(ALSO KNOWN AS LEGAL TENDER NOTES)
(Large Size) NOTE NO. 4

Face Design: Portrait of President Washington in center. Red seal to left, red "1" to the right, red serial numbers.

Back Design: "United States of America" and "ONE DOLLAR" in center. Figures "1" to right and left. This was the last issue of large size "ONE DOLLAR" United States Notes. The last series of large size notes were kept in use until 1929 when the first issue of small size notes were released.

SERIES	SIGNATURES	SEAL	A.B.P.	GOOD	V. FINE	UNC.
☐1923	Speelman-White	Red	8.00	14.50	42.00	220.00

ONE DOLLAR NOTES (1928) UNITED STATES NOTES
(ALSO KNOWN AS LEGAL TENDER NOTES)
(Small Size) **NOTE NO. 5**

Face Design: Red seal to left — red serial numbers, large "ONE" to right. This is the only issue of the $1.00 United States Note, small size. At the present time only the $100.00 United States Note is current.

Back Design: Large "ONE" in center with "ONE DOLLAR" overprint, back printed in green.

SERIES SIGNATURES	SEAL	A.B.P.	GOOD	V. FINE	UNC.
☐ 1928 Woods-Woodin	Red	7.50	13.75	33.00	110.00

ONE DOLLAR NOTES (1863-1875) NATIONAL BANK NOTES
FIRST CHARTER PERIOD (Large Size) — NOTE NO. 6

Face Design: Name of National Bank top center, maidens at altar below.

Back Design: Landing of Pilgrims—center, state seal of state issuing bank to left eagle and flag.

SERIES	SIGNATURES	SEAL	A.B.P.	GOOD	V. FINE	UNC.
☐Original*	Colby-Spinner	Red w/r	45.00	82.00	250.00	1025.00
☐Original*	Jeffries-Spinner	Red w/r	125.00	300.00	1165.00	3250.00
☐Original*	Allison-Spinner	Red w/r	45.00	82.00	250.00	1050.00
☐1875	Allison-New	Red w/s	45.00	82.00	225.00	1075.00
☐1875	Allison-Wyman	Red w/s	45.00	82.00	225.00	1075.00
☐1875	Allison-Gilfillan	Red w/s	45.00	82.00	225.00	1075.00
☐1875	Scofield-Gilfillan	Red w/s	45.00	82.00	225.00	1075.00

w/r—with Rays, w/s—with Scallops

*Early notes of the First Charter Period did not have the series imprinted on them. They are known by the date on the bill which was usually the date of charter or organization, or as the Original Series. These notes had a seal with rays or small notches. In 1875 the series was imprinted in red and the seal was changed to have scallops around the border. The charter number was added to later issues of notes of the original series and to all notes of the 1875 series.

ONE DOLLAR NOTES (1886) SILVER CERTIFICATES
(Large Size) NOTE NO. 7

Face Design:
Portrait of
Martha Washington

Back Design

SERIES	SIGNATURES	SEAL	A.B.P.	GOOD	V. FINE	UNC.
☐1886	Rosecrans-Jordan	Red Sm.	23.00	42.00	195.00	800.00
☐1886	Rosecrans-Hyatt	Red Sm.	23.00	42.00	195.00	800.00
☐1886	Rosecrans-Hyatt	Red Lg.	23.00	42.00	195.00	800.00
☐1886	Rosecrans-Huston	Red Lg.	27.00	50.00	210.00	850.00
☐1886	Rosecrans-Huston	Brown Lg.	27.00	50.00	210.00	850.00
☐1886	Rosecrans-Nebeker	Brown Lg.	27.00	52.00	250.00	850.00
☐1886	Rosecrans-Nebeker	Red Sm.	37.00	75.00	275.00	900.00

ONE DOLLAR NOTES (1891) SILVER CERTIFICATES
(Large Size)

NOTE NO. 8

Back Design:
Face Design:
Same as Note
No. 7.

SERIES	SIGNATURES	SEAL	A.B.P.	GOOD	V. FINE	UNC.
☐1891	Rosecrans-Nebeker	Red Sm.	22.00	45.00	140.00	815.00
☐1891	Tillman-Morgan	Red Sm.	21.00	43.00	135.00	795.00

28 / ONE DOLLAR NOTES

ONE DOLLAR NOTES (1896) SILVER CERTIFICATES
(Large Size)   NOTE NO. 9

The Educational Note

Face Design: History instructing youth. To the right, panoramic view of the Capitol and Washington Monument. Constitution on tablet, names of famous Americans on top and side borders.

Back Design: Portrait of Martha Washington to left and President Washington to right with large numeral "1" in center.

There is a story that when this note was issued people objected to it because they said, No "1" (ONE) SHOULD STAND BETWEEN GEORGE AND MARTHA WASHINGTON. The set consists of $1.00, $2.00, and $5.00 denominations. They all have very beautiful engravings, and they are truly the most beautiful notes ever issued by our government. They were first released in 1896 and replaced by a new issue in 1899. They were short lived because of objections to the unclad female on the $5.00 note.

SERIES	SIGNATURES	SEAL	A.B.P.	GOOD	V. FINE	UNC.
☐ 1896	Tilman-Morgan	Red	30.00	57.50	200.00	1000.00
☐ 1896	Bruce-Roberts	Red	30.00	57.50	200.00	1000.00

ONE DOLLAR NOTES / 29

ONE DOLLAR NOTES (1899) SILVER CERTIFICATES
(Large Size) NOTE NO. 10

Face Design: Eagle on flag and Capitol background over portraits ø Presidents Lincoln and Grant.

Back Design

SERIES	SIGNATURES	SEAL	A.B.P.	GOOD	V. FINE	UNC.
\multicolumn{7}{l}{"SERIES OF 1899" is above upper right serial number.}					
☐1899	Lyons-Roberts	Blue	10.00	21.00	38.00	185.00
\multicolumn{7}{l}{"SERIES OF 1899" is below upper right serial number.}					
☐1899	Lyons-Roberts	Blue	8.75	15.00	35.00	170.00
☐1899	Lyons-Treat	Blue	8.75	15.00	35.00	170.00
☐1899	Vernon-Treat	Blue	8.00	14.00	34.00	165.00
☐1899	Vernon-McClung	Blue	8.00	14.00	32.00	165.00
\multicolumn{7}{l}{"SERIES OF 1899" is vertical to right of blue seal on the following notes:}					
☐1899	Napier-McClung	Blue	8.00	14.00	33.00	150.00
☐1899	Napier-Thompson	Blue	28.00	55.00	190.00	550.00
☐1899	Parker-Burke	Blue	8.00	14.00	33.00	155.00
☐1899	Teehee-Burke	Blue	7.00	13.50	30.00	145.00
☐1899	Elliott-Burke	Blue	7.00	13.50	30.00	145.00
☐1899	Elliott-White	Blue	7.00	13.50	30.00	145.00
☐1899	Speelman-White	Blue	7.00	13.50	30.00	145.00

30 / ONE DOLLAR NOTES

ONE DOLLAR NOTES (1923) SILVER CERTIFICATES
(Large Size)   **NOTE NO. 11**

Face Design: Portrait of President Washington in center, blue seal left, blue "1 DOLLAR" right, blue numbers.

Back Design: Same as Note No. 4

SERIES	SIGNATURES	SEAL	A.B.P.	GOOD	V. FINE	UNC.
☐ 1923	Speelman-White	Blue	5.00	10.00	17.00	55.00
☐ 1923	Woods-White	Blue	6.00	11.00	21.00	62.50
☐ 1923	Woods-Tate	Blue	11.75	22.00	58.00	225.00

ONE DOLLAR NOTES (1928) SILVER CERTIFICATES
(Small Size)   **NOTE NO. 12**

Face Design: Portrait of President Washington, blue seal to the left, "ONE" to right, blue seal and numbers. "ONE SILVER DOLLAR" under portrait.

Back Design

First issue series of 1928. United States paper money was reduced in 1928 from the old large size to the size presently in use. This was mostly an economy measure. Unlike large size notes, the small notes have a letter designation after the date to denote a minor change in design or change of one or both signatures.

SERIES	SIGNATURES	SEAL	A.B.P.	GOOD	V. FINE	UNC.
☐ 1928	Tate-Mellon	Blue	1.35	2.25	6.25	16.00
☐ 1928A	Woods-Mellon	Blue	1.35	2.00	5.00	14.00
☐ 1928B	Woods-Mills	Blue	1.35	3.00	6.50	16.00
☐ 1928C	Woods-Woodin	Blue	18.00	32.00	95.00	525.00
☐ 1928D	Julian-Woodin	Blue	18.00	32.00	105.00	315.00
☐ 1928E	Julian-Morgenthau	Blue	57.50	115.00	320.00	1085.00

32 / ONE DOLLAR NOTES

ONE DOLLAR NOTES (1934) SILVER CERTIFICATES
(Small Size)   NOTE NO. 13

Face Design: Portrait of President Washington, blue "1" to left. "ONE" and blue seal to right. "ONE DOLLAR IN SILVER", under portrait.
        Back Design: Same as Note No. 12.

SERIES	SIGNATURES	SEAL	A.B.P.	GOOD	V. FINE	UNC.
☐1934	Julian-Morgenthau	Blue	1.20	1.60	4.60	22.50

ONE DOLLAR NOTES (1935) SILVER CERTIFICATES
(Small Size)   NOTE NO. 14

Face Design: Portrait of President Washington in center. Gray "1" to left, blue seal right, and blue numbers. "ONE DOLLAR IN SILVER", under portrait.

SERIES	SIGNATURES	SEAL	A.B.P.	GOOD	V. FINE	UNC.
	The following Notes are Without "IN GOD WE TRUST" on back.					
☐1935	Julian-Morgenthau	Blue	1.75	3.25	7.75	13.25
☐1935A	Julian-Morgenthau	Blue	1.15	1.40	2.75	5.50
☐1935A	Julian-Morgenthau	Brown	3.00	6.00	15.00	60.00

This note was a special issue for use in war zones in the Pacific area during World War II. Brown serial numbers and HAWAII stamped on front and back.

ONE DOLLAR NOTES / 33

ONE DOLLAR NOTES (1935) SILVER CERTIFICATES
(Small Size)   **NOTE NO. 14**

SERIES	SIGNATURES	SEAL	A.B.P.	GOOD	V. FINE	UNC.
☐1935A	Julian-Morgenthau	Yellow	4.00	7.00	18.00	90.00

The above note was a special issue for use in war zones in the North African and European areas during World War II. Blue serial numbers and yellow seal.

☐1935A	Julian-Morgenthau	Blue	8.00	14.00	37.00	150.00

Red "R" between the Treasury Seal and signatures of Morgenthau. This was an experimental issue to test wearing qualities of differently treated paper.

☐1935A	Julian-Morgenthau	Blue	6.00	11.00	28.00	130.00

Above note with red "S" between Treasury Seal and signature of Morgenthau. Experimental issue. "R" was for regular paper, "S" for special paper.

☐1935B	Julian-Vinson	Blue	1.15	1.50	3.25	11.50
☐1935C	Julian-Snyder	Blue	1.15	1.35	2.50	5.50
☐1935D	Clark-Snyder	Blue	1.10	1.25	2.00	5.00

Wide design on back. This and all notes of 1935 prior to this, have the wide design. See fig. I.

☐1935D	Clark-Snyder	Blue	1.10	1.25	2.00	4.75

Narrow design on back. This and all $1.00 notes following have narrow design. See fig. II.

FIG. I WIDE DESIGN

FIG. II. NARROW DESIGN
This change was made during the 1935-D Series.

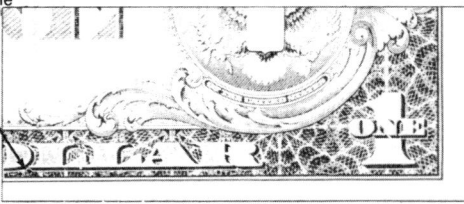

34 / ONE DOLLAR NOTES

ONE DOLLAR NOTES (1935) SILVER CERTIFICATES
(Small Size) NOTE NO. 14

SERIES	SIGNATURES	SEAL	A.B.P.	GOOD	V. FINE	UNC.
☐ 1935E	Priest-Humphrey	Blue	1.15	1.35	1.90	4.25
☐ 1935F	Priest-Anderson	Blue	1.10	1.25	1.60	3.65
☐ 1935G	Smith-Dillon	Blue	1.10	1.25	1.60	3.65

"IN GOD WE TRUST" added. All notes following have the motto.

☐ 1935G	Smith-Dillon	Blue	1.15	1.40	2.15	4.75
☐ 1935H	Granahan-Dillon	Blue	1.15	1.40	2.15	4.75

ONE DOLLAR NOTES (1957) SILVER CERTIFICATES
(Small Size) NOTE NO. 14

The following three notes are the last issue of the $1.00 Silver Certificates. The reason for the change in series from 1935H to 1957 was due to printing improvements. The 1935 series, up until the issue of Clark and Snyder, was printed in sheets of 12 subjects to a sheet. During the term of Clark and Snyder notes were printed 18 subjects to a sheet. Starting with the series of 1957, new high speed rotary presses were installed and notes were printed 32 subjects to a sheet.

SERIES	SIGNATURES	SEAL	A.B.P.	GOOD	V. FINE	UNC.
☐ 1957	Priest-Anderson	Blue	1.05	1.20	1.45	3.20
☐ 1957A	Smith-Dillon	Blue	1.05	1.20	1.45	3.20
☐ 1957B	Granahan-Dillon	Blue	1.05	1.20	1.45	3.20

The redemption of Silver Certificates by the U.S. Treasury Department ended on June 24, 1968. These notes are now worth only their face value, plus the premium value to collectors. Notes in used condition are not regarded as collectors' items and many dealers decline to buy or sell them.

ONE DOLLAR NOTES (1890) TREASURY OR COIN NOTES
(Large Size) **NOTE NO. 15**

Face Design: Portrait of Stanton, Secretary of War during the Civil War.

Back Design: Green large ornate "ONE". Entire back is beautifully engraved.

SERIES	SIGNATURES	SEAL	A.B.P.	GOOD	V. FINE	UNC.
☐ 1890	Rosecrans-Huston	Brown	45.00	75.00	320.00	2675.00
☐ 1890	Rosecrans-Nebeker	Brown	45.00	75.00	310.00	2550.00
☐ 1890	Rosecrans-Nebeker	Red	40.00	70.00	290.00	2200.00

36 / ONE DOLLAR NOTES

ONE DOLLAR NOTES (1891) TREASURY OR COIN NOTES
(Large Size)   NOTE NO. 16

Face Design: Is similar to Note No. 15.

Back Design: More unengraved area, numerous "ONE's" and "1's".

SERIES	SIGNATURES	SEAL	A.B.P.	GOOD	V. FINE	UNC.
☐1891	Rosecrans-Nebeker	Red	23.00	39.00	120.00	485.00
☐1891	Tillman-Morgan	Red	23.00	39.00	120.00	485.00
☐1891	Bruce-Roberts	Red	23.00	39.00	120.00	485.00

ONE DOLLAR NOTES / 37

ONE DOLLAR NOTES (1918) FEDERAL RESERVE BANK NOTES
(Large Size) **NOTE NO. 17**

Face Design: Portrait of President Washington, signature to left of center. Bank and City center, blue seal to right. Signatures of Government Officials above. Signatures of Bank Officials below. Federal Reserve district letter and numbers in four corners.

Back Design: Flying eagle and flag in center. All are series 1918, and have blue seals and blue numbers.

38 / ONE DOLLAR NOTES

ONE DOLLAR NOTES (1918) FEDERAL RESERVE BANK NOTES
(Large Size)   NOTE NO. 17

BANK & CITY	GOV'T SIGNATURES	BANK SIGNATURES	A.B.P.	GOOD	V. FINE	UNC.
☐Boston	Teehee-Burke	Bullen-Morss	5.00	11.00	35.00	165.00
☐Boston	Teehee-Burke	Willet-Morss	11.00	22.00	90.00	340.00
☐Boston	Elliot-Burke	Willet-Morss	5.00	11.00	35.00	165.00
☐New York	Teehee-Burke	Sailer-Strong	5.00	11.00	35.00	165.00
☐New York	Teehee-Burke	Hendricks-Strong	5.00	11.00	35.00	165.00
☐New York	Elliott-Burke	Hendricks-Strong	5.00	11.00	35.00	165.00
☐Philadelphia	Teehee-Burke	Hardt-Passmore	5.00	11.00	35.00	165.00
☐Philadelphia	Teehee-Burke	Dyer-Passmore	5.00	11.00	35.00	165.00
☐Philadelphia	Elliott-Burke	Dyer-Passmore	6.00	12.00	39.00	165.00
☐Philadelphia	Elliott-Burke	Dyer-Norris	5.00	11.00	35.00	165.00
☐Cleveland	Teehee-Burke	Baxter-Fancher	5.00	11.00	35.00	165.00
☐Cleveland	Teehee-Burke	Davis-Fancher	5.00	11.00	35.00	165.00
☐Cleveland	Elliott-Burke	Davis-Fancher	5.00	11.00	35.00	165.00
☐Richmond	Teehee-Burke	Keesee-Seay	5.00	11.00	35.00	165.00
☐Richmond	Elliott-Burke	Keesee-Seay	5.00	11.00	35.00	165.00
☐Atlanta	Teehee-Burke	Pike-McCord	5.00	11.00	35.00	165.00
☐Atlanta	Teehee-Burke	Bell-McCord	6.00	12.00	39.00	165.00
☐Atlanta	Teehee-Burke	Bell-Wellborn	5.00	11.00	35.00	165.00
☐Atlanta	Elliott-Burke	Bell-Wellborn	5.00	11.00	35.00	165.00
☐Chicago	Teehee-Burke	McCloud-McDougal	5.00	11.00	35.00	165.00
☐Chicago	Teehee-Burke	Cramer-McDougal	5.00	11.00	35.00	165.00
☐Chicago	Elliott-Burke	Cramer-McDougal	5.00	11.00	35.00	165.00
☐St. Louis	Teehee-Burke	Attebery-Wells	5.00	11.00	36.00	170.00
☐St. Louis	Teehee-Burke	Attebery-Biggs	5.00	11.00	35.00	170.00
☐St. Louis	Elliott-Burke	Attebery-Biggs	5.00	11.00	35.00	165.00
☐St. Louis	Elliott-Burke	White-Biggs	5.00	11.00	35.00	165.00
☐Minneapolis	Teehee-Burke	Cook-Wold	10.00	20.00	65.00	250.00
☐Minneapolis	Teehee-Burke	Cook-Young	42.00	85.00	475.00	1025.00
☐Minneapolis	Elliott-Burke	Cook-Young	9.00	21.00	75.00	270.00
☐Kansas City	Teehee-Burke	Anderson-Miller	5.00	11.00	35.00	165.00
☐Kansas City	Elliott-Burke	Anderson-Miller	5.00	11.00	35.00	165.00
☐Kansas City	Elliott-Burke	Helm-Miller	5.00	11.00	35.00	165.00
☐Dallas	Teehee-Burke	Talley-VanZandt	5.00	11.00	35.00	165.00
☐Dallas	Elliott-Burke	Talley-VanZandt	14.00	28.00	112.00	265.00
☐Dallas	Elliott-Burke	Lawder-VanZandt	5.00	11.00	35.00	170.00
☐San Francisco	Teehee-Burke	Clerk-Lynch	5.00	11.00	35.00	165.00
☐San Francisco	Teehee-Burke	Clerk-Calkins	5.00	11.00	35.00	165.00
☐San Francisco	Elliott-Burke	Clerk-Calkins	5.00	11.00	35.00	170.00
☐San Francisco	Elliott-Burke	Ambrose-Calkins	5.00	11.00	35.00	170.00

ONE DOLLAR NOTES (1963) FEDERAL RESERVE NOTES
(Small Size)   **NOTE NO. 18**

Face Design: Portrait of President Washington in center, black Federal reserve seal with city and district letter to left, green Treasury Seal to right. Green serial numbers, Federal Reserve numbers in four corners.

Back Design: Same as all $1.00 Notes from 1935.

SERIES OF 1963 GRANAHAN-DILLON — GREEN SEAL

DISTRICT	A.B.P.	UNC.	DISTRICT	A.B.P.	UNC.
☐ 1A Boston	1.60	3.25	☐ 7G Chicago	1.60	3.25
☐ 2B New York	1.60	3.25	☐ 8H St. Louis	1.60	3.25
☐ 3C Philadelphia	1.60	3.25	☐ 9I Minneapolis	1.60	3.25
☐ 4D Cleveland	1.60	3.25	☐ 10J Kansas City	1.60	3.25
☐ 5E Richmond	1.60	3.25	☐ 11K Dallas	1.60	3.25
☐ 6F Atlanta	1.60	3.25	☐ 12L San Francisco	1.60	3.25

The Dallas note of this series as shown, with the letter "K" in the black seal and the numbers "11" in the four corners does not have any more significance or value than any other notes with their respective district letter and corresponding number.

A false rumor was circulated several years ago that the "K" was for Kennedy, the "11" was for November, the month in which he was assassinated, and that the note was issued by the Dallas bank to commemorate the occasion. The entire story is apocryphal.

This note is in no way associated with the late President Kennedy. The notes were authorized by the act of June 4, 1963. This was five months before Kennedy was assassinated. The Federal Reserve district for Dallas is K-11.

SERIES OF 1963A GRANAHAN-FOWLER — GREEN SEAL

DISTRICT	A.B.P.	UNC.	DISTRICT	A.B.P.	UNC.
☐ 1A Boston	1.60	3.25	☐ 7G Chicago	1.60	3.25
☐ 2B New York	1.60	3.25	☐ 8H St. Louis	1.60	3.25
☐ 3C Philadelphia	1.60	3.25	☐ 9I Minneapolis	1.60	3.25
☐ 4D Cleveland	1.60	3.25	☐ 10J Kansas City	1.60	3.25
☐ 5E Richmond	1.60	3.25	☐ 11K Dallas	1.60	3.25
☐ 6F Atlanta	1.60	3.25	☐ 12L San Francisco	1.60	3.25

40 / ONE DOLLAR NOTES

ONE DOLLAR NOTES (1963-B) FEDERAL RESERVE
(WITH SIGNATURE OF JOSEPH W. BARR)

(Small Size)   NOTE NO. 18

Joseph W. Barr served as Secretary of the Treasury from December 20th, 1968 to January 20th, 1969, filling the unexpired term of Henry H. Fowler. His signature appears on the $1.00 Federal Reserve notes of the series of 1963-B only.

During the one month term of Joseph W. Barr about 471 million notes were printed with his signature. These notes were for the following Federal Reserve Banks.

NOTES ISSUED

REGULAR NUMBERS	A.B.P.	UNC.	STAR NUMBERS	A.B.P.	UNC.
☐ 2B New York 123,040,000	1.35	2.75	3,680,000	1.60	2.75
☐ 5E Richmond 93,600,000	1.35	2.75	3,040,000	1.60	2.75
☐ 7G Chicago 91,040,000	1.35	2.75	2,400,000	1.60	2.75
☐10J Kansas City 44,800,000	1.35	2.75	None Printed		
☐12L San Francisco . 106,400,000	1.35	2.75	3,040,000	1.60	2.75
458,880,000			**12,160,000**		

ONE DOLLAR NOTES (1969) FEDERAL RESERVE NOTES
(WORDING IN GREEN TREASURY SEAL CHANGED FROM LATIN TO ENGLISH)

The former design had the Latin inscription: *Thesaur. Amer. Septent. Sigil.*,. which has several translations. It was the Seal of the North American Treasury.

This new design drops the Latin and states "The Department of The Treasury 1789". First used on the $100 Note of the Series of 1966.

FORMER DESIGN   NEW DESIGN

ONE DOLLAR NOTES (1969) FEDERAL RESERVE NOTES
(Small Size)   **NOTE NO. 18A**

SERIES OF 1969—ELSTON-KENNEDY, GREEN SEAL
Boston......2.70	Cleveland....2.70	Chicago......2.70	Kansas City...2.70
New York....2.70	Richmond....2.70	St. Louis.....2.70	Dallas........2.70
Philadelphia..2.70	Atlanta.......2.70	Minneapolis..2.70	San Francisco.2.70

SERIES OF 1969A—KABIS-KENNEDY, GREEN SEAL
Boston......2.70	Cleveland....2.70	Chicago......2.70	Kansas City...2.70
New York....2.70	Richmond....2.70	St. Louis.....2.70	Dallas........2.70
Philadelphia..2.70	Atlanta.......2.70	Minneapolis..2.70	San Francisco.2.70

SERIES OF 1969B—KABIS-CONNALLY, GREEN SEAL
Boston......2.70	Cleveland....2.70	Chicago......2.70	Kansas City...2.70
New York....2.70	Richmond....2.70	St. Louis.....2.70	Dallas........2.70
Philadelphia..2.70	Atlanta.......2.70	Minneapolis..2.70	San Francisco.2.70

SERIES OF 1969C—BANUELOS-CONNALLY, GREEN SEAL
Boston......2.15	Cleveland....2.15	Chicago......2.15	Kansas City...2.15
New York....2.15	Richmond....2.15	St. Louis.....2.15	Dallas........2.15
Philadelphia..2.15	Atlanta.......2.15	Minneapolis..2.15	San Francisco.2.15

SERIES OF 1969D—BANUELOS-CONNALLY, GREEN SEAL
Boston......2.15	Cleveland....2.15	Chicago......2.15	Kansas City...2.15
New York....2.15	Richmond....2.15	St. Louis.....2.15	Dallas........2.15
Philadelphia..2.15	Atlanta.......2.15	Minneapolis..2.15	San Francisco.2.15

SERIES OF 1974—NEFF-SIMON, GREEN SEAL
Boston......2.15	Cleveland....2.15	Chicago......2.15	Kansas City...2.15
New York....2.15	Richmond....2.15	St. Louis.....2.15	Dallas........2.15
Philadelphia..2.15	Atlanta.......2.15	Minneapolis..2.15	San Francisco.2.15

SERIES OF 1977—MORTON-BLUMENTHAL, GREEN SEAL
Boston......2.10	Cleveland....2.10	Chicago......2.10	Kansas City...2.10
New York....2.10	Richmond....2.10	St. Louis.....2.10	Dallas........2.10
Philadelphia..2.10	Atlanta.......2.10	Minneapolis..2.10	San Francisco.2.10

SERIES OF 1977A—MORTON-MILLER, GREEN SEAL
Boston......2.10	Cleveland....2.10	Chicago......2.10	Kansas City...2.10
New York....2.10	Richmond....2.10	St. Louis.....2.10	Dallas........2.10
Philadelphia..2.10	Atlanta.......2.10	Minneapolis..2.10	San Francisco.2.10

SERIES OF 1981—BUCHANAN-REGAN, GREEN SEAL
Boston......1.50	Cleveland....1.50	Chicago......1.50	Kansas City...1.50
New York....1.50	Richmond....1.50	St. Louis.....1.50	Dallas........1.50
Philadelphia..1.50	Atlanta.......1.50	Minneapolis..1.50	San Francisco.1.50

SERIES OF 1981A—ORTEGA-REGAN, GREEN SEAL
Issued for all Federal Reserve Banks..CURRENT

TWO DOLLAR NOTES

ORDER OF ISSUE

	FIRST ISSUE — LAST ISSUE	PAGE
1. UNITED STATES NOTES	1862—1963A	43
2. NATIONAL BANK NOTES	1875-only	48
3. SILVER CERTIFICATES	1886—1899	49
4. TREASURY OR COIN NOTES	1890—1891	53
5. FEDERAL RESERVE BANK NOTES	1918 only	54
6. FEDERAL RESERVE NOTES	1976	56

TWO DOLLAR NOTES / 43

TWO DOLLAR NOTES (1862) UNITED STATES NOTES
(ALSO KNOWN AS LEGAL TENDER NOTE)

(Large Size) **NOTE NO. 19**

ALEXANDER HAMILTON (1754-1804)

Face Design: Portrait of Hamilton, cloverleaf twos in upper corners, medallion with "11" in lower left, medallion with "1, 2, 3," right of portrait.

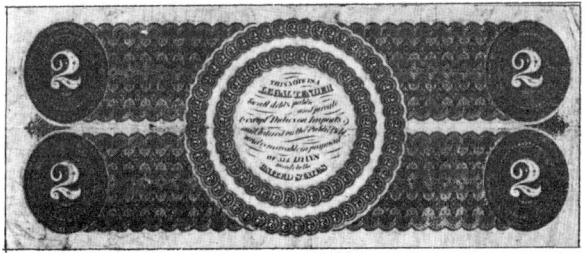

Back Design: "2" in each corner, with "2" motif repeated in scallop circles around obligation, back is printed green.

SERIES SIGNATURES	SEAL	A.B.P.	GOOD	V. FINE	UNC.
☐1862 Chittenden-Spinner TYPE I: American Banknote Company vertical in left border	Red	40.00	80.00	225.00	1075.00
☐1862 Chittenden-Spinner TYPE II: National Banknote Company vertical in left border	Red	32.00	60.00	200.00	950.00

44 / TWO DOLLAR NOTES

TWO DOLLAR NOTES (1869) UNITED STATES NOTES
(ALSO KNOWN AS LEGAL TENDER NOTE)

(Large Size) NOTE NO. 20

Face Design: Portrait of President Jefferson to left, Capitol in center, large red seal to right.

Back Design: Roman II left, Arabic "2" center, "TWO," right. This is the companion note to the $1.00 "RAINBOW NOTE". (see NOTE NO. 2).

SERIES	SIGNATURES	SEAL	A.B.P.	GOOD	V. FINE	UNC.
☐ 1869	Allison-Spinner	Red	36.00	70.00	320.00	1310.00

TWO DOLLAR NOTES (1874) UNITED STATES NOTES
(ALSO KNOWN AS LEGAL TENDER NOTE)

(Large Size)

NOTE NO. 21

Face Design:
Portrait of
President Jefferson
same as
previous
Note. No. 20

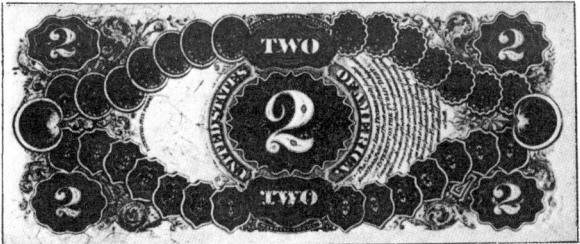

Back Design: Completely revised.

SERIES SIGNATURES	SEAL	A.B.P.	GOOD	V. FINE	UNC.
☐ 1874 Allison-Spinner	Red	42.00	85.00	210.00	700.00
☐ 1875 Allison-New	Red	17.50	32.00	90.00	430.00
☐ SERIES A Allison-New	Red	52.00	100.00	300.00	590.00
☐ SERIES B Allison-New	Red	52.00	100.00	310.00	615.00
☐ 1875 Allison-Wyman	Red	16.00	30.00	90.00	400.00
☐ 1878 Allison-Gilfillan	Red	20.00	40.00	130.00	675.00
☐ 1878 Scofield-Gilfillan	Red	600.00	1150.00	2625.00	6350.00
☐ 1880 Scofield-Gilfillan	Brown	11.00	22.00	63.00	290.00
☐ 1880 Bruce-Gilfillan	Brown	11.00	22.00	63.00	270.00
☐ 1880 Bruce-Wyman	Brown	12.00	23.00	68.00	275.00
☐ 1880 Rosecrans-Huston	Red	38.00	69.00	175.00	650.00
☐ 1880 Rosecrans-Huston	Brown	33.00	65.00	165.00	650.00
☐ 1880 Rosecrans-Nebeker	Red	14.00	27.00	65.00	290.00
☐ 1880 Tilman-Morgan	Red	13.00	25.00	63.00	260.00
☐ 1917 Teehee-Burke	Red	7.25	15.00	37.00	185.00
☐ 1917 Elliott-Burke	Red	7.00	14.00	34.00	142.50
☐ 1917 Elliott-White	Red	7.00	14.00	34.00	142.50
☐ 1917 Speelman-White	Red	7.00	14.00	34.00	142.50

46 / TWO DOLLAR NOTES

TWO DOLLAR NOTES (1928) UNITED STATES NOTES
(ALSO KNOWN AS LEGAL TENDER NOTES)

(Small Size) **NOTE NO. 22**

Face Design: Portrait of President Jefferson, red seal left, "TWO" right, red serial numbers.

Back Design: Jefferson Home—Monticello

SERIES	SIGNATURES	SEAL	A.B.P.	GOOD	V. FINE	UNC.
☐ 1928	Tate-Mellon	Red	3.50	6.25	17.00	38.00
☐ 1928A	Woods-Mellon	Red	5.75	11.00	45.00	145.00
☐ 1928B	Woods-Mills	Red	27.00	52.00	160.00	465.00
☐ 1928C	Julian-Morgenthau	Red	2.50	4.25	9.00	45.00
☐ 1928D	Julian-Morgenthau	Red	2.50	4.25	9.00	25.00
☐ 1928E	Julian-Vinson	Red	2.75	5.00	17.00	50.00
☐ 1928F	Julian-Snyder	Red	2.75	5.00	8.50	29.00
☐ 1928G	Clark-Snyder	Red	2.25	3.50	6.50	21.75

TWO DOLLAR NOTES / 47
TWO DOLLAR NOTES (1953) UNITED STATES NOTES
(ALSO KNOWN AS LEGAL TENDER NOTES)
(Small Size) **NOTE NO. 23**

Face Design: Portrait of President Jefferson, gray "2" to left, red seal to right over "TWO"

Back Design: Same as Note No. 22.

SERIES	SIGNATURES	SEAL	A.B.P.	GOOD	V. FINE	UNC.
☐ 1953	Priest-Humphrey	Red	2.30	— —	5.00	9.00
☐ 1953A	Priest-Anderson	Red	2.10	— —	4.25	8.00
☐ 1953B	Smith-Dillon	Red	2.10	— —	4.25	6.75
☐ 1953C	Granahan-Dillon	Red	2.10	— —	4.50	7.75

Back Design: "IN GOD WE TRUST" on back.
Face Design: Same as previous note.

SERIES	SIGNATURES	SEAL	A.B.P.	GOOD	V. FINE	UNC.
☐ 1963	Granahan-Dillon	Red	2.10	— —	3.80	6.00
☐ 1963A	Granahan-Fowler	Red	2.10	— —	3.80	6.35

Production of Two Dollar United States Notes was discontinued on Aug. 10, 1966.

48 / TWO DOLLAR NOTES

TWO DOLLAR NOTES (1875) NATIONAL BANK NOTES
FIRST CHARTER PERIOD (Large Size) **NOTE NO. 24**

Face Design: This note is known as "The Lazy Two Note" due to the unusual "lying down" shape of the "2" shown on the face. Liberty with flag and red seal.

Back Design: Sir Walter Raleigh in England, 1585 exhibiting corn and smoking tobacco from America, state seal and eagle.

SERIES	SIGNATURES	SEAL	A.B.P.	GOOD	V. FINE	UNC.
☐ Original	Colby-Spinner	Red	105.00	215.00	465.00	2475.00
☐ Original	Jeffries-Spinner	Red	400.00	800.00	2000.00	5250.00
☐ Original	Allison-Spinner	Red	105.00	215.00	465.00	2475.00
☐ 1875	Allison-New	Red	105.00	215.00	465.00	2475.00
☐ 1875	Allison-Wyman	Red	105.00	215.00	465.00	2475.00
☐ 1875	Allison-Gilfillan	Red	105.00	215.00	465.00	2475.00
☐ 1875	Scofield-Gilfillan	Red	105.00	215.00	465.00	2475.00

TWO DOLLAR NOTES (1886) SILVER CERTIFICATES
(Large Size) **NOTE NO. 25**

Face Design: General Hancock portrait left. Treasury seal to the right of center.

Back Design: "2" left and right, very ornate engraving, obligation in center of Note. Note is printed in green.

SERIES	SIGNATURES	SEAL	A.B.P.	GOOD	V. FINE	UNC.
☐1886	Rosecrans-Jordan	Red	32.00	60.00	200.00	1235.00
☐1886	Rosecrans-Hyatt	Red Sm.	28.00	53.00	190.00	1195.00
☐1886	Rosecrans-Hyatt	Red Lg.	28.00	53.00	190.00	1195.00
☐1886	Rosecrans-Huston	Red	28.00	53.00	190.00	1195.00
☐1886	Rosecrans-Huston	Brown	31.00	58.00	197.50	1220.00

50 / TWO DOLLAR NOTES

TWO DOLLAR NOTES (1891) SILVER CERTIFICATES
(Large Size)   NOTE NO. 26

Face Design: Portrait of William Windom, Secretary of the Treasury 1881-1884 and 1889-1891, red seal right.

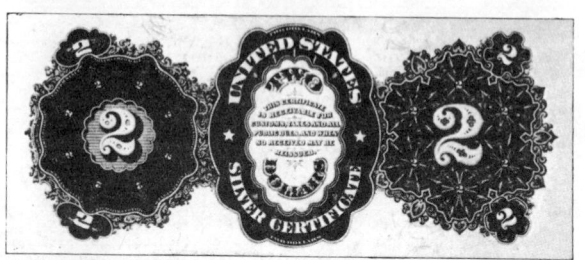

Back Design: "2" left and right, scalloped design center with obligation, printed in green.

SERIES	SIGNATURES	SEAL	A.B.P.	GOOD	V. FINE	UNC.
☐ 1891	Rosecrans-Nebeker	Red	48.00	97.50	315.00	1925.00
☐ 1891	Tillman-Morgan	Red	48.00	97.50	315.00	1925.00

TWO DOLLAR NOTES / 51

TWO DOLLAR NOTES (1896) SILVER CERTIFICATES
(Large Size) **NOTE NO. 27**

Face Design: Science presenting Steam and Electricity to Industry and Commerce.

Back Design: Portraits of Robert Fulton and Samuel F. B. Morse.

THIS IS THE SECOND NOTE OF THE POPULAR EDUCATIONAL SERIES

SERIES	SIGNATURES	SEAL	A.B.P.	GOOD	V. FINE	UNC.
☐1896	Tillman-Morgan	Red	50.00	100.00	415.00	2050.00
☐1896	Bruce-Roberts	Red	50.00	100.00	400.00	2050.00

52 / TWO DOLLAR NOTES

TWO DOLLAR NOTES (1899) SILVER CERTIFICATES
(Large Size) NOTE NO. 28

Face Design: Portrait of President Washington between figures of Trade and Agriculture, blue "2" left, blue seal right.

Back Design

SERIES	SIGNATURES	SEAL	A.B.P.	GOOD	V. FINE	UNC.
☐1899	Lyons-Roberts	Blue	18.00	35.00	100.00	450.00
☐1899	Lyons-Treat	Blue	18.00	35.00	95.00	325.00
☐1899	Vernon-Treat	Blue	18.00	35.00	80.00	285.00
☐1899	Vernon-McClung	Blue	18.00	35.00	80.00	285.00
☐1899	Napier-McClung	Blue	18.00	35.00	80.00	285.00
☐1899	Napier-Thompson	Blue	35.00	70.00	250.00	1320.00
☐1899	Parker-Burke	Blue	18.00	35.00	82.00	340.00
☐1899	Teehee-Burke	Blue	18.00	35.00	82.00	285.00
☐1899	Elliott-Burke	Blue	18.00	35.00	82.00	285.00
☐1899	Speelman-White	Blue	18.00	35.00	82.00	285.00

TWO DOLLAR NOTES (1890-1891) TREASURY OR COIN NOTES
(Large Size) **NOTE NO. 29**

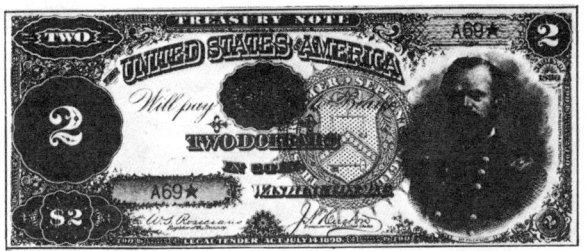

Face Design: Portrait of General James McPherson.

Back Design: Large "TWO" center, over obligation. Large "2" on engraved background right. Intricate engraving, printed green.

SERIES	SIGNATURES	SEAL	A.B.P.	GOOD	V. FINE	UNC.
☐ 1890	Rosecrans-Huston	Brown	65.00	140.00	470.00	3120.00
☐ 1890	Rosecrans-Nebeker	Brown	65.00	130.00	470.00	3120.00
☐ 1890	Rosecrans-Nebeker	Red	40.00	90.00	430.00	3175.00

TWO DOLLAR NOTES (1890-1891) TREASURY OR COIN NOTES
(Large Size) **NOTE NO. 30**

Face Design: Similar to NOTE NO. 29
Back Design: Revised.

SERIES	SIGNATURES	SEAL	A.B.P.	GOOD	V. FINE	UNC.
☐ 1891	Rosecrans-Nebeker	Red	38.00	75.00	235.00	850.00
☐ 1891	Tillman-Morgan	Red	38.00	75.00	235.00	850.00
☐ 1891	Bruce-Roberts	Red	38.00	75.00	235.00	850.00

54 / TWO DOLLAR NOTES

TWO DOLLAR NOTES (1918) FEDERAL RESERVE BANK NOTES
(Large Size)   NOTE NO. 31

Face Design: Portrait of President Jefferson to left, name of Bank in center, blue seal to the right, blue numbers, Federal Reserve district letter and number in four corners.

Back Design: American battleship of World War I.

TWO DOLLAR NOTES / 55

TWO DOLLAR NOTES (1918) FEDERAL RESERVE BANK NOTES
(Large Size)   NOTE NO. 31

BANK & CITY	GOV'T SIGNATURES	BANK SIGNATURES	A.B.P.	GOOD	V. FINE	UNC.
☐ Boston	Teehee-Burke	Bullen-Morss	18.00	42.00	120.00	525.00
☐ Boston	Teehee-Burke	Willet-Morss	18.00	42.00	120.00	525.00
☐ Boston	Elliot-Burke	Willet-Morss	18.00	42.00	120.00	525.00
☐ New York	Teehee-Burke	Sailer-Strong	18.00	42.00	120.00	525.00
☐ New York	Teehee-Burke	Hendricks-Strong	18.00	42.00	120.00	525.00
☐ New York	Elliott-Burke	Hendricks-Strong	18.00	42.00	120.00	525.00
☐ Philadelphia	Teehee-Burke	Hardt-Passmore	17.00	37.00	115.00	525.00
☐ Philadelphia	Teehee-Burke	Dyer-Passmore	17.00	37.00	115.00	525.00
☐ Philadelphia	Elliott-Burke	Dyer-Passmore	21.00	45.00	125.00	540.00
☐ Philadelphia	Elliott-Burke	Dyer-Norris	17.00	37.00	115.00	525.00
☐ Cleveland	Teehee-Burke	Baxter-Fancher	17.00	37.00	115.00	525.00
☐ Cleveland	Teehee-Burke	Davis-Fancher	17.00	37.00	115.00	525.00
☐ Cleveland	Elliott-Burke	Davis-Fancher	17.00	37.00	115.00	525.00
☐ Richmond	Teehee-Burke	Keesee-Seay	17.00	37.00	115.00	525.00
☐ Richmond	Elliott-Burke	Keesee-Seay	17.00	37.00	115.00	525.00
☐ Atlanta	Teehee-Burke	Pike-McCord	17.00	37.00	115.00	525.00
☐ Atlanta	Teehee-Burke	Bell-McCord	21.00	45.00	125.00	530.00
☐ Atlanta	Elliott-Burke	Bell-Wellborn	17.00	37.00	115.00	525.00
☐ Chicago	Teehee-Burke	McCloud-McDougal	17.00	37.00	115.00	525.00
☐ Chicago	Teehee-Burke	Cramer-McDougal	17.00	37.00	115.00	525.00
☐ Chicago	Elliott-Burke	Cramer-McDougal	17.00	37.00	115.00	525.00
☐ St. Louis	Teehee-Burke	Attebery-Wells	17.00	37.00	115.00	525.00
☐ St. Louis	Teehee-Burke	Attebery-Biggs	19.00	42.00	120.00	530.00
☐ St. Louis	Elliott-Burke	Attebery-Biggs	19.00	42.00	120.00	530.00
☐ St. Louis	Elliott-Burke	White-Biggs	19.00	42.00	120.00	530.00
☐ Minneapolis	Teehee-Burke	Cook-Wold	19.00	42.00	120.00	530.00
☐ Minneapolis	Elliott-Burke	Cook-Young	19.00	42.00	120.00	530.00
☐ Kansas City	Teehee-Burke	Anderson-Miller	17.00	37.00	115.00	530.00
☐ Kansas City	Elliott-Burke	Helm-Miller	20.00	45.00	125.00	535.00
☐ Dallas	Teehee-Burke	Talley-VanZandt	20.00	45.00	125.00	535.00
☐ Dallas	Elliott-Burke	Talley-VanZandt	20.00	45.00	125.00	535.00
☐ San Francisco	Teehee-Burke	Clerk-Lynch	17.00	37.00	115.00	535.00
☐ San Francisco	Elliott-Burke	Clerk-Calkins	17.00	42.00	115.00	530.00
☐ San Francisco	Elliott-Burke	Ambrose-Calkins	17.00	42.00	115.00	530.00

56 / TWO DOLLAR NOTES

TWO DOLLAR (1976) FEDERAL RESERVE NOTES
(Small Size)　　　　　　　　　　　　　　　　　　　　　　**NOTE NO. 31A**

Face Design: Portrait of President Jefferson

Back Design: Signing Of The Declaration of Independence

SERIES OF 1976 NEFF-SIMON — GREEN SEAL

DISTRICT	A.B.P.	UNC.	DISTRICT	A.B.P.	UNC.
☐ 1A Boston	2.10	4.25	☐ 7G Chicago	2.10	4.25
☐ 2B New York	2.10	4.25	☐ 8H St. Louis	2.10	4.25
☐ 3C Philadelphia	2.10	4.25	☐ 9I Minneapolis	2.10	4.25
☐ 4D Cleveland	2.10	4.25	☐ 10J Kansas City	2.10	4.25
☐ 5E Richmond	2.10	4.25	☐ 11K Dallas	2.10	4.25
☐ 6F Atlanta	2.10	4.25	☐ 12L San Francisco	2.10	4.25

FIVE DOLLAR NOTES

ORDER OF ISSUE

	FIRST ISSUE	LAST ISSUE	PAGE
1. DEMAND NOTES	1861 only		58
2. UNITED STATES NOTES	1862—	1963	59
3. NATIONAL BANK NOTES	1863—	1929	64
4. NATIONAL GOLD BANK NOTES	1870—	1874	71
5. SILVER CERTIFICATES	1886—	1953	72
6. TREASURY OR COIN NOTES	1890—	1891	79
7. FEDERAL RESERVE NOTES	1914—	present	80
8. FEDERAL RESERVE BANK NOTES	1915—	1929	88

58 / FIVE DOLLAR NOTES

FIVE DOLLAR NOTES (1861) DEMAND NOTES
(Large Size) NOTE NO. 32

Face Design: Left, Statue of America by Crawford atop United States Capitol. Center, numeral "5" in green. Right, Portrait of Alexander Hamilton, statesman, first Secretary of the Treasury.

Back Design: Numerous small "Fives" in ovals. This note has no Treasury Seal. The signatures are those of Treasury Department employees who signed for the Officials.

PAYABLE AT	A.B.P.	GOOD	V. GOOD
☐ Boston (I)	235.00	460.00	925.00
☐ New York (I)	235.00	460.00	925.00
☐ Philadelphia (I)	235.00	460.00	925.00
☐ Cincinnati (I)	1250.00	2800.00	4450.00
☐ St. Louis (I)	785.00	1675.00	3500.00
☐ Boston (II)	195.00	390.00	595.00
☐ New York (II)	195.00	390.00	595.00
☐ Philadelphia (II)	195.00	390.00	595.00
☐ Cincinnati (II)	825.00	1850.00	3175.00
☐ St. Louis (II)	535.00	1175.00	1950.00

FIVE DOLLAR NOTES / 59

FIVE DOLLAR NOTES (1862) UNITED STATES NOTES
(ALSO KNOWN AS LEGAL TENDER NOTES)
(Large Size) **NOTE NO. 33**

Face Design: Similar to Note No. 32

Back Design: Note No. 33 First Obligation

Back Design: Note No. 33A Second Obligation

SERIES	SIGNATURES	SEAL	A.B.P.	GOOD	V. FINE	UNC.
☐ 1862	Crittenden-Spinner*	Red	28.00	55.00	175.00	1075.00
☐ 1862	Crittenden-Spinner**	Red	28.00	55.00	175.00	1100.00
☐ 1863	Crittenden-Spinner**	Red	28.00	55.00	175.00	1085.00

*FIRST OBLIGATION—**SECOND OBLIGATION

60 / FIVE DOLLAR NOTES

FIVE DOLLAR NOTES (1869) UNITED STATES NOTES
(ALSO KNOWN AS LEGAL TENDER NOTES)

(Large Size) NOTE NO. 34

Face Design: Portrait of President Jackson on left. Pioneer and family in center.

Back Design: Color, green. This is a companion note to the $1.00 and $2.00 notes of 1869 Rainbow Notes.

SERIES	SIGNATURES	SEAL	A.B.P.	GOOD	V. FINE	UNC.
☐ 1869	Allison-Spinner	Red	25.00	57.50	200.00	795.00

FIVE DOLLAR NOTES / 61

FIVE DOLLAR NOTES (1875-1907) UNITED STATES
(ALSO KNOWN AS LEGAL TENDER NOTES)
(Large Size) **NOTE NO. 35**

Back Design: Revised
Face Design: Similar to previous Note.

SERIES	SIGNATURES	SEAL	A.B.P.	GOOD	V. FINE	UNC.
☐1875	Allison-New	Red	16.00	25.00	105.00	365.00
☐1875A	Allison-New	Red	24.00	52.00	125.00	575.00
☐1875B	Allison-New	Red	24.00	52.00	125.00	600.00
☐1875	Allison-Wyman	Red	22.00	47.00	120.00	545.00
☐1878	Allison-Gilfillan	Red	21.00	45.00	130.00	570.00
☐1880	Scofield-Gilfillan	Brown	17.00	35.00	70.00	340.00
☐1880	Bruce-Gilfillan	Brown	17.00	35.00	70.00	340.00
☐1880	Bruce-Wyman	Brown	17.00	35.00	70.00	340.00
☐1880	Bruce-Wyman	Red	16.00	32.00	85.00	500.00
☐1880	Rosecrans-Jordan	Red	17.00	35.00	85.00	515.00
☐1880	Rosecrans-Hyatt	Red	18.00	37.00	120.00	565.00
☐1880	Rosecrans-Huston	Red	22.00	45.00	130.00	590.00
☐1880	Rosecrans-Huston	Brown	15.00	30.00	95.00	380.00
☐1880	Rosecrans-Nebeker	Brown	22.00	45.00	95.00	380.00
☐1880	Rosecrans-Nebeker	Red	14.00	28.00	60.00	320.00
☐1880	Tilman-Morgan	Red	14.00	28.00	60.00	320.00
☐1880	Bruce-Roberts	Red	14.00	28.00	60.00	320.00
☐1880	Lyons-Roberts	Red	14.00	28.00	60.00	320.00
☐1907	Vernon-Treat	Red	7.50	15.00	43.00	170.00
☐1907	Vernon-McClung	Red	7.50	15.00	43.00	170.00
☐1907	Napier-McClung	Red	7.50	15.00	43.00	170.00
☐1907	Napier-Thompson	Red	27.00	53.00	230.00	600.00
☐1907	Parker-Burke	Red	7.50	15.00	43.00	145.00
☐1907	Teehee-Burke	Red	7.50	15.00	43.00	145.00
☐1907	Elliott-Burke	Red	7.50	15.00	43.00	145.00
☐1907	Elliot-White	Red	7.50	15.00	43.00	145.00
☐1907	Speelman-White	Red	7.50	15.00	43.00	145.00
☐1907	Woods-White	Red	7.50	15.00	43.00	145.00

62 / FIVE DOLLAR NOTES

FIVE DOLLAR NOTES (1928) UNITED STATES NOTES
(ALSO KNOWN AS LEGAL TENDER NOTES)
(Small Size) NOTE NO. 36

Face Design: Portrait of President Lincoln center. Red seal to left, red serial numbers.

Back Design: Lincoln Memorial in Washington, D.C.

SERIES	SIGNATURES	SEAL	A.B.P.	GOOD	V. FINE	UNC.
☐ 1928	Woods-Mellon	Red	5.20	6.00	9.00	30.00
☐ 1928A	Woods-Mills	Red	5.20	6.25	12.50	67.00
☐ 1928B	Julian-Morgenthau	Red	5.20	6.00	10.00	32.00
☐ 1928C	Julian-Morgenthau	Red	5.20	6.00	11.00	22.00
☐ 1928D	Julian-Vinson	Red	5.75	10.00	23.00	112.00
☐ 1928E	Julian-Snyder	Red	5.20	6.00	9.75	18.75
☐ 1928F	Clark-Snyder	Red	5.20	6.00	9.75	18.75

FIVE DOLLAR NOTES (1953-1963) UNITED STATES NOTES
(Small Size) NOTE NO. 37

Face Design: Similar to previous note. Portrait of President Lincoln center. Red seal is moved to the right, red numbers.
Back Design: Similar to previous Note.

SERIES	SIGNATURES	SEAL	A.B.P.	GOOD	V. FINE	UNC.
☐ 1953	Priest-Humphrey	Red	5.20	5.50	9.00	15.25
☐ 1953A	Priest-Anderson	Red		5.25	8.25	12.75
☐ 1953B	Smith-Dillon	Red		5.25	8.25	12.75
☐ 1953C	Granahan-Dillon	Red		5.25	8.25	12.75

FIVE DOLLAR NOTES (1953-1963) UNITED STATES NOTES
(ALSO KNOWN AS LEGAL TENDER NOTES)
(Small Size) NOTE NO. 37A

SERIES OF 1963

Back Design: The following notes have "IN GOD WE TRUST" on the back.
Face Design: Similar to previous Note.

SERIES	SIGNATURES	SEAL	A.B.P.	GOOD	V. FINE	UNC.
☐ 1963	Granahan-Dillon	Red		5.20	6.75	11.25

Production of Five Dollar United States Notes ended in 1967.

64 / FIVE DOLLAR NOTES

FIVE DOLLAR NOTES (1863-1875) NATIONAL BANK NOTES
FIRST CHARTER PERIOD (Large Size) NOTE NO. 38

Face Design: The Columbus Note. The face shows Columbus in sight of land and Columbus presenting an Indian Princess.

Back Design: Christopher Columbus landing at San Salvador 1492. Also the State seal left, and American Eagle right.

SERIES	SIGNATURES	SEAL	A.B.P.	GOOD	V. FINE	UNC.
☐Original	Chittenden-Spinner	Red	37.00	72.00	335.00	1675.00
☐Original	Colby-Spinner	Red	37.00	72.00	335.00	1675.00
☐Original	Jeffries-Spinner	Red	150.00	350.00	1300.00	3000.00
☐Original	Allison-Spinner	Red	37.00	72.00	335.00	1695.00
☐1875	Allison-New	Red	39.00	80.00	310.00	1695.00
☐1875	Allison-Wyman	Red	39.00	80.00	310.00	1695.00
☐1875	Allison-Gilfillan	Red	39.00	80.00	310.00	1695.00
☐1875	Scofield-Gilfillan	Red	39.00	80.00	310.00	1695.00
☐1875	Bruce-Gilfillan	Red	39.00	80.00	310.00	1695.00
☐1875	Bruce-Wyman	Red	39.00	80.00	310.00	1695.00
☐1875	Bruce-Jordan	Red		EXTREMELY RARE		
☐1875	Rosecrans-Huston	Red	42.00	85.00	315.00	1670.00
☐1875	Rosecrans-Jordan	Red	42.00	85.00	315.00	1670.00

FIVE DOLLAR NOTES / 65

FIVE DOLLAR NOTES (1882) NATIONAL BANK NOTES
SECOND CHARTER PERIOD (Large Size)   NOTE NO. 39

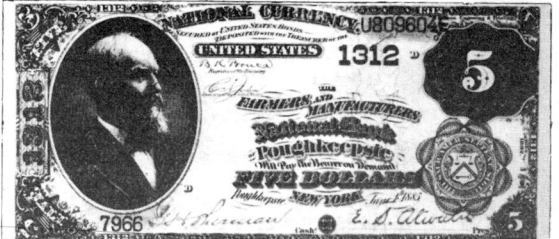

First Issue brown seal and brown backs.

Face Design: Portrait of President Garfield left. Name of Bank and City center, brown seal to right. Brown charter number.

Back Design: Brown border-design similar to previous note. Center oval now has the Bank's charter number in green. The top signatures are those of the Treasury Officials. Bottom signatures, usually hand written or probably rubber stamped, are Bank Officials.

SERIES	SIGNATURES	SEAL	A.B.P.	GOOD	V. FINE	UNC.
☐1882	Bruce-Gilfillan	Brown	27.00	52.00	145.00	525.00
☐1882	Bruce-Wyman	Brown	27.00	52.00	145.00	525.00
☐1882	Bruce-Jordan	Brown	27.00	52.00	145.00	525.00
☐1882	Rosecrans-Jordan	Brown	27.00	52.00	145.00	525.00
☐1882	Rosecrans-Hyatt	Brown	27.00	52.00	145.00	525.00
☐1882	Rosecrans-Huston	Brown	27.00	52.00	145.00	575.00
☐1882	Rosecrans-Nebeker	Brown	27.00	52.00	145.00	525.00
☐1882	Rosecrans-Morgan	Brown	70.00	150.00	450.00	1125.00
☐1882	Tillman-Morgan	Brown	27.00	52.00	145.00	525.00
☐1882	Tillman-Roberts	Brown	27.00	52.00	145.00	525.00
☐1882	Bruce-Roberts	Brown	27.00	52.00	145.00	525.00
☐1882	Lyons-Roberts	Brown	27.00	52.00	145.00	525.00
☐1882	Lyons-Treat	(Unknown in any collection)				
☐1882	Vernon-Treat	Brown	34.00	65.00	165.00	575.00

66 / FIVE DOLLAR NOTES

FIVE DOLLAR NOTES (1882) NATIONAL BANK NOTES
SECOND CHARTER PERIOD (Large Size) NOTE NO. 40

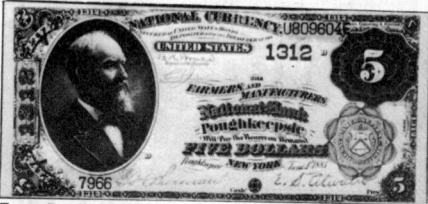

Face Design: Similar to preceding portrait of President Garfield.

Back Design: Back is now green with date 1882-1908 in center.

SERIES	SIGNATURES	SEAL	A.B.P.	GOOD	V. FINE	UNC.
☐ 1882	Rosecrans-Huston	Blue	23.50	50.00	160.00	625.00
☐ 1882	Rosecrans-Nebeker	Blue	23.50	50.00	160.00	625.00
☐ 1882	Rosecrans-Morgan	Blue	90.00	180.00	815.00	2000.00
☐ 1882	Tillman-Morgan	Blue	23.50	50.00	160.00	625.00
☐ 1882	Tillman-Roberts	Blue	23.50	50.00	160.00	625.00
☐ 1882	Bruce-Roberts	Blue	23.50	50.00	160.00	625.00
☐ 1882	Lyons-Roberts	Blue	23.50	50.00	160.00	625.00
☐ 1882	Vernon-Treat	Blue	23.50	50.00	160.00	625.00
☐ 1882	Vernon-McClung	RARE				
☐ 1882	Napier-McClung	RARE				

FIVE DOLLAR NOTES / 67

FIVE DOLLAR NOTES (1882) NATIONAL BANK NOTES
SECOND CHARTER PERIOD, Third Issue (Large Size)   **NOTE NO. 41**

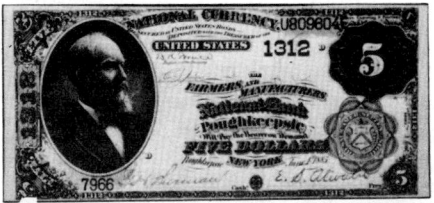

Face Design: Same as Note No. 39. Blue Seal.

Back Design: Similar to Note No. 40, "FIVE DOLLARS" replaces 1882-1908.

SERIES	SIGNATURES	SEAL	A.B.P.	GOOD	V. FINE	UNC.
☐1882	Tillman-Morgan	Blue	36.00	70.00	350.00	1625.00
☐1882	Tillman-Roberts	Blue	57.00	110.00	475.00	1785.00
☐1882	Bruce-Roberts	Blue	57.00	110.00	475.00	1785.00
☐1882	Lyons-Roberts	Blue	36.00	70.00	350.00	1600.00
☐1882	Vernon-Treat	Blue	41.00	80.00	350.00	1600.00
☐1882	Napier-McClung	Blue	41.00	80.00	350.00	1600.00
☐1882	Teehee-Burke	Blue			EXTREMELY RARE	

68 / FIVE DOLLAR NOTES

FIVE DOLLAR NOTES (1902) NATIONAL BANK NOTES
THIRD CHARTER PERIOD (Large Size)   **NOTE NO. 42**

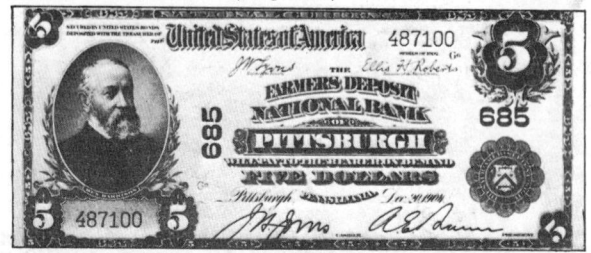

First Issue — red seal and charter numbers.
Face Design: Portrait of President Harrison left, name of Bank and City center, Treasury Seal to right, red seal and Charter number.

Back Design: Landing of Pilgrims.

SERIES	SIGNATURES	SEAL	A.B.P.	GOOD	V. FINE	UNC.
☐ 1902	Lyons-Roberts	Red	25.00	50.00	170.00	800.00
☐ 1902	Lyons-Treat	Red	31.00	60.00	180.00	800.00
☐ 1902	Vernon-Treat	Red	34.00	75.00	210.00	800.00

FIVE DOLLAR NOTES / 69

FIVE DOLLAR NOTES (1902) NATIONAL BANK NOTES
THIRD CHARTER PERIOD (Large Size)   **NOTE NO. 42A**

Second Issue — seal, Charter numbers and serial numbers are now changed to blue, back of note now has 1902-1908 added.

SERIES	SIGNATURES	SEAL	A.B.P.	GOOD	V. FINE	UNC.
☐ 1902	Lyons-Roberts	Blue	10.00	20.00	50.00	300.00
☐ 1902	Lyons-Treat	Blue	10.00	20.00	50.00	300.00
☐ 1902	Vernon-Treat	Blue	10.00	20.00	50.00	300.00
☐ 1902	Vernon-McClung	Blue	10.00	20.00	50.00	300.00
☐ 1902	Napier-McClung	Blue	10.00	20.00	50.00	300.00
☐ 1902	Napier-Thompson	Blue	23.00	45.00	130.00	590.00
☐ 1902	Napier-Burke	Blue	10.00	20.00	50.00	300.00
☐ 1902	Parker-Burke	Blue	10.00	20.00	50.00	300.00
☐ 1902	Teehee-Burke	Blue	28.00	60.00	145.00	510.00

FIVE DOLLAR NOTES (1902) NATIONAL BANK NOTES
Third Charter Period (Large Size)   **NOTE NO. 42B**

Third Issue—blue seal and numbers. The following Notes do not have date of 1902-1908 on the back.

SERIES	SIGNATURES	SEAL	A.B.P.	GOOD	V. FINE	UNC.
☐ 1902	Lyons-Roberts	Blue	8.25	17.00	42.00	215.00
☐ 1902	Lyons-Treat	Blue	8.25	17.00	42.00	215.00
☐ 1902	Vernon-Treat	Blue	8.25	17.00	42.00	215.00
☐ 1902	Vernon-McClung	Blue	8.25	17.00	42.00	215.00
☐ 1902	Napier-McClung	Blue	8.25	17.00	42.00	215.00
☐ 1902	Napier-Thompson	Blue	8.25	17.00	42.00	215.00
☐ 1902	Napier-Burke	Blue	8.25	17.00	42.00	215.00
☐ 1902	Parker-Burke	Blue	8.25	17.00	42.00	215.00
☐ 1902	Teehee-Burke	Blue	8.25	17.00	42.00	215.00
☐ 1902	Elliott-Burke	Blue	8.25	17.00	42.00	215.00
☐ 1902	Elliott-White	Blue	8.25	17.00	42.00	215.00
☐ 1902	Speelman-White	Blue	8.35	17.00	42.00	215.00
☐ 1902	Woods-White	Blue	8.25	17.00	42.00	215.00
☐ 1902	Woods-Tate	Blue	11.00	21.00	45.00	240.00
☐ 1902	Jones-Wood	Blue	42.00	85.00	220.00	675.00

70 / FIVE DOLLAR NOTES

FIVE DOLLAR NOTES (1929) NATIONAL BANK NOTES
(Small Size) NOTE NO. 43

TYPE I

TYPE II

Face Design: Portrait of President Lincoln in center, name of Bank to left, brown seal to the right. TYPE I — Charter number in black. TYPE II — Similar, Charter number added in brown.

Back Design: Lincoln Memorial.

SERIES	SIGNATURES	SEAL	A.B.P.	GOOD	V. FINE	UNC.
☐1929 TYPE I	Jones-Woods	Brown	5.10	6.50	19.00	70.00
☐1929 TYPE II	Jones-Woods	Brown	5.15	7.50	24.00	95.00

FIVE DOLLAR NOTES (1870) NATIONAL GOLD BANK NOTES
(Large Size) **NOTE NO. 38A**

Face Design: Vignettes of Columbus sighting land. Presentation of an Indian Princess. Red seal. Signatures, Allison-Spinner.

Back Design: California State Seal left, gold coins center, American Eagle right.

DATE	NAME OF BANK	CITY	A.B.P.	GOOD	V. GOOD
☐1870	First National Gold Bank	San Francisco	275.00	585.00	1125.00
☐1872	National Gold Bank and Trust Company	San Francisco	275.00	585.00	1125.00
☐1872	National Gold Bank of D.O. Mills and Company	Sacramento	370.00	815.00	1250.00
☐1873	First National Gold Bank	Santa Barbara	360.00	770.00	1250.00
☐1873	First National Gold Bank	Stockton	360.00	770.00	1250.00
☐1874	Farmers Nat'l Gold Bank	San Jose	360.00	770.00	1250.00

72 / FIVE DOLLAR NOTES

FIVE DOLLAR NOTES (1886-1891) SILVER CERTIFICATES
(Large Size) **NOTE NO. 45**

Face Design: Portrait of President Grant.

Back Design: Five silver dollars.

SERIES	SIGNATURES	SEAL	A.B.P.	GOOD	V. FINE	UNC.
☐1886	Rosecrans-Jordan	Red	65.00	135.00	410.00	2425.00
☐1886	Rosecrans-Hyatt	Red Sm.	65.00	135.00	400.00	2425.00
☐1886	Rosecrans-Hyatt	Red Lg.	75.00	155.00	450.00	2425.00
☐1886	Rosecrans-Huston	Red Lg.	70.00	150.00	430.00	245.00
☐1886	Rosecrans-Huston	Brown	82.00	165.00	500.00	2425.00
☐1886	Rosecrans-Nebeker	Brown	82.00	165.00	510.00	2425.00
☐1886	Rosecrans-Nebeker	Red Sm.	67.00	140.00	415.00	2425.00

FIVE DOLLAR NOTES / 73

FIVE DOLLAR NOTES (1891) SILVER CERTIFICATES
(Large Size) **NOTE NO. 46**

Face Design: Similar to previous Note.

Back Design: Revised.

SERIES	SIGNATURES	SEAL	A.B.P.	GOOD	V. FINE	UNC.
☐ 1891	Rosecrans-Nebeker	Red	42.00	90.00	315.00	2250.00
☐ 1891	Tillman-Morgan	Red	53.00	125.00	700.00	3375.00

74 / FIVE DOLLAR NOTES

FIVE DOLLAR NOTES (1896) SILVER CERTIFICATES
(Large Size)   **NOTE NO. 47**

Face Design: Portrait of General Grant and General Sheridan.

LAST NOTE OF THE POPULAR EDUCATIONAL SERIES

Back Design: Five Females representing electricity as the dominant force in the world.

SERIES	SIGNATURES	SEAL	A.B.P.	GOOD	V. FINE	UNC.
☐ 1896	Tillman-Morgan	Red	72.00	145.00	620.00	3375.00
☐ 1896	Bruce-Roberts	Red	72.00	145.00	620.00	3375.00
☐ 1896	Lyons-Roberts	Red	75.00	150.00	630.00	3415.00

FIVE DOLLAR NOTES / 75

FIVE DOLLAR NOTES (1899) SILVER CERTIFICATES
(Large Size) **NOTE NO. 48**

Face Design: Portrait of Indian Chief.

Back Design: Green "V" and "5"

SERIES	SIGNATURES	SEAL	A.B.P.	GOOD	V. FINE	UNC.
☐ 1899	Lyons-Roberts	Blue	26.00	52.00	180.00	935.00
☐ 1899	Lyons-Treat	Blue	26.00	52.00	180.00	935.00
☐ 1899	Vernon-Treat	Blue	26.00	52.00	180.00	935.00
☐ 1899	Vernon-McClung	Blue	26.00	52.00	180.00	935.00
☐ 1899	Napier-McClung	Blue	26.00	52.00	180.00	935.00
☐ 1899	Napier-Thompson	Blue	48.00	95.00	425.00	2750.00
☐ 1899	Parker-Burke	Blue	26.00	52.00	180.00	935.00
☐ 1899	Teehee-Burke	Blue	26.00	52.00	180.00	935.00
☐ 1899	Elliott-Burke	Blue	26.00	52.00	180.00	935.00
☐ 1899	Elliott-White	Blue	26.00	52.00	180.00	935.00
☐ 1899	Speelman-White	Blue	26.00	52.00	180.00	935.00

76 / FIVE DOLLAR NOTES

FIVE DOLLAR NOTES (1923) SILVER CERTIFICATES
(Large Size)   **NOTE NO. 49**

Face Design: Portrait of President Lincoln in oval, nicknamed "Porthole Note", blue seal left, blue "5" right.

Back Design: Obverse of Great Seal of the United States.

SERIES	SIGNATURES	SEAL	A.B.P.	GOOD	V. FINE	UNC.
☐1923	Speelman-White	Blue	29.00	57.50	250.00	925.00

FIVE DOLLAR NOTES (1934) SILVER CERTIFICATES
(Small Size) **NOTE NO. 50**

First Issue — small size of $5.00 Silver Certificates 1934.
Face Design: Portrait of President Lincoln, blue "5" to left, blue seal to right.

Back Design: All small size $5.00 notes have the same back design.

SERIES	SIGNATURES	SEAL	A.B.P.	GOOD	V. FINE	UNC.
☐1934	Julian-Morgenthau	Blue	5.20	6.00	12.00	25.00
☐1934A	Jullian-Morgenthau	Blue	5.20	6.00	9.00	17.50
☐1934A	Jullian-Morgenthau	Yellow	5.50	8.00	22.00	200.00

This note, with Yellow Treasury Seal was a Special Issue during World War II, for military use in combat areas of North Africa and Europe.

☐1934B	Julian-Vinson	Blue	5.20	6.50	14.00	48.00
☐1934C	Julian-Snyder	Blue	5.20	6.00	9.00	21.00
☐1934D	Clark-Snyder	Blue	5.20	6.00	8.50	16.75

78 / FIVE DOLLAR NOTES

FIVE DOLLAR NOTES (1953) SILVER CERTIFICATES
(Small Size)   **NOTE NO. 51**

Face Design: The following Notes are similar to the previous Note. The face design has been revised. Gray "5" replaces blue "5" to left of Lincoln. Blue seal is slightly smaller.

Back Design: Same as previous Note.

SERIES	SIGNATURES	SEAL	A.B.P.	GOOD	V. FINE	UNC.
☐1953	Priest-Humphrey	Blue		5.25	6.00	15.85
☐1953A	Priest-Anderson	Blue		5.25	6.00	15.85
☐1953B	Smith-Dillon	Blue		5.25	6.00	15.85

Production of Five Dollar Silver Certificates ended in 1962.

FIVE DOLLAR NOTES / 79
FIVE DOLLAR NOTES (1890) TREASURY NOTES
(Large Size) **NOTE NO. 52**

Face Design: Portrait of General George Henry Thomas (1816-1870) the "Rock of Chickamaugua".

Back Design: NOTE NO. 52

SERIES	SIGNATURES	SEAL	A.B.P.	GOOD	V. FINE	UNC.
☐ 1890	Rosecrans-Huston	Brown	50.00	100.00	475.00	1875.00
☐ 1890	Rosecrans-Nebeker	Brown	50.00	100.00	475.00	1875.00
☐ 1890	Rosecrans-Nebeker	Red	45.00	95.00	475.00	1850.00

Back Design: NOTE NO. 53.
Face Design: Same as previous Note.

SERIES	SIGNATURES	SEAL	A.B.P.	GOOD	V. FINE	UNC.
☐ 1891	Rosecrans-Nebeker	Red	35.00	70.00	200.00	775.00
☐ 1891	Tillman-Morgan	Red	35.00	70.00	200.00	775.00
☐ 1891	Bruce-Roberts	Red	35.00	70.00	200.00	775.00
☐ 1891	Lyons-Roberts	Red	40.00	80.00	330.00	1025.00

80 / FIVE DOLLAR NOTES

FIVE DOLLAR NOTES (1914) FEDERAL RESERVE NOTES
(Large Size)   **NOTE NO. 54**

Face Design: Portrait of President Lincoln center, Federal Reserve Seal left, Treasury Seal right.

Back Design: Scene of Columbus in sight of land left, Landing of Pilgrims right.

Series of 1914—red Treasury Seal and red numbers.

SERIES	CITY	SIGNATURES	SEAL	A.B.P.	GOOD	V. FINE	UNC.
☐ 1914	Boston	Burke-McAdoo	Red	11.00	21.75	50.00	325.00
☐ 1914	New York	Burke-McAdoo	Red	11.00	21.75	50.00	325.00
☐ 1914	Philadelphia	Burke-McAdoo	Red	11.00	21.75	50.00	325.00
☐ 1914	Cleveland	Burke-McAdoo	Red	11.00	21.75	50.00	325.00
☐ 1914	Richmond	Burke-McAdoo	Red	11.00	21.75	50.00	325.00
☐ 1914	Atlanta	Burke-McAdoo	Red	11.00	21.75	50.00	325.00
☐ 1914	Chicago	Burke-McAdoo	Red	11.00	21.75	50.00	325.00
☐ 1914	St. Louis	Burke-McAdoo	Red	11.00	21.75	50.00	325.00
☐ 1914	Minneapolis	Burke-McAdoo	Red	11.00	21.75	50.00	325.00
☐ 1914	Kansas City	Burke-McAdoo	Red	11.00	21.75	50.00	325.00
☐ 1914	Dallas	Burke-McAdoo	Red	11.00	21.75	50.00	325.00
☐ 1914	San Francisco	Burke-McAdoo	Red	11.00	21.75	50.00	325.00

FIVE DOLLAR NOTES (1914) FEDERAL RESERVE NOTES
Series of 1914—blue Treasury Seal and blue numbers. NOTE NO. 54A

SERIES	CITY	SIGNATURES	SEAL	A.B.P.	GOOD	V. FINE	UNC.
☐1914	Boston	Burke-McAdoo	Blue	5.50	9.00	18.00	115.00
☐1914	Boston	Burke-Glass	Blue	6.00	11.00	21.00	115.00
☐1914	Boston	Burke-Huston	Blue	5.50	9.00	18.00	115.00
☐1914	Boston	White-Mellon	Blue	5.50	9.00	18.00	115.00
☐1914	New York	Burke-McAdoo	Blue	5.50	9.00	18.00	115.00
☐1914	New York	Burke-Glass	Blue	6.00	12.00	21.00	115.00
☐1914	New York	Burke-Huston	Blue	5.50	9.00	18.00	115.00
☐1914	New York	White-Mellon	Blue	5.50	9.00	18.00	115.00
☐1914	Philadelphia	Burke-McAdoo	Blue	5.50	9.00	18.00	115.00
☐1914	Philadelphia	Burke-Glass	Blue	6.00	11.50	22.00	125.00
☐1914	Philadelphia	Burke-Huston	Blue	5.50	9.00	18.00	115.00
☐1914	Philadelphia	White-Mellon	Blue	5.50	9.00	18.00	115.00
☐1914	Cleveland	Burke-McAdoo	Blue	5.50	9.00	18.00	115.00
☐1914	Cleveland	Burke-Glass	Blue	6.00	12.00	21.00	115.00
☐1914	Cleveland	Burke-Huston	Blue	5.50	9.00	18.00	115.00
☐1914	Cleveland	White-Mellon	Blue	5.50	9.00	18.00	115.00
☐1914	Richmond	Burke-McAdoo	Blue	6.00	12.00	17.00	115.00
☐1914	Richmond	Burke-Glass	Blue	6.00	12.00	21.00	125.00
☐1914	Richmond	Burke-Huston	Blue	6.00	11.00	18.00	115.00
☐1914	Richmond	White-Mellon	Blue	6.00	11.00	18.00	115.00
☐1914	Atlanta	Burke-McAdoo	Blue	5.50	9.00	18.00	115.00
☐1914	Atlanta	Burke-Glass	Blue	6.50	13.00	23.00	125.00
☐1914	Atlanta	Burke-Huston	Blue	5.50	9.00	18.00	115.00
☐1914	Atlanta	White-Mellon	Blue	5.50	9.00	18.00	115.00
☐1914	Chicago	Burke-McAdoo	Blue	5.50	9.00	18.00	115.00
☐1914	Chicago	Burke-Glass	Blue	6.00	12.00	21.00	115.00
☐1914	Chicago	Burke-Huston	Blue	5.50	9.00	18.00	115.00
☐1914	Chicago	White-Mellon	Blue	5.50	9.00	18.00	115.00
☐1914	St. Louis	Burke-McAdoo	Blue	5.50	9.00	18.00	115.00
☐1914	St. Louis	Burke-Glass	Blue	6.00	12.00	22.00	115.00
☐1914	St. Louis	Burke-Huston	Blue	5.50	9.00	18.00	115.00
☐1914	St. Louis	White-Mellon	Blue	5.50	9.00	18.00	115.00
☐1914	Minneapolis	Burke-McAdoo	Blue	5.50	9.00	18.00	115.00
☐1914	Minneapolis	Burke-Glass	Blue	6.50	13.00	24.00	125.00
☐1914	Minneapolis	Burke-Huston	Blue	5.50	9.00	18.00	115.00
☐1914	Minneapolis	White-Mellon	Blue	5.50	9.00	18.00	115.00
☐1914	Kansas City	Burke-McAdoo	Blue	5.50	9.00	18.00	115.00
☐1914	Kansas City	Burke-Glass	Blue	6.00	12.00	21.00	115.00
☐1914	Kansas City	Burke-Huston	Blue	5.50	9.00	18.00	115.00
☐1914	Kansas City	White-Mellon	Blue	5.50	9.00	18.00	115.00
☐1914	Dallas	Burke-McAdoo	Blue	6.50	13.00	23.00	125.00
☐1914	Dallas	Burke-Glass	Blue	6.50	13.00	21.00	125.00
☐1914	Dallas	Burke-Huston	Blue	5.50	9.00	18.00	115.00
☐1914	Dallas	White-Mellon	Blue	5.50	9.00	18.00	115.00
☐1914	San Francisco	Burke-McAdoo	Blue	6.00	12.00	21.00	115.00
☐1914	San Francisco	Burke-Glass	Blue	6.00	12.00	21.00	115.00
☐1914	San Francisco	Burke-Huston	Blue	6.00	12.00	21.00	115.00
☐1914	San Francisco	White-Mellon	Blue	6.00	12.00	21.00	115.00

82 / FIVE DOLLAR NOTES

FIVE DOLLAR NOTES (1928) FEDERAL RESERVE NOTES
(Small Size)   **NOTE NO. 55**

Face Design: Portrait of President Lincoln center, black
Federal Reserve Seal with numeral for district in center.
City of issuing bank in seal circle.
Green Treasury Seal to right.
Back Design: Similar to Note No. 50,
Lincoln Memorial in Washington, D.C.

SERIES OF 1928 — SIGNATURES OF TATE AND MELLON, GREEN SEAL

BANK	A.B.P.	GOOD	V.FINE	UNC.	BANK	A.B.P.	GOOD	V.FINE	UNC.
☐Boston	5.50	7.00	14.00	40.00	☐Chicago	5.50	7.00	14.00	40.00
☐New York	5.50	7.00	11.00	33.00	☐St. Louis	5.50	7.00	14.00	40.00
☐Philadelphia	5.50	7.00	14.00	40.00	☐Minneapolis	5.50	7.00	14.00	40.00
☐Cleveland	5.50	7.00	14.00	40.00	☐Kansas City	5.50	7.00	14.00	40.00
☐Richmond	5.50	7.00	14.00	40.00	☐Dallas	5.50	7.00	14.00	40.00
☐Atlanta	5.50	7.00	14.00	40.00	☐San Francisco	5.50	7.00	14.00	40.00

SERIES OF 1928A — SIGNATURES OF WOODS-MELLON, GREEN SEAL

BANK	A.B.P.	GOOD	V.FINE	UNC.	BANK	A.B.P.	GOOD	V.FINE	UNC.
☐Boston	5.50	7.00	14.00	37.00	☐Chicago	5.50	7.00	14.00	37.00
☐New York	5.50	7.00	14.00	37.00	☐St. Louis	5.50	7.00	14.00	37.00
☐Philadelphia	5.50	7.00	14.00	37.00	☐Minneapolis	5.50	7.00	14.00	37.00
☐Cleveland	5.50	7.00	14.00	37.00	☐Kansas City	5.50	7.00	14.00	37.00
☐Richmond	5.50	7.00	14.00	37.00	☐Dallas	5.50	7.00	14.00	37.00
☐Atlanta	5.50	7.00	14.00	37.00	☐San Francisco	5.50	7.00	14.00	37.00

SERIES OF 1928B—SIGNATURES OF WOODS-MELLON, GREEN SEAL
BLACK FEDERAL RESERVE SEAL NOW HAS A LETTER FOR DISTRICT IN PLACE OF THE NUMERAL
(Small Size)

BANK	A.B.P.	GOOD	V.FINE	UNC.	BANK	A.B.P.	GOOD	V.FINE	UNC.
☐Boston	5.15	6.75	14.00	37.00	☐Chicago	5.15	6.75	14.00	37.00
☐New York	5.15	6.75	14.00	37.00	☐St. Louis	5.15	6.75	14.00	37.00
☐Philadelphia	5.15	6.75	14.00	37.00	☐Minneapolis	5.15	6.75	14.00	37.00
☐Cleveland	5.15	6.75	14.00	37.00	☐Kansas City	5.15	6.75	14.00	37.00
☐Richmond	5.15	6.75	14.00	37.00	☐Dallas	5.15	6.75	14.00	37.00
☐Atlanta	5.15	6.75	14.00	37.00	☐San Francisco	5.15	6.75	14.00	37.00

FIVE DOLLAR NOTES / 83

FIVE DOLLAR NOTES (1928) FEDERAL RESERVE NOTES
SERIES OF 1928C — SIGNATURES OF WOODS-MILLS, GREEN SEAL

BANK	A.B.P.	GOOD	V.FINE	UNC.	BANK	A.B.P.	GOOD	V.FINE	UNC.
☐ Cleveland	15.00	40.00	85.00	280.00	☐ San				
☐ Atlanta	15.00	40.00	85.00	280.00	Francisco	18.50	40.00	85.00	310.00

This series not issued by other banks.

SERIES OF 1928D — SIGNATURES OF WOODS-WOODIN, GREEN SEAL

BANK	A.B.P.	GOOD	V.FINE	UNC.
☐ Atlanta	50.00	80.00	200.00	550.00

This series not issued by other banks.

SERIES OF 1934 — JULIAN-MORGENTHAU, GREEN SEAL
("Redeemable in Gold" removed from obligation over Federal Reserve Seal.)

Note: The Green Treasury Seal on this note is known in a light and dark color. The light seal is worth about 10% to 20% more in most cases.

BANK	A.B.P.	V.FINE	UNC.	BANK	A.B.P.	V.FINE	UNC.
☐ Boston	5.50	9.50	34.00	☐ Kansas City	5.50	9.50	34.00
☐ New York	5.50	9.50	34.00	☐ Dallas	5.50	9.50	34.00
☐ Philadelphia	5.50	9.50	34.00	☐ San Francisco	5.50	9.50	34.00
☐ Cleveland	5.50	9.50	34.00	☐ San Francisco*	8.00	28.00	185.00
☐ Richmond	5.50	9.50	34.00				
☐ Atlanta	5.50	9.50	34.00	*This note with BROWN Treasury			
☐ Chicago	5.50	9.50	34.00	Seal and surcharged HAWAII. For			
☐ St. Louis	5.50	9.50	34.00	use in Pacific area of Operations			
☐ Minneapolis	5.50	9.50	34.00	during World War II.			

(Small Size)   NOTE NO. 56

SERIES OF 1934-1934A
1934A-JULIAN-MORGENTHAU, Surprinted HAWAII, used in Pacific area during World War II. Used with Brown Treasury Seal.

SERIES OF 1934A — JULIAN-MORGENTHAU, GREEN SEAL

BANK	A.B.P.	V.FINE	UNC.	BANK	A.B.P.	V.FINE	UNC.
☐ Boston	5.25	7.00	25.00	☐ San Francisco	5.50	9.00	26.00
☐ New York	5.25	7.00	23.00	☐ San Francisco*	7.00	21.00	180.00
☐ Philadelphia	5.25	7.00	21.00				
☐ Cleveland	5.25	7.00	23.00	*This note with BROWN			
☐ Richmond	5.50	7.00	26.00	Treasury Seal and surcharged			
☐ Atlanta	5.50	7.00	23.00	HAWAII. For use in Pacific area			
☐ Chicago	5.50	9.00	21.00	of operations during World War II.			
☐ St. Louis	5.50	9.00	25.00				

84 / FIVE DOLLAR NOTES

FIVE DOLLAR NOTES (1934) FEDERAL RESERVE NOTES
(Small Size)   NOTE NO. 56

Face Design: Same as Note No. 55. **Back Design:** Same as Note No. 50

SERIES OF 1934B — SIGNATURES OF JULIAN-VINSON, GREEN SEAL

BANK & CITY	A.B.P.	V.FINE	UNC.	BANK & CITY	A.B.P.	V.FINE	UNC.
☐Boston	6.00	12.00	33.75	☐Chicago	5.75	10.00	33.75
☐New York	5.75	10.00	33.75	☐St. Louis	6.00	14.50	33.75
☐Philadelphia	5.75	10.00	33.75	☐Minneapolis	6.00	14.50	33.75
☐Cleveland	5.75	10.00	33.75	☐Kansas City	6.00	14.50	33.75
☐Richmond	6.00	12.00	33.75	☐Dallas		Not Issued	
☐Atlanta	6.00	12.00	33.75	☐San Francisco	6.00	12.00	38.00

SERIES OF 1934C — SIGNATURES OF JULIAN-SNYDER, GREEN SEAL

BANK & CITY	A.B.P.	V.FINE	UNC.	BANK & CITY	A.B.P.	V.FINE	UNC.
☐Boston	5.25	8.00	24.00	☐Chicago	5.25	8.00	24.00
☐New York	5.25	8.00	24.00	☐St. Louis	5.25	8.00	24.00
☐Philadelphia	5.25	8.00	24.00	☐Minneapolis	5.25	8.00	24.00
☐Cleveland	5.25	8.00	24.00	☐Kansas City	5.25	8.00	24.00
☐Richmond	5.25	8.00	24.00	☐Dallas	5.25	8.00	24.00
☐Atlanta	5.25	8.00	24.00	☐San Francisco	5.25	8.00	24.00

SERIES OF 1934D — SIGNATURES OF CLARK-SNYDER, GREEN SEAL

BANK & CITY	A.B.P.	V.FINE	UNC.	BANK & CITY	A.B.P.	V.FINE	UNC.
☐Boston	5.15	6.50	17.00	☐Chicago	5.15	6.50	15.00
☐New York	5.15	6.50	14.00	☐St. Louis	5.50	8.00	18.00
☐Philadelphia	5.15	6.50	16.00	☐Minneapolis	5.50	8.00	19.00
☐Cleveland	5.15	6.50	18.00	☐Kansas City	5.50	6.00	19.00
☐Richmond	5.20	6.50	18.00	☐Dallas	5.75	9.00	21.00
☐Atlanta	5.30	7.00	18.00	☐San Francisco	5.25	7.00	18.00

FIVE DOLLAR NOTES (1950) FEDERAL RESERVE NOTES
BLACK FEDERAL RESERVE SEAL AND GREEN TREASURY SEALS
ARE NOW SMALLER
(Small Size)   NOTE NO. 57

Face Design: Similar to Note No. 55.   **Back Design:** Similar to Note No. 50.

FIVE DOLLAR NOTES (1950-1963) FEDERAL RESERVE NOTES
(Small Size)   **NOTE NO. 57**

SERIES OF 1950 — SIGNATURES OF CLARK-SNYDER, GREEN SEAL

BANK & CITY	A.B.P.	V.FINE	UNC.	BANK & CITY	A.B.P.	V.FINE	UNC.
☐Boston	5.15	7.00	15.75	☐Chicago	5.15	7.00	16.00
☐New York	5.15	7.00	13.75	☐St. Louis	5.15	7.00	17.00
☐Philadelphia	5.15	7.00	15.00	☐Minneapolis	5.15	7.00	17.50
☐Cleveland	5.15	7.00	15.00	☐Kansas City	5.15	7.00	17.00
☐Richmond	5.15	7.00	14.75	☐Dallas	5.15	7.00	17.00
☐Atlanta	5.15	7.00	15.00	☐San Francisco	5.15	7.00	16.00

SERIES OF 1950A — PRIEST-HUMPHREY, GREEN SEAL

Boston......14.25	Cleveland...14.25	Chicago.....14.25	Kansas City..14.25
New York...14.25	Richmond...14.25	St. Louis....14.75	Dallas......14.25
Philadelphia..14.25	Atlanta......14.25	Minneapolis..14.75	San Francisco 14.25

SERIES OF 1950B — PRIEST-ANDERSON, GREEN SEAL

Boston......13.60	Cleveland...13.00	Chicago.....12.00	Kansas City..14.25
New York...13.00	Richmond...13.00	St. Louis....14.50	Dallas......13.80
Philadelphia..13.00	Atlanta......13.00	Minneapolis..15.00	San Francisco 14.35

SERIES OF 1950C — SMITH-DILLON, GREEN SEAL

Boston......12.50	Cleveland...12.85	Chicago.....13.75	Kansas City..13.65
New York...12.25	Richmond...12.85	St. Louis....12.85	Dallas......15.75
Philadelphia..12.85	Atlanta......12.85	Minneapolis..13.75	San Francisco 14.25

SERIES OF 1950D — GRANAHAN-DILLON, GREEN SEAL

Boston......12.30	Cleveland...12.30	Chicago.....12.30	Kansas City..12.75
New York...12.30	Richmond...12.30	St. Louis....12.30	Dallas......12.75
Philadelphia..12.30	Atlanta......12.30	Minneapolis..12.75	San Francisco 12.30

SERIES OF 1950E — GRANAHAN-FOWLER, GREEN SEAL

New York ...16.25   Chicago.....17.00   San Francisco 16.50
This Note was issued by only three banks.

FIVE DOLLAR NOTES (1963) FEDERAL RESERVE NOTES
("IN GOD WE TRUST" IS ADDED ON THE BACK)
(Small Size) **NOTE NO. 57A**

SERIES OF 1963 — GRANAHAN-DILLON, GREEN SEAL

Boston......13.25	Cleveland...12.25	Chicago.....12.35	Kansas City..15.50
New York...12.25	Richmond...NONE	St. Louis....12.50	Dallas.......14.25
Philadelphia..11.75	Atlanta......12.25	Minneapolis..NONE	San Francisco 13.50

SERIES OF 1963A — GRANAHAN-FOWLER, GREEN SEAL

Boston......10.75	Cleveland...10.75	Chicago.....10.75	Kansas City..12.25
New York...12.00	Richmond...NONE	St. Louis....10.75	Dallas.......11.35
Philadelphia..10.75	Atlanta......10.75	Minneapolis..10.75	San Francisco 11.35

FIVE DOLLAR NOTES (1969) FEDERAL RESERVE NOTES
(WORDING IN GREEN TREASURY SEAL CHANGED FROM LATIN TO ENGLISH)
(Small Size) **NOTE NO. 57B**

SERIES OF 1969 — ELSTON-KENNEDY, GREEN SEAL

Boston........9.50	Cleveland....9.50	Chicago.....10.00	Kansas City..10.75
New York...9.50	Richmond....9.50	St. Louis....9.50	Dallas.......10.50
Philadelphia..9.50	Atlanta......9.50	Minneapolis..10.00	San Francisco 10.25

SERIES OF 1969A — KABIS-CONNALLY, GREEN SEAL

Boston........8.75	Cleveland....8.75	Chicago.....8.75	Kansas City..8.75
New York....8.75	Richmond....8.75	St. Louis....8.75	Dallas.......8.75
Philadelphia...8.75	Atlanta......8.75	Minneapolis..8.75	San Francisco .8.75

FIVE DOLLAR NOTES (1969) FEDERAL RESERVE NOTES
(WORDING IN GREEN TREASURY SEAL CHANGED FROM LATIN TO ENGLISH)
(Small Size) **NOTE NO. 57B**

SERIES OF 1969B — BANUELOS-CONNALLY, GREEN SEAL

Boston 8.25	Cleveland 8.25	Chicago 8.25	Kansas City ... 8.25
New York 8.25	Richmond 8.25	St. Louis 8.25	Dallas 8.25
Philadelphia ... 8.25	Atlanta 8.25	Minneapolis ... 8.25	San Francisco .8.25

SERIES OF 1969C — BANUELOS-SHULTZ, GREEN SEAL

Boston 8.00	Cleveland 8.00	Chicago 8.00	Kansas City ... 8.00
New York 8.00	Richmond 8.00	St. Louis 8.00	Dallas 8.00
Philadelphia ... 8.00	Atlanta 8.00	Minneapolis ... 8.00	San Francisco .8.00

SERIES OF 1974 — NEFF-SIMON, GREEN SEAL

Boston 7.75	Cleveland 7.75	Chicago 7.75	Kansas City ... 7.75
New York 7.75	Richmond 7.75	St. Louis 7.75	Dallas 7.75
Philadelphia ... 7.75	Atlanta 7.75	Minneapolis ... 7.75	San Francisco .7.75

SERIES OF 1977 — MORTON-BLUMENTHAL, GREEN SEAL

Boston 7.25	Cleveland 7.25	Chicago 7.25	Kansas City ... 7.25
New York 7.25	Richmond 7.25	St. Louis 7.25	Dallas 7.25
Philadelphia ... 7.25	Atlanta 7.25	Minneapolis ... 7.25	San Francisco .7.25

SERIES OF 1977A — MORTON-MILLER, GREEN SEAL

Boston 6.75	Cleveland 6.75	Chicago 6.75	Kansas City ... 6.75
New York 6.75	Richmond 6.75	St. Louis 6.75	Dallas 6.75
Philadelphia ... 6.75	Atlanta 6.75	Minneapolis ... 6.75	San Francisco .6.75

SERIES OF 1981 — BUCHANAN-REGAN, GREEN SEAL

Boston 5.50	Cleveland 5.50	Chicago 5.50	Kansas City ... 5.50
New York 5.50	Richmond 5.50	St. Louis 5.50	Dallas 5.50
Philadelphia ... 5.50	Atlanta 5.50	Minneapolis ... 5.50	San Francisco .5.50

SERIES OF 1981A — ORTEGA-REGAN, GREEN SEAL

Issued for all Federal Reserve Banks .... CURRENT.

88 / FIVE DOLLAR NOTES

FIVE DOLLAR NOTES (1918) FEDERAL RESERVE BANK NOTES
(ALL WITH BLUE SEAL AND BLUE SERIAL NUMBERS)
(Large Size) **NOTE NO. 58**

Face Design: Portrait of President Lincoln with Reserve City in center.
Back Design: Same as Note No. 54.

BANK & CITY	SERIES	GOVERNMENT SIGNATURES	BANK SIGNATURES	A.B.P.	GOOD	V. FINE	UNC.
☐ Boston	1918	Teehee-Burke	Bullen-Morse	135.00	300.00	1000.00	2500.00
☐ New York	1918	Teehee-Burke	Hendricks-Strong	16.00	33.00	110.00	385.00
☐ Phila.	1918	Teehee-Burke	Hardt-Passmore	16.00	33.00	110.00	385.00
☐ Phila.	1918	Teehee-Burke	Dyer-Passmore	16.00	33.00	110.00	385.00
☐ Cleveland	1918	Teehee-Burke	Baxter-Fancher	16.00	33.00	110.00	370.00
☐ Cleveland	1918	Teehee-Burke	Davis-Fancher	16.00	33.00	110.00	370.00
☐ Cleveland	1918	Elliott-Burke	Davis-Fancher	16.00	34.00	110.00	370.00
☐ Atlanta	1915	Teehee-Burke	Bell-Wellborn	30.00	60.00	130.00	465.00
☐ Atlanta	1915	Teehee-Burke	Pike-McCord	16.00	27.00	110.00	410.00
☐ Atlanta	1918	Teehee-Burke	Pike-McCord	16.00	33.00	115.00	385.00
☐ Atlanta	1918	Teehee-Burke	Bell-Wellborn	16.00	33.00	115.00	385.00
☐ Atlanta	1918	Elliott-Burke	Bell-Wellborn	16.00	33.00	115.00	385.00
☐ Chicago	1915	Teehee-Burke	McLallen-McDougal	16.00	33.00	112.00	400.00
☐ Chicago	1918	Teehee-Burke	McCloud-McDougal	16.00	33.00	115.00	370.00
☐ Chicago	1918	Teehee-Burke	Cramer-McDougal	16.00	33.00	115.00	385.00
☐ St. Louis	1918	Teehee-Burke	Attebery-Wells	16.00	33.00	115.00	385.00
☐ St. Louis	1918	Teehee-Burke	Attebery-Biggs	16.00	33.00	115.00	385.00
☐ St. Louis	1918	Elliott-Burke	White-Biggs	16.00	33.00	115.00	385.00
☐ Minn.	1918	Teehee-Burke	Cook-Wold	16.00	33.00	115.00	410.00
☐ Kan. City	1915	Teehee-Burke	Anderson-Miller	16.00	33.00	115.00	400.00
☐ Kan. City	1915	Teehee-Burke	Cross-Miller	15.00	29.00	90.00	370.00
☐ Kan. City	1915	Teehee-Burke	Helm-Miller	15.00	29.00	90.00	370.00
☐ Kan. City	1918	Teehee-Burke	Anderson-Miller	16.00	33.00	112.00	385.00
☐ Kan. City	1918	Elliott-Burke	Helm-Miller	16.00	33.00	112.00	385.00
☐ Dallas	1915	Teehee-Burke	Hoopes-VanZandt	16.00	33.00	105.00	370.00
☐ Dallas	1918	Teehee-Burke	Talley-VanZandt	17.00	34.00	130.00	385.00
☐ Dallas	1918	Teehee-Burke	Talley-VanZandt	16.00	29.00	80.00	370.00
☐ San Fran.	1915	Teehee-Burke	Clerk-Lynch	13.00	36.00	120.00	400.00
☐ San Fran.	1918	Teehee-Burke	Clerk-Lynch	16.00	48.00	130.00	465.00

FIVE DOLLAR NOTES (1929) FEDERAL RESERVE BANK NOTES
(Small Size)
NOTE NO. 59

Face Design: Portrait of President Lincoln.

SERIES 1929—brown seal.

BANK & CITY	SIGNATURES	A.B.P.	GOOD	V. FINE	UNC.
☐ Boston	Jones-Woods	5.15	5.50	17.00	65.00
☐ New York	Jones-Woods	5.15	6.00	15.00	60.00
☐ Philadelphia	Jones-Woods	5.15	5.50	16.00	75.00
☐ Cleveland	Jones-Woods	5.15	5.50	15.00	58.00
☐ Atlanta	Jones-Woods	5.15	6.00	19.00	105.00
☐ Chicago	Jones-Woods	5.15	5.50	13.00	60.00
☐ St. Louis	Jones-Woods	6.00	11.00	165.00	355.00
☐ Minneapolis	Jones-Woods	5.15	6.00	25.00	105.00
☐ Kansas City	Jones-Woods	5.15	5.50	15.00	72.00
☐ Dallas	Jones-Woods	5.15	5.50	19.00	65.00
☐ San Francisco	Jones-Woods	10.00	21.00	800.00	2150.00

TEN DOLLAR NOTES

ORDER OF ISSUE

	FIRST ISSUE	LAST ISSUE	PAGE
1. DEMAND	1861 only		91
2. UNITED STATES NOTES	1862	1923	92
3. NATIONAL BANK NOTES	1863	1929	196
4. NATIONAL GOLD BANK NOTES	1870	1875	101
5. SILVER CERTIFICATES	1878	1953B	102
6. REFUNDING CERTIFICATE	1879		106
7. GOLD CERTIFICATES	1882	1928	107
8. TREASURY OR COIN NOTES	1890	1891	109
9. FEDERAL RESERVE NOTES	1914	present	110
10. FEDERAL RESERVE BANK NOTES	1915	1929	116

TEN DOLLAR NOTES / 91

TEN DOLLAR NOTES (1861) DEMAND NOTES
NO TREASURY SEAL

(Large Size) **NOTE NO. 60**

Face Design: Portrait of President Lincoln left, female figure with sword and shield.

Back Design: Ornate designs of "TEN".

CITY	A.B.P.	GOOD	V.GOOD
☐ Boston (I)	315.00	745.00	1425.00
☐ New York (I)	315.00	745.00	1425.00
☐ Philadelphia (I)	315.00	745.00	1425.00
☐ Cincinnati (I)	1300.00	2675.00	RARE
☐ St. Louis (I)	1250.00	2625.00	RARE
☐ Boston (II)	300.00	625.00	950.00
☐ New York (II)	300.00	625.00	950.00
☐ Philadelphia (II)	300.00	625.00	950.00
☐ Cincinnati (II)	965.00	1900.00	2875.00
☐ St. Louis (II)	965.00	1900.00	2875.00

92 / TEN DOLLAR NOTES

TEN DOLLAR NOTES (1862-1863) UNITED STATES NOTES
(ALSO KNOWN AS LEGAL TENDER NOTES)
(Large Size) **NOTE NO. 61**

Back Design
Face Design: Similar to previous Note.

SERIES	SIGNATURES	SEAL	A.B.P.	GOOD	V. FINE	UNC.
☐ 1862	Chittenden-Spinner*	Red	65.00	125.00	350.00	1425.00
☐ 1862	Chittenden-Spinner**	Red	70.00	140.00	380.00	1460.00
☐ 1863	Chittenden-Spinner**	Red	70.00	140.00	400.00	1460.00

*First Obligation: Similar to Note No. 33   **Second Obligation: Shown above.

TEN DOLLAR NOTES (1869) UNITED STATES NOTES
(Large Size) **NOTE NO. 62**

Face Design: Portrait of Daniel Webster left, presentation of Indian Princess right. (This note is nicknamed "Jackass Note", because the EAGLE between the signatures resembles a donkey when it is held upside down.)

SERIES	SIGNATURES	SEAL	A.B.P.	GOOD	V. FINE	UNC.
☐ 1869	Allison-Spinner	Red	42.00	85.00	385.00	1320.00

TEN DOLLAR NOTES (1875-1880) UNITED STATES NOTES
(Large Size) NOTE NO. 63

Face Design: Similar to previous Note.

Back Design: Revised

SERIES	SIGNATURES	SEAL	A.B.P.	GOOD	V. FINE	UNC.
☐ 1875	Allison-New	Red	22.00	45.00	210.00	1050.00
☐ Same as above — SERIES A		Red	27.00	55.00	230.00	1075.00
☐ 1878	Allison-Gilfillan	Red	29.00	50.00	215.00	1250.00
☐ 1880	Scofield-Gilfillan	Brown	22.00	45.00	150.00	985.00
☐ 1880	Bruce-Gilfillan	Brown	22.00	45.00	150.00	985.00
☐ 1880	Bruce-Wyman	Brown	22.00	45.00	150.00	985.00
☐ 1880	Bruce-Wyman	Red Plain	22.00	45.00	150.00	985.00
☐ 1880	Rosecrans-Jordan	Red Plain	22.00	45.00	150.00	985.00
☐ 1880	Rosecrans-Hyatt	Red Plain	22.00	45.00	150.00	985.00
☐ 1880	Rosecrans-Hyatt	Red Spikes	23.00	47.00	160.00	985.00
☐ 1880	Rosecrans-Huston	Red Spikes	22.00	45.00	150.00	985.00
☐ 1880	Rosecrans-Huston	Brown	22.00	45.00	150.00	985.00
☐ 1880	Rosecrans-Nebeker	Brown	22.00	45.00	150.00	985.00
☐ 1880	Rosecrans-Nebeker	Red	19.00	40.00	145.00	750.00
☐ 1880	Tillman-Morgan	Red	19.00	40.00	145.00	750.00
☐ 1880	Bruce-Roberts	Red	19.00	40.00	145.00	750.00
☐ 1880	Lyons-Roberts	Red	19.00	40.00	145.00	750.00

94 / TEN DOLLAR NOTES
TEN DOLLAR NOTES (1901) UNITED STATES NOTES
LEGAL TENDER (Large Size) — NOTE NO. 64

Face Design: American Bison (buffalo) center, portrait of Lewis left, portrait of Clark right.

Back Design: Female allegorical figure in arch.

SERIES	SIGNATURES	SEAL	A.B.P.	GOOD	V. FINE	UNC.
☐ 1901	Lyons-Roberts	Red	25.00	52.00	235.00	1250.00
☐ 1901	Lyons-Treat	Red	25.00	52.00	235.00	1250.00
☐ 1901	Vernon-Treat	Red	25.00	52.00	235.00	1250.00
☐ 1901	Vernon-McClung	Red	25.00	52.00	235.00	1250.00
☐ 1901	Napier-McClung	Red	25.00	52.00	235.00	1250.00
☐ 1901	Parker-Burke	Red	25.00	52.00	235.00	1250.00
☐ 1901	Teehee-Burke	Red	25.00	52.00	235.00	1250.00
☐ 1901	Elliott-White	Red	25.00	52.00	235.00	1250.00
☐ 1901	Speelman-White	Red	25.00	52.00	235.00	1250.00

TEN DOLLAR NOTES / 95

TEN DOLLAR NOTES (1923) UNITED STATES NOTES
(Large Size)   NOTE NO. 65

Face Design: Portrait of President Jackson center, red seal left, red "X" to right.

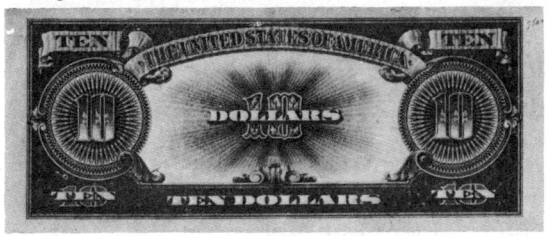

Back Design

SERIES	SIGNATURES	SEAL	A.B.P.	GOOD	V. FINE	UNC.
☐1923	Speelman-White	Red	55.00	110.00	525.00	2400.00

96 / TEN DOLLAR NOTES

TEN DOLLAR NOTES (1863-1875) NATIONAL BANK NOTES
FIRST CHARTER PERIOD (Large Size) NOTE NO. 66

Face Design: Benjamin Franklin and kite left, name of bank and city center. Effigy of Liberty and Eagle right.

Back Design: Border green, center black. DeSoto on horseback at Mississippi River.

SERIES	SIGNATURES	SEAL	A.B.P.	GOOD	V. FINE	UNC.
☐Original	Chittenden-Spinner	Red	55.00	115.00	270.00	2150.00
☐Original	Colby-Spinner	Red	55.00	115.00	270.00	2150.00
☐Original	Jeffries-Spinner	Red	175.00	400.00	1150.00	RARE
☐Original	Allison-Spinner	Red	56.00	115.00	270.00	2175.00
☐1875	Allison-New	Red	48.00	100.00	250.00	1725.00
☐1875	Allison-Wyman	Red	48.00	100.00	250.00	1725.00
☐1875	Allison-Gilfillan	Red	48.00	100.00	250.00	1725.00
☐1875	Scofield-Gilfillan	Red	48.00	100.00	250.00	1725.00
☐1875	Bruce-Gilfillan	Red	48.00	100.00	250.00	1725.00
☐1875	Bruce-Wyman	Red	48.00	100.00	250.00	1725.00
☐1875	Rosecrans-Huston	Red	48.00	100.00	250.00	1725.00
☐1875	Rosecrans-Nebeker	Red	48.00	100.00	250.00	1725.00

TEN DOLLAR NOTES (1882) NATIONAL BANK NOTES
SECOND CHARTER PERIOD (Large Size)   **NOTE NO. 68**

First Issue—brown seal and brown backs.

Face Design: Similar to previous Notes No. 66-67.
Back Design: Similar to Note No. 39, but border in brown with green Charter Number.

SERIES	SIGNATURES	SEAL	A.B.P.	GOOD	V. FINE	UNC.
☐1882	Bruce-Gilfillan	Brown	28.00	60.00	165.00	775.00
☐1882	Bruce-Wyman	Brown	28.00	60.00	165.00	775.00
☐1882	Bruce-Jordan	Brown	30.00	65.00	170.00	775.00
☐1882	Rosecrans-Jordan	Brown	28.00	60.00	165.00	775.00
☐1882	Rosecrans-Hyatt	Brown	28.00	60.00	165.00	775.00
☐1882	Rosecrans-Huston	Brown	28.00	60.00	165.00	775.00
☐1882	Rosecrans-Nebeker	Brown	28.00	60.00	165.00	775.00
☐1882	Rosecrans-Morgan	Brown	95.00	200.00	750.00	1500.00
☐1882	Tillman-Morgan	Brown	28.00	60.00	165.00	775.00
☐1882	Tillman-Roberts	Brown	28.00	60.00	165.00	775.00
☐1882	Bruce-Roberts	Brown	28.00	60.00	165.00	775.00
☐1882	Lyons-Roberts	Brown	28.00	60.00	165.00	775.00
☐1882	Lyons-Treat	Brown	30.00	65.00	170.00	800.00
☐1882	Vernon-Treat	Brown	30.00	65.00	170.00	800.00

Second Issue—blue seal, Greenback with date 1882-1908

Face Design: Similar to Note No. 66.   **Back Design:** Similar to Note No. 40
(Large Size)   **NOTE NO. 69**

SERIES	SIGNATURES	SEAL	A.B.P.	GOOD	V. FINE	UNC.
☐1882	Rosecrans-Huston	Blue	23.75	49.00	140.00	820.00
☐1882	Rosecrans-Nebeker	Blue	23.75	49.00	140.00	820.00
☐1882	Rosecrans-Morgan	Blue	85.00	175.00	550.00	1750.00
☐1882	Tillman-Morgan	Blue	23.75	49.00	140.00	820.00
☐1882	Tillman-Roberts	Blue	23.75	49.00	140.00	820.00
☐1882	Bruce-Roberts	Blue	23.75	49.00	140.00	820.00
☐1882	Lyons-Roberts	Blue	23.75	49.00	140.00	820.00
☐1882	Vernon-Treat	Blue	23.75	49.00	140.00	820.00
☐1882	Vernon-McClung	Blue	23.75	49.00	160.00	820.00
☐1882	Napier-McClung	Blue	23.75	49.00	160.00	820.00

98 / TEN DOLLAR NOTES

TEN DOLLAR NOTES (1882) NATIONAL BANK NOTES
NOTE NO. 70

Third Issue—blue seal, Greenback with value in block letters.

Face Design: Similar to previous Notes (See Note No. 66)
Back Design: Similar to Note No. 41.

SERIES	SIGNATURES	SEAL	A.B.P.	GOOD	V. FINE	UNC.
☐ 1882	Tillman-Roberts	Blue	55.00	115.00	375.00	2000.00
☐ 1882	Lyons-Roberts	Blue	55.00	115.00	375.00	2000.00
☐ 1882	Vernon-Treat	Blue	55.00	115.00	375.00	2000.00
☐ 1882	Napier-McClung	Blue	55.00	115.00	375.00	2000.00

NOTE: These Notes may exist with other signatures, but are very rare.

TEN DOLLAR NOTES (1902) NATIONAL BANK NOTES
THIRD CHARTER PERIOD (Large Size) — NOTE NO. 71

First Issue—red seal and red Charter numbers

Face Design: Portrait of President McKinley left, name of bank and City in center.

SERIES	SIGNATURES	SEAL	A.B.P.	GOOD	V. FINE	UNC.
☐ 1902	Lyons-Roberts	Red	35.00	70.00	180.00	825.00
☐ 1902	Lyons-Treat	Red	44.00	90.00	180.00	825.00
☐ 1902	Vernon-Treat	Red	47.00	100.00	180.00	825.00

TEN DOLLAR NOTES (1902) NATIONAL BANK NOTES
THIRD CHARTER PERIOD (Large Size)   **NOTE NO. 71A**

Second Issue—blue seal and numbers, 1902-1908 on the back.
Back Design: Same as Note No. 70, date 1902-1908.
Face Design: Same as Note No. 71.

SERIES	SIGNATURES	SEAL	A.B.P.	GOOD	V. FINE	UNC.
☐1902	Lyons-Roberts	Blue	14.00	25.00	55.00	275.00
☐1902	Lyons-Treat	Blue	14.00	25.00	55.00	275.00
☐1902	Vernon-Treat	Blue	14.00	25.00	55.00	275.00
☐1902	Vernon-McClung	Blue	14.00	25.00	55.00	275.00
☐1902	Napier-McClung	Blue	14.00	25.00	55.00	275.00
☐1902	Napier-Thompson	Blue	15.00	30.00	65.00	400.00
☐1902	Napier-Burke	Blue	14.00	25.00	55.00	275.00
☐1902	Parker-Burke	Blue	14.00	25.00	55.00	275.00
☐1902	Teehee-Burke	Blue	14.00	27.00	60.00	275.00

Third Issue—blue seal and numbers, without date on back.

SERIES	SIGNATURES	SEAL	A.B.P.	GOOD	V. FINE	UNC.
☐1902	Lyons-Roberts	Blue	13.00	26.00	45.00	250.00
☐1902	Lyons-Treat	Blue	13.00	26.00	45.00	250.00
☐1902	Vernon-Treat	Blue	13.00	26.00	45.00	250.00
☐1902	Vernon-McClung	Blue	13.00	26.00	45.00	250.00
☐1902	Napier-McClung	Blue	13.00	26.00	45.00	250.00
☐1902	Napier-Thompson	Blue	16.00	32.00	55.00	285.00
☐1902	Napier-Burke	Blue	12.75	26.00	45.00	250.00
☐1902	Parker-Burke	Blue	12.75	26.00	45.00	250.00
☐1902	Teehee-Burke	Blue	12.75	26.00	45.00	250.00
☐1902	Elliott-Burke	Blue	12.75	26.00	45.00	250.00
☐1902	Elliott-White	Blue	12.75	26.00	45.00	250.00
☐1902	Speelman-White	Blue	12.75	26.00	45.00	250.00
☐1902	Woods-White	Blue	13.00	27.00	50.00	250.00
☐1902	Woods-Tate	Blue	14.00	28.00	50.00	250.00
☐1902	Jones-Woods	Blue	58.00	115.00	275.00	925.00

100 / TEN DOLLAR NOTES

TEN DOLLAR NOTES (1929) NATIONAL BANK NOTES
(Small Size)   **NOTE NO. 72**

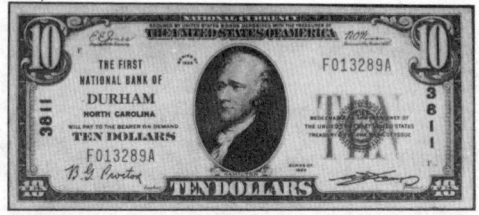

Face Design—TYPE I: Portrait of Hamilton center, name of Bank left, brown seal right, Charter number black.

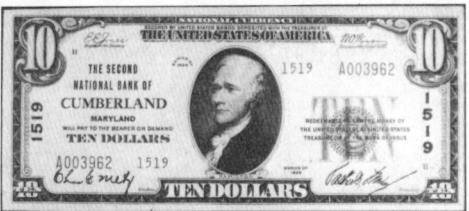

Face Design—TYPE II: Charter number added in brown.

Back Design: United States Treasury Building.

SERIES	SIGNATURES	SEAL	A.B.P.	GOOD	V. FINE	UNC.
☐ 1929—TYPE I	Jones-Woods	Brown	10.25	11.25	20.00	87.00
☐ 1929—TYPE II	Jones-Woods	Brown	10.75	12.00	25.00	110.00

TEN DOLLAR NOTES / 101

TEN DOLLAR NOTES (1870-1875) NATIONAL GOLD BANK NOTES
(Large Size) NOTE NO. 67

Face Design: Similar to Note No. 66

Back Design: State Seal left, gold coins center, American Eagle right.

SIGNATURES OF ALLISON-SPINNER, RED TREASURY SEAL

SERIES	NAME OF BANK	CITY	A.B.P.	GOOD	V. GOOD
☐1870	First National Gold Bank	San Francisco	310.00	625.00	2125.00
☐1872	National Gold Bank and Trust Company	San Francisco	295.00	610.00	2125.00
☐1872	National Gold Bank of D.O. Mills and Company	Sacramento	360.00	775.00	2315.00
☐1873	First National Gold Bank	Santa Barbara	400.00	850.00	2315.00
☐1873	First National Gold Bank	Stockton	345.00	750.00	2315.00
☐1874	Farmers Nat'l Gold Bank	San Jose	350.00	765.00	2315.00
☐1874	First National Gold Bank	Petaluma	350.00	765.00	2315.00
☐1875	First National Gold Bank	Oakland	350.00	765.00	2315.00

102 / TEN DOLLAR NOTES

TEN DOLLAR NOTES (1880) SILVER CERTIFICATES
(Large Size) NOTE NO. 73

Face Design: Portrait of Robert Morris left.

Back Design: Printed in black ink, large letters "SILVER".

SERIES	SIGNATURES	SEAL	A.B.P.	GOOD	V. FINE	UNC.
☐1880	Scofield-Gilfillan	Brown	80.00	175.00	800.00	3325.00
☐1880	Bruce-Gilfillan	Brown	80.00	225.00	800.00	3325.00
☐1880	Bruce-Wyman	Brown	80.00	225.00	800.00	3325.00
☐1880	Bruce-Wyman	Red	110.00	225.00	1125.00	3750.00

TEN DOLLAR NOTES (1886) SILVER CERTIFICATES
(Large Size) **NOTE NO. 74**

Face Design: Portrait of Thomas A. Hendricks in center.

Back Design

SERIES	SIGNATURES	SEAL	A.B.P.	GOOD	V. FINE	UNC.
☐1886	Rosecrans-Jordan	Small Red	60.00	120.00	370.00	2925.00
☐1886	Rosecrans-Hyatt	Small Red	60.00	120.00	370.00	2925.00
☐1886	Rosecrans-Hyatt	Large Red	65.00	130.00	420.00	2800.00
☐1886	Rosecrans-Huston	Large Red	65.00	130.00	440.00	2800.00
☐1886	Rosecrans-Huston	Large Brown	60.00	120.00	390.00	2715.00
☐1886	Rosecrans-Nebeker	Large Brown	60.00	120.00	390.00	2715.00
☐1886	Rosecrans-Nebeker	Small Red	75.00	155.00	510.00	2975.00

TEN DOLLAR NOTES (1891-1908) SILVER CERTIFICATES
(Large Size)
NOTE NO. 75

Face Design: Same as Note No. 74.

Back Design

SERIES	SIGNATURES	SEAL	A.B.P.	GOOD	V. FINE	UNC.
☐1891	Rosecrans-Nebeker	Red	30.00	62.00	180.00	1800.00
☐1891	Tillman-Morgan	Red	30.00	62.00	180.00	1800.00
☐1891	Bruce-Roberts	Red	30.00	62.00	180.00	1800.00
☐1891	Lyons-Roberts	Red	30.00	62.00	180.00	1800.00
☐1908	Vernon-Treat	Blue	27.00	55.00	165.00	1275.00
☐1908	Vernon-McClung	Blue	27.00	55.00	165.00	1275.00
☐1908	Parker-Burke	Blue	27.00	55.00	165.00	1275.00

104 / TEN DOLLAR NOTES

TEN DOLLAR NOTES (1933) SILVER CERTIFICATES
(Small Size)   **NOTE NO. 76**

Face Design: Portrait of President Hamilton, center. Blue seal to left, blue numbers.

Back Design: Green United States Treasury Building.

SERIES	SIGNATURES	SEAL	A.B.P.	GOOD	V. FINE	UNC.
☐1933	Julian-Woodin	Blue	155.00	290.00	715.00	5275.00

TEN DOLLAR NOTES (1934) SILVER CERTIFICATES
(Small Size)   **NOTE NO. 77**

Face Design: Blue "10" to left of portrait. Treasury Seal is now to right.

Back Design: Similar to previous issue.

TEN DOLLAR NOTES (1934) SILVER CERTIFICATES
(Small Size) **NOTE NO. 77**

SERIES	SIGNATURES	SEAL	A.B.P.	GOOD	V. FINE	UNC.
☐ 1934	Julian-Morgenthau	Blue	10.50	13.00	20.00	45.00
☐ 1934	Julian-Morgenthau*	Yellow	135.00	315.00	1150.00	6300.00
☐ 1934A	Julian-Morgenthau	Blue	10.50	13.00	20.00	57.00
☐ 1934A	Julian-Morgenthau*	Yellow	11.00	15.00	25.00	130.00
☐ 1934B	Julian-Vinson	Blue	13.00	25.00	130.00	915.00
☐ 1934C	Julian-Snyder	Blue	10.50	13.00	17.00	40.00
☐ 1934D	Clark-Snyder	Blue	10.50	13.00	17.00	35.00

NOTE: *Silver Certificates with a yellow seal were a special issue for use in combat areas of North Africa and Europe during World War II.

TEN DOLLAR NOTES (1953) SILVER CERTIFICATES
(Small Size) **NOTE NO. 78**

Face Design: Gray "10" to left of portrait, Treasury Seal is smaller.
Back Design: Back similar to previous note.

SERIES	SIGNATURES	SEAL	A.B.P.	GOOD	V. FINE	UNC.
☐ 1953	Priest-Humphrey	Blue	10.25	——	17.50	45.00
☐ 1953A	Priest-Anderson	Blue	10.25	——	21.00	78.00
☐ 1953B	Smith-Dillon	Blue	10.25	——	23.00	57.50

ABOVE NOTE ONLY 720,000 ISSUED

NOTE: Last issue of $10.00 Silver Certificates. These were not issued with "In God We Trust" on the back. Production ended in 1962.

TEN DOLLAR NOTES

TEN DOLLAR (1879) REFUNDING CERTIFICATE
NOTE NO. 78A

Face Design: Portrait of President Franklin.

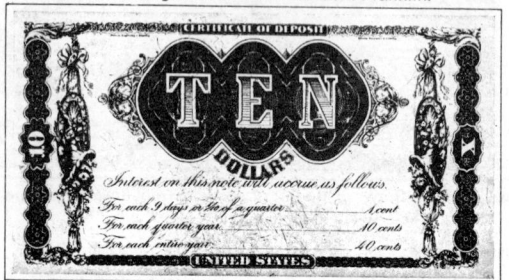

Back Design: Large "TEN", ornate cornucopia border.

SERIES SIGNATURES	SEAL	A.B.P.	GOOD	FINE
☐ 1879 Scofield-Gilfillan, PAY TO ORDER	Red	900.00	2250.00	5750.00
☐ 1879 Scofield-Gilfillan, PAY TO BEARER	Red	275.00	650.00	1375.00

TEN DOLLAR NOTES / 107
TEN DOLLAR NOTES (1907) GOLD CERTIFICATES
(Large Size) NOTE NO. 79

Face Design: Portrait of Hillegas center, yellow "X" left, yellow seal right, yellow numbers.

Back Design: The backs are a bright yellow color.

SERIES	SIGNATURES	SEAL	A.B.P.	GOOD	V. FINE	UNC.
☐1907	Vernon-Treat	Gold	12.00	24.00	65.00	410.00
☐1907	Vernon-McClung	Gold	12.00	24.00	65.00	410.00
☐1907	Napier-McClung	Gold	12.00	24.00	65.00	410.00
☐1907	Napier-Thompson	Gold	20.00	39.00	130.00	875.00
☐1907	Parker-Burke	Gold	12.00	24.00	65.00	410.00
☐1907	Teehee-Burke	Gold	12.00	24.00	65.00	410.00
☐1922	Speelman-White	Gold	12.00	24.00	65.00	410.00

108 / TEN DOLLAR NOTES

TEN DOLLAR NOTES (1928) GOLD CERTIFICATES
(Small Size) NOTE NO. 80

Face Design: Portrait of President Hamilton center, yellow seal to left, yellow numbers.

Back Design: Printed in green ink.

SERIES	SIGNATURES	SEAL	A.B.P.	GOOD	V. FINE	UNC.
☐1928	Woods-Mellon	Gold	10.25	12.00	40.00	275.00

TEN DOLLAR NOTES (1890) TREASURY NOTES
(Large Size) NOTE NO. 81

Face Design: Portrait of General Philip Sheridan.

Back Design: Very ornate large "TEN."

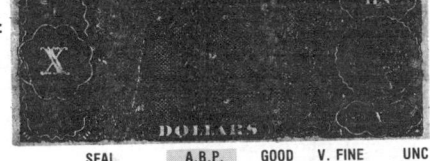

SERIES	SIGNATURES	SEAL	A.B.P.	GOOD	V. FINE	UNC.
☐ 1890	Rosecrans-Huston	Lg. Brown	57.00	115.00	450.00	3225.00
☐ 1890	Rosecrans-Nebeker	Lg. Brown	57.00	115.00	450.00	3225.00
☐ 1890	Rosecrans-Nebeker	Sm. Red	52.00	105.00	410.00	3000.00

TEN DOLLAR NOTES (1891) TREASURY NOTES
(Large Size)
NOTE NO. 81A

Face Design: Same as No. 81
Back Design: Ornate small "TEN."

SERIES	SIGNATURES	SEAL	A.B.P.	GOOD	V. FINE	UNC.
☐ 1891	Rosecrans-Nebeker	Sm. Red	42.00	90.00	210.00	985.00
☐ 1891	Tillman-Morgan	Sm. Red	42.00	90.00	220.00	985.00
☐ 1891	Bruce-Roberts	Sm. Red	42.00	90.00	220.00	985.00

110 / TEN DOLLAR NOTES

TEN DOLLAR NOTES (1914) FEDERAL RESERVE NOTES
(Large Size)
NOTE NO. 82

Face Design: Portrait of President Jackson center, Federal Reserve Seal left, Treasury Seal right.

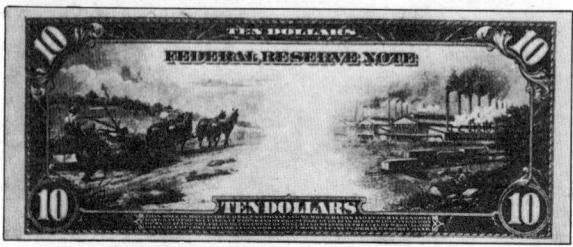

Back Design: Scenes of farming and industry.
SIGNATURES OF BURKE-McADOO, RED SEALS AND RED SERIAL NUMBERS

SERIES	CITY	SEAL	A.B.P.	GOOD	V. FINE	UNC.
☐1914	Boston	Red	13.00	25.00	70.00	460.00
☐1914	New York	Red	11.50	21.00	65.00	450.00
☐1914	Philadelphia	Red	11.50	21.00	65.00	450.00
☐1914	Cleveland	Red	11.50	21.00	65.00	450.00
☐1914	Richmond	Red	11.50	21.00	65.00	450.00
☐1914	Atlanta	Red	11.50	21.00	65.00	450.00
☐1914	Chicago	Red	11.50	21.00	65.00	450.00
☐1914	St. Louis	Red	11.50	21.00	65.00	450.00
☐1914	Minneapolis	Red	11.50	21.00	65.00	450.00
☐1914	Kansas City	Red	11.50	21.00	65.00	450.00
☐1914	Dallas	Red	13.00	25.00	70.00	475.00
☐1914	San Francisco	Red	13.00	25.00	70.00	475.00

TEN DOLLAR NOTES (1914) FEDERAL RESERVE NOTES
(Large Size)

NOTE NO. 82A

BANK & CITY	SIGNATURES	SEAL	A.B.P.	V. FINE	UNC.
☐ Boston	Burke-McAdoo	Blue	13.00	29.00	130.00
☐ Boston	Burke-Glass	Blue	16.00	31.00	185.00
☐ Boston	Burke-Huston	Blue	13.00	29.00	130.00
☐ Boston	White-Mellon	Blue	13.00	29.00	130.00
☐ New York	Burke-McAdoo	Blue	13.00	29.00	130.00
☐ New York	Burke-Glass	Blue	16.00	31.00	185.00
☐ New York	Burke-Huston	Blue	13.00	26.00	130.00
☐ New York	White-Mellon	Blue	13.00	26.00	130.00
☐ Philadelphia	Burke-McAdoo	Blue	13.00	26.00	130.00
☐ Philadelphia	Burke-Glass	Blue	13.00	26.00	130.00
☐ Philadelphia	Burke-Huston	Blue	13.00	26.00	130.00
☐ Philadelphia	White-Mellon	Blue	13.00	26.00	130.00
☐ Cleveland	Burke-McAdoo	Blue	13.00	26.00	130.00
☐ Cleveland	Burke-Glass	Blue	13.00	26.00	130.00
☐ Cleveland	Burke-Huston	Blue	13.00	26.00	130.00
☐ Cleveland	White-Mellon	Blue	13.00	26.00	130.00
☐ Richmond	Burke-McAdoo	Blue	13.00	26.00	130.00
☐ Richmond	Burke-Glass	Blue	13.00	26.00	130.00
☐ Richmond	Burke-Huston	Blue	13.00	26.00	130.00
☐ Richmond	White-Mellon	Blue	13.00	26.00	130.00
☐ Atlanta	Burke-McAdoo	Blue	13.00	26.00	130.00
☐ Atlanta	Burke-Glass	Blue	16.00	31.00	145.00
☐ Atlanta	Burke-Huston	Blue	13.00	27.00	130.00
☐ Atlanta	White-Mellon	Blue	13.00	27.00	130.00
☐ Chicago	Burke-McAdoo	Blue	13.00	27.00	130.00
☐ Chicago	Burke-Glass	Blue	13.00	27.00	130.00
☐ Chicago	Burke-Huston	Blue	13.00	27.00	130.00
☐ Chicago	White-Mellon	Blue	13.00	27.00	130.00
☐ St. Louis	Burke-McAdoo	Blue	13.00	27.00	130.00
☐ St. Louis	Burke-Glass	Blue	13.00	27.00	130.00
☐ St. Louis	Burke-Huston	Blue	13.00	27.00	130.00
☐ St. Louis	White-Mellon	Blue	13.00	27.00	130.00
☐ Minneapolis	Burke-McAdoo	Blue	13.00	27.00	130.00
☐ Minneapolis	Burke-Glass	Blue	13.00	27.00	130.00
☐ Minneapolis	Burke-Huston	Blue	13.00	27.00	130.00
☐ Minneapolis	White-Mellon	Blue	13.00	27.00	130.00
☐ Kansas City	Burke-McAdoo	Blue	13.00	27.00	130.00
☐ Kansas City	Burke-Glass	Blue	16.00	31.00	160.00
☐ Kansas City	Burke-Huston	Blue	13.00	28.00	130.00
☐ Kansas City	White-Mellon	Blue	13.00	28.00	130.00
☐ Dallas	Burke-McAdoo	Blue	13.00	28.00	130.00
☐ Dallas	Burke-Glass	Blue	13.00	28.00	130.00
☐ Dallas	Burke-Huston	Blue	13.00	28.00	130.00
☐ Dallas	White-Mellon	Blue	13.00	28.00	130.00
☐ San Francisco	Burke-McAdoo	Blue	13.00	28.00	130.00
☐ San Francisco	Burke-Glass	Blue	21.00	40.00	235.00
☐ San Francisco	Burke-Huston	Blue	14.00	29.00	135.00
☐ San Francisco	White-Mellon	Blue	14.00	29.00	135.00

112 / TEN DOLLAR NOTES

TEN DOLLAR NOTES (1928-1928A) FEDERAL RESERVE NOTES
(Small Size) **NOTE NO. 83**

Face Design: Portrait of President Hamilton center, black Federal Reserve Seal left, with number, green Treasury Seal to the right.

Back Design: United States Treasury Building.

SERIES OF 1928 — SIGNATURES OF TATE-MELLON, GREEN SEAL

BANK & CITY	A.B.P.	V.FINE	UNC.	BANK & CITY	A.B.P.	V.FINE	UNC.
☐Boston	11.25	18.00	45.00	☐Chicago	11.25	20.00	46.00
☐New York	11.25	18.00	45.00	☐St. Louis	11.25	18.00	50.00
☐Philadelphia	11.25	18.00	45.00	☐Minneapolis	11.25	18.00	50.00
☐Cleveland	11.25	18.00	45.00	☐Kansas City	11.25	18.00	50.00
☐Richmond	11.25	18.00	47.00	☐Dallas	11.25	18.00	50.00
☐Atlanta	11.25	18.00	47.00	☐San Francisco	11.25	18.00	45.00

SERIES OF 1928A — SIGNATURES OF WOODS-MELLON, GREEN SEAL

BANK & CITY	A.B.P.	V.FINE	UNC.	BANK & CITY	A.B.P.	V.FINE	UNC.
☐Boston	11.25	17.00	37.00	☐Chicago	11.25	17.00	36.00
☐New York	11.25	17.00	37.00	☐St. Louis	11.50	19.00	42.00
☐Philadelphia	11.25	17.00	37.00	☐Minneapolis	11.50	19.00	45.00
☐Cleveland	11.25	17.00	37.00	☐Kansas City	11.50	19.00	41.00
☐Richmond	11.25	17.00	40.00	☐Dallas	11.50	17.00	41.00
☐Atlanta	11.25	18.00	38.00	☐San Francisco	11.50	19.00	38.00

TEN DOLLAR NOTES / 113

TEN DOLLAR NOTES (1928B-1928C) FEDERAL RESERVE NOTES
(Small Issue) **NOTE NO. 83A**

Face Design: Alexander Hamilton Black Federal Reserve Seal left has letter instead of number.

Back Design: Same as Note No. 83.

SERIES OF 1928B — SIGNATURES OF WOODS-MELLON, GREEN SEAL

BANK & CITY	A.B.P.	V.FINE	UNC.	BANK & CITY	A.B.P.	V.FINE	UNC.
☐Boston	10.20	15.00	32.00	☐Chicago	11.00	17.00	32.00
☐New York	10.20	15.00	32.00	☐St. Louis	11.00	17.00	32.00
☐Philadelphia	10.20	17.00	32.00	☐Minneapolis	11.00	17.00	32.00
☐Cleveland	10.50	16.00	32.00	☐Kansas City	11.00	17.00	32.00
☐Richmond	11.00	17.00	32.00	☐Dallas	11.00	17.00	33.75
☐Atlanta	11.00	17.00	32.00	☐San Francisco	11.00	17.00	32.00

SERIES OF 1928C — SIGNATURES OF WOODS-MILLS, GREEN SEAL

BANK & CITY	A.B.P.	V.FINE	UNC.	BANK & CITY	A.B.P.	V.FINE	UNC.
☐New York	13.00	26.00	97.50	☐Atlanta	13.00	26.00	97.50
☐Cleveland	13.00	26.00	97.50	☐Chicago	13.00	26.00	97.50
☐Richmond	13.00	26.00	97.50				

TEN DOLLAR NOTES (1934) FEDERAL RESERVE NOTES
(Small Size) **NOTE NO. 83B**

SERIES OF 1934 — SIGNATURES OF JULIAN-MORGENTHAU, GREEN SEAL

BANK & CITY	A.B.P.	V.FINE	UNC.	BANK & CITY	A.B.P.	V.FINE	UNC.
☐Boston	10.50	14.00	30.00	☐Chicago	10.50	14.00	29.00
☐New York	10.50	14.00	29.00	☐St. Louis	10.50	14.00	29.00
☐Philadelphia	10.50	14.00	28.00	☐Minneapolis	10.50	14.00	30.00
☐Cleveland	10.50	14.00	28.00	☐Kansas City	10.50	14.00	30.00
☐Richmond	10.50	14.00	29.00	☐Dallas	10.50	14.00	30.00
☐Atlanta	10.50	15.00	29.00	☐San Francisco	10.50	14.00	30.75

NOTE: The green Treasury Seal on this note is known in a light and dark color. The light seal is worth about 10% to 20% more in most cases. "Redeemable In Gold" removed from obligation over Federal Reserve Seal.

114 / TEN DOLLAR NOTES

TEN DOLLAR NOTES (1934) FEDERAL RESERVE NOTES
(Small Size)   NOTE NO. 83B

SERIES OF 1934A—SIGNATURES OF JULIAN-MORGENTHAU, GREEN SEAL

BANK & CITY	A.B.P.	V.FINE	UNC.	BANK & CITY	A.B.P.	V.FINE	UNC.
☐ Boston	10.50	13.75	26.00	☐ Chicago	10.50	13.75	25.00
☐ New York	10.50	13.75	26.00	☐ St. Louis	10.50	13.75	31.00
☐ Philadelphia	10.50	13.75	26.00	☐ Minneapolis	10.50	13.75	31.00
☐ Cleveland	10.50	13.75	28.00	☐ Kansas City	10.50	13.75	25.00
☐ Richmond	10.50	13.75	29.00	☐ Dallas	10.50	13.75	25.00
☐ Atlanta	10.50	13.75	29.00	☐ San Francisco*	14.00	25.00	250.00

*San Francisco - 1934A with brown seal and overprinted HAWAII on face and back. Special issue for use in combat areas during World War II. Value in V. Fine $45.00, Value in Unc. $220.00.

SERIES OF 1934B — SIGNATURES OF JULIAN-VINSON, GREEN SEAL

BANK & CITY	A.B.P.	V.FINE	UNC.	BANK & CITY	A.B.P.	V.FINE	UNC.
☐ Boston	10.75	15.00	29.00	☐ Chicago	10.75	15.00	29.00
☐ New York	10.75	15.00	29.00	☐ St. Louis	10.75	15.00	29.00
☐ Philadelphia	10.75	15.00	29.00	☐ Minneapolis	10.75	15.00	29.00
☐ Cleveland	10.75	15.00	31.00	☐ Kansas City	10.75	16.00	31.00
☐ Richmond	10.75	15.00	29.00	☐ Dallas	10.75	15.00	31.00
☐ Atlanta	10.75	15.00	29.00	☐ San Francisco	10.75	15.00	29.00

SERIES OF 1934C — SIGNATURES OF JULIAN-SNYDER, GREEN SEAL

BANK & CITY	A.B.P.	V.FINE	UNC.	BANK & CITY	A.B.P.	V.FINE	UNC.
☐ Boston	10.25	12.75	21.75	☐ Chicago	10.25	12.75	21.00
☐ New York	10.25	12.75	21.00	☐ St. Louis	10.25	12.75	21.00
☐ Philadelphia	10.25	12.75	21.00	☐ Minneapolis	10.25	12.75	22.00
☐ Cleveland	10.25	13.00	23.00	☐ Kansas City	10.25	12.75	22.00
☐ Richmond	10.25	12.75	21.00	☐ Dallas	10.25	12.75	22.00
☐ Atlanta	10.25	12.75	21.00	☐ San Francisco	10.25	12.75	21.00

SERIES OF 1934D — SIGNATURES OF CLARK-SNYDER, GREEN SEAL

BANK & CITY	A.B.P.	V.FINE	UNC.	BANK & CITY	A.B.P.	V.FINE	UNC.
☐ Boston	10.25	12.75	21.50	☐ Chicago	10.25	12.75	21.50
☐ New York	10.25	12.75	21.50	☐ St. Louis	10.25	12.75	21.50
☐ Philadelphia	10.25	12.75	21.50	☐ Minneapolis	10.25	12.75	23.00
☐ Cleveland	10.25	12.75	22.00	☐ Kansas City	10.25	12.75	23.50
☐ Richmond	10.25	12.75	21.50	☐ Dallas	10.25	12.75	22.00
☐ Atlanta	10.25	12.75	21.50	☐ San Francisco	10.25	12.75	21.50

TEN DOLLAR NOTES (1950) FEDERAL RESERVE NOTES
(Small Size)   NOTE NO. 83C

SERIES OF 1950 — CLARK-SNYDER SIGNATURES, GREEN SEAL

                                                                     UNC.
Issued for all Federal Reserve Banks 21.00

TEN DOLLAR NOTES / 115

TEN DOLLAR NOTES (1950) FEDERAL RESERVE NOTES
(Small Size) **NOTE NO. 83C**

SERIES OF 1950A — SIGNATURES OF PRIEST-HUMPHREY, GREEN SEAL
Issued for all Federal Reserve Banks...19.00

SERIES OF 1950B — SIGNATURES OF PRIEST-ANDERSON, GREEN SEAL
Issued for all Federal Reserve Banks...18.00

SERIES OF 1950C — SIGNATURES OF SMITH-DILLON, GREEN SEAL
Issued for all Federal Reserve Banks...17.15

SERIES OF 1950D — SIGNATURES OF GRANAHAN-DILLON, GREEN SEAL
Issued for all Federal Reserve Banks...17.00

SERIES OF 1950E — SIGNATURES OF GRANAHAN-FOWLER, GREEN SEAL

BANK	UNC.	BANK	UNC.
☐ New York	18.00	☐ San Francisco	18.00
☐ Chicago	18.00	ONLY DISTRICTS USED	

TEN DOLLAR NOTES (1963) FEDERAL RESERVE NOTES
(Small Size) ("IN GOD WE TRUST" ADDED ON BACK) **NOTE NO. 83D**

SERIES OF 1963 — SIGNATURES OF GRANAHAN-DILLON, GREEN SEAL
Issued for all banks except Minneapolis..17.00

SERIES OF 1963A — SIGNATURES OF GRANAHAN-FOWLER, GREEN SEAL
Issued for all Federal Reserve Banks...16.50

TEN DOLLAR NOTES (1969) FEDERAL RESERVE NOTES
(WORDING IN GREEN TREASURY SEAL CHANGED FROM LATIN TO ENGLISH)
(Small Size) **NOTE NO. 83E**

SERIES OF 1969 — SIGNATURES OF ELSTON-KENNEDY
Issued for all Federal Reserve Banks...16.50

SERIES OF 1969A — SIGNATURES OF KABIS-CONNALLY
Issued for all Federal Reserve Banks...16.25

SERIES OF 1969B — SIGNATURES OF BANUELOS-CONNALLY
Issued for all Federal Reserve Banks...14.75

SERIES OF 1969C — SIGNATURES OF BANUELOS-SHULTZ
Issued for all Federal Reserve Banks...14.25

SERIES OF 1974 — SIGNATURES OF NEFF-SIMON
Issued for all Federal Reserve Banks...14.25

SERIES OF 1977 — SIGNATURES OF MORTON-BLUMENTHAL
Issued for all Federal Reserve Banks...14.25

SERIES OF 1977A — SIGNATURES OF MORTON-MILLER
Issued for all Federal Reserve Banks...14.25

SERIES OF 1981 — SIGNATURES OF BUCHANAN-REGAN, GREEN SEAL
Issued for all Federal Reserve Banks...12.00

SERIES OF 1981A — SIGNATURES OF ORTEGA-REGAN, GREEN SEAL
Issued for all Federal Reserve Banks...CURRENT

116 / TEN DOLLAR NOTES

TEN DOLLAR NOTES (1915-1918) FEDERAL RESERVE BANK
(Large Size) **NOTE NO. 84**

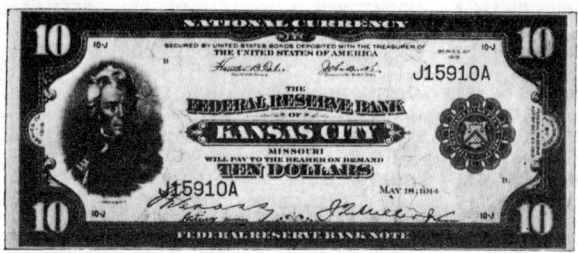

Face Design: Portrait of President Jackson to left, Bank and City in center, blue seal to the right.

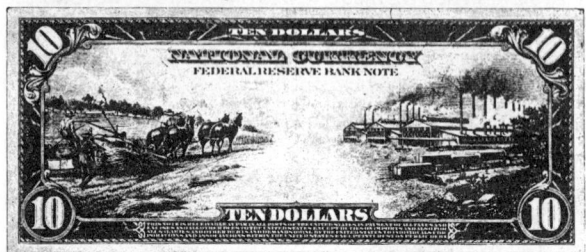

Back Design: Similar to Note No. 82.

BANK & CITY	SERIES	GOVERNMENT SIGNATURES	BANK SIGNATURES	A.B.P.	GOOD	V. FINE	UNC.
☐ New York	1918	Teehee-Burke	Hendricks-Strong	45.00	95.00	375.00	2750.00
☐ Atlanta	1915	Teehee-Burke	Bell-Wellborn	60.00	130.00	450.00	2300.00
☐ Atlanta	1918	Elliott-Burke	Bell-Wellborn	45.00	95.00	375.00	2775.00
☐ Chicago	1915	Teehee-Burke	McLallen-McDougal	45.00	85.00	330.00	1500.00
☐ Chicago	1918	Teehee-Burke	McCloud-McDougal	45.00	90.00	360.00	2600.00
☐ St. Louis	1918	Teehee-Burke	Attebery-Wells	55.00	100.00	415.00	2725.00
☐ Kan. City	1915	Teehee-Burke	Anderson-Miller	42.00	87.00	330.00	1500.00
☐ Kan. City	1915	Teehee-Burke	Cross-Miller	42.00	87.00	330.00	1500.00
☐ Kan. City	1915	Teehee-Burke	Helm-Miller	42.00	87.00	330.00	1500.00
☐ Dallas	1915	Teehee-Burke	Hoopes-VanZandt	42.00	87.00	330.00	1675.00
☐ Dallas	1915	Teehee-Burke	Gilbert-VanZandt	80.00	170.00	550.00	2275.00
☐ Dallas	1915	Teehee-Burke	Talley-VanZandt	42.00	85.00	330.00	1675.00

TEN DOLLAR NOTES / 117

TEN DOLLAR NOTES (1929) FEDERAL RESERVE BANK NOTES
(Small Size)
NOTE NO. 85

Face Design: Portrait of President Hamilton

Back Design: Same as all small size $10.00 Notes.

SIGNATURES OF JONES-WOODS, BROWN SEAL

BANK	SEAL	A.B.P.	GOOD	V. FINE	UNC.
☐ Boston	Brown	10.50	12.00	23.00	55.00
☐ New York	Brown	10.50	12.00	22.00	45.00
☐ Philadelphia	Brown	10.50	12.00	23.00	60.00
☐ Cleveland	Brown	10.50	12.00	22.00	50.00
☐ Richmond	Brown	10.50	12.00	22.00	57.00
☐ Atlanta	Brown	10.50	12.00	24.00	62.00
☐ Chicago	Brown	10.50	12.00	21.00	48.00
☐ St. Louis	Brown	10.50	12.00	22.00	60.00
☐ Minneapolis	Brown	10.50	12.00	24.00	78.00
☐ Kansas City	Brown	10.50	12.00	23.00	68.00
☐ Dallas	Brown	110.00	210.00	550.00	1875.00
☐ San Francisco	Brown	10.50	12.00	24.00	85.00

TWENTY DOLLAR NOTES

ORDER OF ISSUE

	FIRST ISSUE	LAST ISSUE	PAGE
1. DEMAND NOTES	1861 only		119
2. UNITED STATES NOTES	1862	1880	120
3. NATIONAL BANK NOTES	1863	1929	122
4. SILVER CERTIFICATES	1878	1891	126
5. GOLD CERTIFICATES	1882	1928	129
6. TREASURY OR COIN NOTES	1890	1891	132
7. FEDERAL RESERVE NOTES	1914	present	133
8. FEDERAL RESERVE BANK NOTES	1915	1929	138

TWENTY DOLLAR NOTES / 119

TWENTY DOLLAR NOTES (1861) DEMAND NOTES
(Large Size)
NOTE NO. 86

Face Design: Liberty with sword and shield.

Back Design: Intricate design of numerals "20", Demand Notes have no Treasury Seal.

SERIES	PAYABLE AT	A.B.P.	GOOD	V.GOOD
☐1861	Boston (I)	1900.00	3800.00	7500.00
☐1861	New York (I)	1700.00	3450.00	6425.00
☐1861	Philadelphia (I)	1700.00	3450.00	6425.00
☐1861	Cincinnati (I)	1900.00	3800.00	7500.00
☐1861	St. Louis (I)	(Unknown in any collection)		
☐1861	Boston (II)	1900.00	3800.00	7500.00
☐1861	New York (II)	1700.00	3450.00	6425.00
☐1861	Philadelphia (II)	1550.00	3175.00	6275.00
☐1861	Cincinnati (II)	1900.00	3800.00	7500.00
☐1861	St. Louis (II)	(Unknown in any collection)		

*NOTE: Counterfeits and expertly repaired specimens exist. Use caution in buying.

120 / TWENTY DOLLAR NOTES

TWENTY DOLLAR NOTES (1862-1863) UNITED STATES NOTES
(ALSO KNOWN AS LEGAL TENDER NOTES)
(Large Size) **NOTE NO. 86A**

Face Design: Liberty with sword and shield

Back Design: Second obligation. This Note was also issued with first obligation on the back. See Notes No. 33 and 33A.

SERIES	SIGNATURES	SEAL	A.B.P.	GOOD	V. FINE	UNC.
☐1862	Chittenden-Spinner*	Red	85.00	170.00	500.00	2675.00
☐1862	Chittenden-Spinner**	Red	85.00	170.00	500.00	2675.00
☐1863	Chittenden-Spinner**	Red	78.00	160.00	475.00	2675.00

*First Obligation: Similar to Note No. 33 **Second Obligation: Shown above.

TWENTY DOLLAR NOTES / 121

TWENTY DOLLAR NOTES (1869) UNITED STATES NOTES
(ALSO KNOWN AS LEGAL TENDER NOTES)

(Large Size) **NOTE NO. 87-87A**

Face Design

Back Design No. 87A revised.

Back Design: No. 87.

87 SERIES	SIGNATURES	SEAL	A.B.P.	GOOD	V. FINE	UNC.
☐ 1869	Allison-Spinner	Red	115.00	230.00	775.00	3275.00

87A SERIES Back Design: Revised

☐ 1875	Allison-New	Red	65.00	130.00	360.00	1275.00
☐ 1878	Allison-Gilfillan	Red	67.00	145.00	390.00	1350.00
☐ 1880	Scofield-Gilfillan	Brown Lg.	39.00	80.00	275.00	1225.00
☐ 1880	Bruce-Gilfillan	Brown Lg.	39.00	80.00	275.00	1225.00
☐ 1880	Bruce-Wyman	Brown Lg.	39.00	80.00	275.00	1225.00
☐ 1880	Bruce-Wyman	Red Lg.	39.00	80.00	275.00	1225.00
☐ 1880	Rosecrans-Jordan	Red Lg.	39.00	80.00	275.00	1225.00
☐ 1880	Rosecrans-Hyatt	Red Plain	39.00	80.00	275.00	1225.00
☐ 1880	Rosecrans-Hyatt	Red Spikes	39.00	80.00	275.00	1225.00
☐ 1880	Rosecrans-Huston	Red Lg.	39.00	80.00	270.00	1225.00
☐ 1880	Rosecrans-Huston	Brown Lg.	39.00	80.00	270.00	1225.00
☐ 1880	Rosecrans-Nebeker	Brown Lg.	39.00	80.00	270.00	1225.00
☐ 1880	Rosecrans-Nebeker	Red Sm.	34.00	70.00	250.00	865.00
☐ 1880	Tillman-Morgan	Red Sm.	34.00	70.00	250.00	865.00
☐ 1880	Bruce-Roberts	Red Sm.	34.00	70.00	250.00	865.00
☐ 1880	Lyons-Roberts	Red Sm.	34.00	70.00	250.00	865.00
☐ 1880	Vernon-Treat	Red Sm.	34.00	70.00	250.00	865.00
☐ 1880	Vernon-McClung	Red Sm.	34.00	70.00	250.00	865.00
☐ 1880	Teehee-Burke	Red Sm.	34.00	70.00	250.00	865.00
☐ 1880	Elliott-White	Red Sm.	34.00	70.00	250.00	865.00

122 / TWENTY DOLLAR NOTES

TWENTY DOLLAR NOTES (1863-1875) NATIONAL BANK NOTE
FIRST CHARTER PERIOD (Large Size) NOTE NO. 88

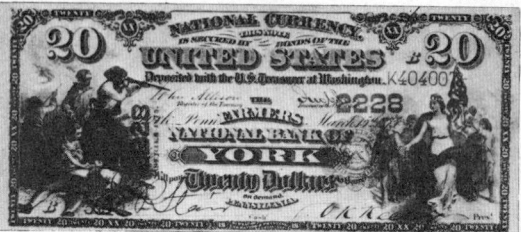

Face Design: Battle of Lexington left, name of Bank in center. Columbia with flag right.

Back Design: Green border, black center picture of baptism of Pocahontas.

SERIES	SIGNATURES	SEAL	A.B.P.	GOOD	V. FINE	UNC.
☐ Original	Chittenden-Spinner	Red	115.00	225.00	675.00	4000.00
☐ Original	Colby-Spinner	Red	105.00	210.00	625.00	3875.00
☐ Original	Jeffries-Spinner	Red	385.00	900.00	2075.00	4750.00
☐ Original	Allison-Spinner	Red	108.00	220.00	630.00	3750.00
☐ 1875	Allison-New	Red	108.00	220.00	630.00	4250.00
☐ 1875	Allison-Wyman	Red	108.00	220.00	630.00	4250.00
☐ 1875	Allison-Gilfillan	Red	108.00	220.00	630.00	4250.00
☐ 1875	Scofield-Gilfillan	Red	108.00	220.00	630.00	4250.00
☐ 1875	Bruce-Gilfillan	Red	108.00	220.00	630.00	4250.00
☐ 1875	Bruce-Wyman	Red	108.00	225.00	780.00	4375.00
☐ 1875	Rosecrans-Huston	Red	108.00	220.00	630.00	4225.00
☐ 1875	Rosecrans-Nebeker	Red	108.00	225.00	780.00	4250.00
☐ 1875	Tillman-Morgan	Red	115.00	235.00	820.00	4450.00

TWENTY DOLLAR NOTES / 123

TWENTY DOLLAR NOTES (1882) NATIONAL BANK NOTES
SECOND CHARTER PERIOD (Large Size)   **NOTE NO. 88A**
First Issue—brown seal and brown backs
Face Design: Similar to Note No. 88.
Back Design: Similar to Note No. 39, border is brown, green Charter number in center.

SERIES	SIGNATURES	SEAL	A.B.P.	GOOD	V. FINE	UNC.
☐ 1882	Bruce-Gilfillan	Brown	27.00	58.00	165.00	950.00
☐ 1882	Bruce-Wyman	Brown	27.00	58.00	165.00	950.00
☐ 1882	Bruce-Jordan	Brown	27.00	58.00	165.00	950.00
☐ 1882	Rosecrans-Jordan	Brown	27.00	58.00	165.00	950.00
☐ 1882	Rosecrans-Hyatt	Brown	27.00	58.00	165.00	950.00
☐ 1882	Rosecrans-Huston	Brown	27.00	58.00	165.00	950.00
☐ 1882	Rosecrans-Nebeker	Brown	27.00	58.00	165.00	950.00
☐ 1882	Rosecrans-Morgan	Brown	130.00	275.00	900.00	2635.00
☐ 1882	Tillman-Morgan	Brown	27.00	58.00	165.00	950.00
☐ 1882	Tillman-Roberts	Brown	27.00	58.00	165.00	950.00
☐ 1882	Bruce-Roberts	Brown	27.00	58.00	165.00	950.00
☐ 1882	Lyons-Roberts	Brown	27.00	58.00	165.00	950.00
☐ 1882	Lyons-Treat	Brown	30.00	65.00	185.00	1225.00
☐ 1882	Vernon-Treat	Brown	30.00	65.00	185.00	1225.00

SECOND CHARTER PERIOD, Second Issue   **NOTE NO. 88B**
Face Design: Similar to Note No. 88. **Back Design:** Similar to Note No. 40.

SERIES	SIGNATURES	SEAL	A.B.P.	GOOD	V. FINE	UNC.
☐ 1882	Rosecrans-Huston	Blue	29.00	60.00	145.00	1225.00
☐ 1882	Rosecrans-Nebeker	Blue	29.00	60.00	145.00	1225.00
☐ 1882	Rosecrans-Morgan	Blue	150.00	330.00	900.00	2450.00
☐ 1882	Tillman-Morgan	Blue	29.00	60.00	145.00	1225.00
☐ 1882	Tillman-Roberts	Blue	29.00	60.00	145.00	1225.00
☐ 1882	Bruce-Roberts	Blue	29.00	60.00	145.00	1225.00
☐ 1882	Lyons-Roberts	Blue	29.00	60.00	145.00	1225.00
☐ 1882	Vernon-Treat	Blue	29.00	60.00	145.00	1225.00
☐ 1882	Napier-McClung	Blue	30.00	65.00	210.00	1250.00

SECOND CHARTER PERIOD, Third Issue (Large Size)   **NOTE NO. 88C**
Face Design: Similar to Note No. 88 with blue seal.
Back Design: Similar to Note No. 41, green back, value in block letters.

SERIES	SIGNATURES	SEAL	A.B.P.	GOOD	V. FINE	UNC.
☐ 1882	Tillman-Morgan	Blue	70.00	140.00	450.00	2375.00
☐ 1882	Lyons-Roberts	Blue	70.00	140.00	450.00	2450.00
☐ 1882	Lyons-Treat	Blue	70.00	140.00	450.00	2450.00
☐ 1882	Vernon-Treat	Blue	70.00	140.00	450.00	2450.00
☐ 1882	Napier-McClung	Blue	70.00	140.00	450.00	2450.00
☐ 1882	Teehee-Burke	Blue	70.00	140.00	450.00	2450.00

124 / TWENTY DOLLAR NOTES

TWENTY DOLLAR NOTES (1902) NATIONAL BANK NOTES
THIRD CHARTER PERIOD, First Issue (Large Size)   NOTE NO. 89

Face Design: Portrait of McCulloch left, name of bank center, Treasury Seal right.

SERIES	SIGNATURES	SEAL	A.B.P.	GOOD	V. FINE	UNC.
☐1902	Lyon-Roberts	Red	34.00	77.00	160.00	1160.00
☐1902	Lyons-Treat	Red	34.00	77.00	160.00	1160.00
☐1902	Vernon-Treat	Red	36.00	77.00	215.00	1725.00

Second Issue—
Date 1902-1908 added on back, Treasury seal and serial numbers blue.

SERIES	SIGNATURES	SEAL	A.B.P.	GOOD	V. FINE	UNC.
☐1902	Lyons-Roberts	Blue	20.75	25.00	50.00	400.00
☐1902	Lyons-Treat	Blue	20.75	25.00	50.00	400.00
☐1902	Vernon-Treat	Blue	20.75	25.00	50.00	400.00
☐1902	Vernon-McClung	Blue	20.75	25.00	50.00	400.00
☐1902	Napier-McClung	Blue	20.75	25.00	50.00	400.00
☐1902	Napier-Thompson	Blue	22.50	33.00	90.00	550.00
☐1902	Napier-Burke	Blue	20.75	25.00	50.00	400.00
☐1902	Parker-Burke	Blue	20.75	25.00	50.00	400.00

Third Issue—
Date 1902-1908 removed from back, seal and serial numbers are blue.

SERIES	SIGNATURES	SEAL	A.B.P.	GOOD	V. FINE	UNC.
☐1902	Lyons-Roberts	Blue	20.75	24.00	49.00	350.00
☐1902	Lyons-Treat	Blue	20.75	24.00	49.00	350.00
☐1902	Vernon-Treat	Blue	20.75	24.00	49.00	385.00
☐1902	Vernon-McClung	Blue	20.75	24.00	49.00	370.00
☐1902	Napier-McClung	Blue	20.75	24.00	49.00	375.00
☐1902	Napier-Thompson	Blue	23.50	35.00	95.00	535.00
☐1902	Napier-Burke	Blue	20.75	24.00	49.00	370.00
☐1902	Parker-Burke	Blue	20.75	24.00	49.00	370.00
☐1902	Teehee-Burke	Blue	20.75	24.00	49.00	370.00
☐1902	Elliott-Burke	Blue	20.75	24.00	49.00	370.00
☐1902	Elliott-White	Blue	20.75	24.00	49.00	370.00
☐1902	Speelman-White	Blue	20.75	24.00	49.00	370.00
☐1902	Woods-White	Blue	21.00	37.00	115.00	370.00
☐1902	Woods-Tate	Blue	23.00	42.00	200.00	545.00
☐1902	Jones-Woods	Blue	200.00	425.00	1175.00	4500.00

TWENTY DOLLAR NOTES / 125

TWENTY DOLLAR NOTES (1929) NATIONAL BANK NOTES
(Small Size) **NOTE NO. 90**

Face Design: TYPE I Portrait of President Jackson in center, name of Bank to left, brown seal right. Charter number in black.

Face Design: TYPE II

Back Design: The White House, similar to all $20.00 small Notes.

SERIES	SIGNATURES	SEAL	A.B.P.	GOOD	V. FINE	UNC.
☐ 1929—TYPE I	Jones-Woods	Brown	20.50	21.00	30.00	100.00
☐ 1929—TYPE II	Jones-Woods	Brown	20.50	22.50	38.00	110.00

126 / TWENTY DOLLAR NOTES

TWENTY DOLLAR NOTES (1880) SILVER CERTIFICATES
(Large Size)   **NOTE NO. 91**

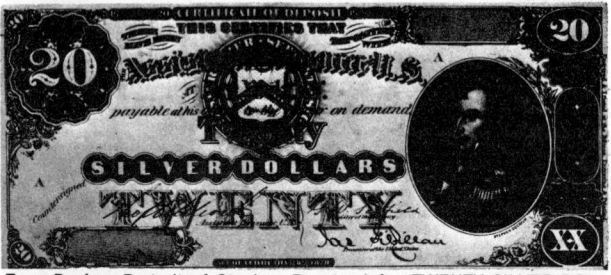

Face Design: Portrait of Stephen Decatur left. "TWENTY SILVER DOLLARS", in center.

Back Design: "SILVER" in large block letters.

SERIES	SIGNATURES	SEAL	A.B.P.	GOOD	V. FINE	UNC.
☐ 1880	Scofield-Gilfillan	Brown	160.00	350.00	1275.00	6275.00
☐ 1880	Bruce-Gilfillan	Brown	140.00	300.00	1025.00	6275.00
☐ 1880	Bruce-Wyman	Brown	140.00	300.00	1025.00	6275.00
☐ 1880	Bruce-Wyman	Red Sm.	305.00	625.00	2800.00	6150.00

This Note was also issued in series of 1878. They are very rare.

TWENTY DOLLAR NOTES (1886) SILVER CERTIFICATES
(Large Size) NOTE NO. 92

Face Design: Portrait of Daniel Manning center, Agriculture left, Industry right.

Back Design: Double diamond design center.

SERIES	SIGNATURES	SEAL	A.B.P.	GOOD	V. FINE	UNC.
☐ 1886	Rosecrans-Hyatt	Red Lg.	160.00	325.00	1600.00	6650.00
☐ 1886	Rosecrans-Huston	Brown Lg.	160.00	325.00	1600.00	6385.00
☐ 1886	Rosecrans-Nebeker	Brown Lg.	160.00	325.00	1600.00	6385.00
☐ 1886	Rosecrans-Nebeker	Red Sm.	220.00	475.00	2200.00	6725.00

128 / TWENTY DOLLAR NOTES

TWENTY DOLLAR NOTES (1891) SILVER CERTIFICATES
(NOT ISSUED IN SMALL SIZE NOTES)

(Large Size) **NOTE NO. 93**

Face Design: Same as Note No. 92.

Back Design: Revised.

SERIES	SIGNATURES	SEAL	A.B.P.	GOOD	V. FINE	UNC.
☐1891	Rosecrans-Nebeker	Red	50.00	105.00	310.00	1875.00
☐1891	Tillman-Morgan	Red	50.00	105.00	310.00	1875.00
☐1891	Bruce-Roberts	Red	50.00	105.00	310.00	1875.00
☐1891	Lyons-Roberts	Red	50.00	105.00	310.00	1875.00
☐1891	Parker-Burke	Blue	42.00	95.00	275.00	2300.00
☐1891	Teehee-Burke	Blue	42.00	95.00	275.00	2300.00

TWENTY DOLLAR NOTES (1882) GOLD CERTIFICATES
(Large Size) **NOTE NO. 94**

Face Design: Portrait of President Garfield right, "TWENTY DOLLARS IN GOLD COIN" center.

Back Design: Large "20" left, Eagle and arrows center, bright orange color.

SERIES	SIGNATURES	SEAL	A.B.P.	GOOD	V. FINE	UNC.
☐ 1882	Bruce-Gilfillan	Brown	650.00	1500.00	6000.00	20000.00
	The above Note has a countersigned signature.					
☐ 1882	Bruce-Gilfillan	Brown	210.00	500.00	2750.00	8500.00
☐ 1882	Bruce-Wyman	Brown	120.00	250.00	1500.00	5000.00
☐ 1882	Rosecrans-Huston	Brown	160.00	310.00	1750.00	7000.00
☐ 1882	Lyons-Roberts	Red	45.00	90.00	310.00	2475.00

130 / TWENTY DOLLAR NOTES

TWENTY DOLLAR NOTES (1905) GOLD CERTIFICATES
(Large Size)   **NOTE NO. 95**

Face Design: Portrait of President Washington center, "XX" left, Treasury Seal right.

Back Design: Eagle and Shield center, printed in bright orange color.

SERIES	SIGNATURES	SEAL	A.B.P.	GOOD	V. FINE	UNC.
☐ 1905	Lyons-Roberts	Red	155.00	310.00	1300.00	10000.00
☐ 1905	Lyons-Treat	Red	155.00	310.00	1300.00	10000.00
☐ 1906	Vernon-Treat	Gold	25.00	52.00	150.00	700.00
☐ 1906	Vernon-McClung	Gold	25.00	52.00	150.00	700.00
☐ 1906	Napier-McClung	Gold	25.00	52.00	150.00	700.00
☐ 1906	Napier-Thompson	Gold	30.00	60.00	250.00	875.00
☐ 1906	Parker-Burke	Gold	25.00	52.00	160.00	700.00
☐ 1906	Teehee-Burke	Gold	25.00	52.00	160.00	700.00
☐ 1922	Speelman-White	Gold	25.00	52.00	140.00	550.00

TWENTY DOLLAR NOTES (1928) GOLD CERTIFICATES
(Small Size)
NOTE NO. 96

Face Design: Portrait of President Jackson center, gold seal left, gold serial numbers.

Back Design: The White House, printed green, similar to all small size $20's.

SERIES	SIGNATURES	SEAL	A.B.P.	V. FINE	UNC.
☐ 1928	Woods-Mellon	Gold	23.00	70.00	300.00

TWENTY DOLLAR NOTES (1890) TREASURY NOTES
(Large Size) NOTE NO. 97

Face Design: Portrait of John Marshall, Chief Justice Supreme Court left, "20" center.

Back Design

SERIES	SIGNATURES	SEAL	A.B.P.	GOOD	V. FINE	UNC.
☐ 1890	Rosecrans-Huston	Brown	155.00	325.00	2000.00	7750.00
☐ 1890	Rosecrans-Nebeker	Brown	155.00	325.00	2000.00	7750.00
☐ 1890	Rosecrans-Nebeker	Red	155.00	325.00	2000.00	7750.00

(Large Size) NOTE NO. 97A

Back Design

Face Design: Same as previous Note.

SERIES	SIGNATURES	SEAL	A.B.P.	GOOD	V. FINE	UNC.
☐ 1891	Tillman-Morgan	Red	225.00	500.00	2750.00	10250.00
☐ 1891	Bruce-Roberts	Red	225.00	500.00	2750.00	10250.00

TWENTY DOLLAR NOTES / 133

TWENTY DOLLAR NOTES (1914) FEDERAL RESERVE NOTES
(Large Size) **NOTE NO. 98**

Face Design: Portrait of President Cleveland center, Federal Reserve Seal left, Treasury Seal right.

Back Design: Scenes of transportation. Locomotive left, Steamship right.

SERIES OF 1914 — SIGNATURES OF BURKE-McADOO, RED TREASURY SEAL

BANK	A.B.P.	V.FINE	UNC.	BANK	A.B.P.	V.FINE	UNC.
☐ Boston	28.00	125.00	650.00	☐ Chicago	26.00	105.00	580.00
☐ New York	26.00	105.00	580.00	☐ St. Louis	26.00	105.00	580.00
☐ Philadelphia	26.00	105.00	580.00	☐ Minneapolis	26.00	105.00	580.00
☐ Cleveland	26.00	105.00	580.00	☐ Kansas City	26.00	105.00	580.00
☐ Richmond	26.00	105.00	580.00	☐ Dallas	26.00	105.00	580.00
☐ Atlanta	26.00	105.00	580.00	☐ San Francisco	26.00	105.00	580.00

SERIES OF 1914 — WITH BLUE TREASURY SEAL AND BLUE SERIAL NUMBERS

This Note was issued with signatures of BURKE-McADOO, BURKE-GLASS, BURKE-HUSTON and WHITE-MELLON.

	A.B.P.	V.FINE	UNC.
Issued to all Federal Reserve Banks	24.00	45.00	200.00

134 / TWENTY DOLLAR NOTES

TWENTY DOLLAR NOTES (1928) FEDERAL RESERVE NOTES
(Small Size) **NOTE NO. 99**

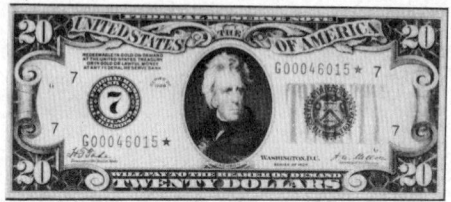

Face Design: Portrait of President Jackson center, black Federal Reserve Seal with numeral for district in center. City of issuing bank in seal circle. Green Treasury Seal right.

Back Design: Picture of the White House, similar to all small size $20.00 notes.

SERIES OF 1928 — SIGNATURES OF TATE-MELLON, GREEN SEAL

BANK	A.B.P.	V.FINE	UNC.	BANK	A.B.P.	V.FINE	UNC.
☐ Boston	22.00	28.00	65.00	☐ Chicago	22.00	28.00	53.00
☐ New York	22.00	28.00	57.00	☐ St. Louis	22.00	32.00	70.00
☐ Philadelphia	22.00	28.00	60.00	☐ Minneapolis	22.00	35.00	80.00
☐ Cleveland	22.00	28.00	60.00	☐ Kansas City	22.00	32.00	80.00
☐ Richmond	22.00	35.00	70.00	☐ Dallas	22.00	32.00	80.00
☐ Atlanta	22.00	32.00	65.00	☐ San Francisco	22.00	30.00	70.00

SERIES OF 1928A — SIGNATURES OF WOODS-MELLON, GREEN SEAL

CITY	A.B.P.	V.FINE	UNC.	CITY	A.B.P.	V.FINE	UNC.
☐ Boston	22.75	40.00	60.00	☐ Chicago	22.75	37.00	70.00
☐ New York	22.75	37.00	70.00	☐ St. Louis	22.75	40.00	65.00
☐ Philadelphia	22.75	37.00	60.00	☐ Minneapolis		NOT ISSUED	
☐ Cleveland	22.75	37.00	65.00	☐ Kansas City	22.75	45.00	85.00
☐ Richmond	22.75	40.00	70.00	☐ Dallas	22.75	35.00	75.00
☐ Atlanta	22.75	40.00	65.00	☐ San Francisco		NOT ISSUED	

TWENTY DOLLAR NOTES (1928) FEDERAL RESERVE NOTES
(Small Size)
NOTE NO. 100

SERIES OF 1928B — SIGNATURES OF WOODS-MELLON, GREEN SEAL FACE AND BACK DESIGN SIMILAR TO PREVIOUS NOTE. NUMERAL IN FEDERAL RESERVE SEAL IS NOW CHANGED TO A LETTER.

BANK	A.B.P.	V.FINE	UNC.	BANK	A.B.P.	V.FINE	UNC.
☐ Boston	21.85	31.50	53.00	☐ Chicago	21.85	31.50	53.00
☐ New York	21.85	31.50	53.00	☐ St. Louis	21.85	31.50	55.00
☐ Philadelphia	21.85	31.50	53.00	☐ Minneapolis	21.85	31.50	55.00
☐ Cleveland	21.85	31.50	53.00	☐ Kansas City	21.85	31.50	55.00
☐ Richmond	21.85	31.50	53.00	☐ Dallas	21.85	31.50	60.00
☐ Atlanta	21.85	31.50	55.00	☐ San Francisco	21.85	31.50	55.00

SERIES OF 1928C — SIGNATURES OF WOODS-MILLS, GREEN SEAL ONLY TWO BANKS ISSUED THIS NOTE.

BANK	A.B.P.	V.FINE	UNC.	BANK	A.B.P.	V.FINE	UNC.
☐ Chicago	28.00	55.00	225.00	☐ San Francisco	28.00	55.00	225.00

TWENTY DOLLAR NOTES (1934) FEDERAL RESERVE NOTES
(Small Size)
NOTE NO. 100A

FACE AND BACK DESIGN SIMILAR TO PREVIOUS NOTE. "REDEEMABLE IN GOLD" REMOVED FROM OBLIGATION OVER FEDERAL RESERVE SEAL. SIGNATURES OF JULIAN-MORGENTHAU, GREEN SEAL.

BANK	GOOD	V.FINE	UNC.	BANK	GOOD	V.FINE	UNC.
☐ Boston	——	29.00	50.00	☐ St. Louis	——	30.00	47.00
☐ New York	——	29.00	47.00	☐ Minneapolis	——	30.00	55.00
☐ Philadelphia	——	29.00	47.00	☐ Kansas City	——	30.00	47.00
☐ Cleveland	——	29.00	47.00	☐ Dallas	——	30.00	47.00
☐ Richmond	——	29.00	47.00	☐ San Francisco	——	30.00	47.00
☐ Atlanta	——	29.00	47.00	☐ *San Francisco			
☐ Chicago	——	29.00	47.00	(HAWAII)	50.00	150.00	925.00

*The San Francisco Federal Reserve Note with brown seal and brown serial numbers, and overprinted "HAWAII" on face and back, was a special issue for the Armed Forces in the Pacific area during World War II.

136 / TWENTY DOLLAR NOTES

TWENTY DOLLAR NOTES (1934A) FEDERAL RESERVE NOTES
(Small Size) NOTE NO. 101

SERIES OF 1934A — SIGNATURES OF JULIAN-MORGENTHAU

BANK	V.FINE	UNC.	BANK	V.FINE	UNC.
☐ Boston	27.00	48.00	☐ St. Louis	27.00	52.00
☐ New York	27.00	48.00	☐ Minneapolis	27.00	58.00
☐ Philadelphia	27.00	48.00	☐ Kansas City	27.00	52.00
☐ Cleveland	27.00	48.00	☐ Dallas	27.00	48.00
☐ Richmond	27.00	48.00	☐ San Francisco	27.00	48.00
☐ Atlanta	27.00	48.00	☐ *San Francisco (HAWAII)	110.00	475.00
☐ Chicago	27.00	48.00			

SERIES OF 1934B — SIGNATURES OF JULIAN-VINSON, GREEN SEAL

BANK	V.FINE	UNC.	BANK	V.FINE	UNC.
☐ Boston	26.50	48.00	☐ Chicago	26.50	38.00
☐ New York	26.50	42.00	☐ St. Louis	26.50	42.00
☐ Philadelphia	26.50	45.00	☐ Minneapolis	26.50	52.00
☐ Cleveland	26.50	45.00	☐ Kansas City	26.50	42.00
☐ Richmond	26.50	42.00	☐ Dallas	26.50	53.00
☐ Atlanta	26.50	38.00	☐ San Francisco	26.50	43.00

SERIES OF 1934C — SIGNATURES OF JULIAN-SNYDER, GREEN SEAL

Back Design: This has been modified with this series, balcony added to the White House.

BANK	V.FINE	UNC.	BANK	V.FINE	UNC.
☐ Boston	26.00	50.00	☐ Chicago	26.00	46.00
☐ New York	26.00	46.00	☐ St. Louis	26.00	46.00
☐ Philadelphia	26.00	46.00	☐ Minneapolis	26.00	53.00
☐ Cleveland	26.00	46.00	☐ Kansas City	26.00	50.00
☐ Richmond	26.00	46.00	☐ Dallas	26.00	50.00
☐ Atlanta	26.00	46.00	☐ San Francisco	26.00	46.00

SERIES OF 1934D — SIGNATURES OF CLARK-SNYDER, GREEN SEAL

BANK	V.FINE	UNC.	BANK	V.FINE	UNC.
☐ Boston	25.00	42.00	☐ Chicago	25.00	42.00
☐ New York	25.00	42.00	☐ St. Louis	25.00	42.00
☐ Philadelphia	25.00	42.00	☐ Minneapolis	25.00	47.00
☐ Cleveland	25.00	42.00	☐ Kansas City	25.00	47.00
☐ Richmond	25.00	42.00	☐ Dallas	25.00	45.00
☐ Atlanta	25.00	42.00	☐ San Francisco	25.00	45.00

TWENTY DOLLAR NOTES (1950) FEDERAL RESERVE NOTES
(Small Size) NOTE NO. 102

SERIES OF 1950 — SIGNATURES OF CLARK-SNYDER, GREEN SEAL
Black Federal Reserve Seal and Green Treaury Seal are slightly smaller.

BANK	UNC.	BANK	UNC.
☐Boston	36.00	☐Chicago	36.00
☐New York	36.00	☐St. Louis	36.00
☐Philadelphia	36.00	☐Minneapolis	36.00
☐Cleveland	36.00	☐Kansas City	36.00
☐Richmond	36.00	☐Dallas	36.00
☐Atlanta	36.00	☐San Francisco	36.00

SERIES OF 1950A — SIGNATURES OF PRIEST-HUMPHREY, GREEN SEAL
Issued for all Federal Reserve Banks...31.25
SERIES OF 1950B — SIGNATURES OF PRIEST-ANDERSON, GREEN SEAL
Issued for all Federal Reserve Banks...31.25
SERIES OF 1950C — SIGNATURES OF SMITH-DILLON, GREEN SEAL
Issued for all Federal Reserve Banks...31.00
SERIES OF 1950D — SIGNATURES OF GRANAHAN-DILLON, GREEN SEAL
Issued for all Federal Reserve Banks...33.50
SERIES OF 1950E — SIGNATURES OF GRANAHAN-FOWLER, GREEN SEAL
Issued only for New York, Chicago and San Francisco 34.25

TWENTY DOLLAR NOTES (1963) FEDERAL RESERVE NOTES
(Small Size) NOTE NO. 102A
SERIES OF 1963 — SIGNATURES OF GRANAHAN-DILLON, GREEN SEAL
Issued for all banks except Minneapolis 32.00
SERIES OF 1963A — SIGNATURES OF GRANAHAN-FOWLER, GREEN SEAL
Issued for all Federal Reserve Banks...29.00
SERIES OF 1969 — SIGNATURES OF ELSTON-KENNEDY, GREEN SEAL
Issued for all Federal Reserve Banks...28.00
SERIES OF 1969A — SIGNATURES OF KABIS-CONNALLY, GREEN SEAL
Issued for all Federal Reserve Banks...27.50
SERIES OF 1969B — SIGNATURES OF BANUELOS-CONNALLY
Issued for all Federal Reserve Banks...27.00
SERIES OF 1969C — SIGNATURES OF BANUELOS-SHULTZ, GREEN SEAL
Issued for all Federal Reserve Banks...27.00
SERIES OF 1974 — SIGNATURES OF NEFF-SIMON, GREEN SEAL
Issued for all Federal Reserve Banks...27.00
SERIES OF 1977 — SIGNATURES OF MORTON-BLUMENTHAL, GREEN SEAL
Issued for all Federal Reserve Banks...25.50
SERIES OF 1977A — SIGNATURES OF MORTON-MILLER, GREEN SEAL
Issued for all Federal Reserve Banks...26.00
SERIES OF 1981 — SIGNATURES OF BUCHANAN-REGAN, GREEN SEAL
Issued for all Federal Reserve Banks...22.00
SERIES OF 1981A — SIGNATURES OF ORTEGA-REGAN, GREEN SEAL
Issued for all Federal Reserve Banks......................................CURRENT

138 / TWENTY DOLLAR NOTES

TWENTY DOLLAR NOTES (1915-1918) FEDERAL RESERVE BANK (ALL HAVE BLUE SEALS)

(Large Size)
NOTE NO. 103

Face Design: Portrait of President Cleveland left, name of Bank and city center, blue Seal right.

Back Design: Locomotive and Steamship, same as Page 140, similar to Note No. 98.

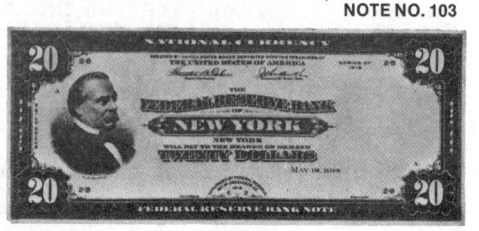

BANK & CITY	SERIES	GOV'T SIGNATURES	BANK SIGNATURES	A.B.P.	GOOD	V. FINE	UNC.
☐ Atlanta	1915	Teehee-Burke	Bell-Wellborn	53.00	110.00	410.00	1725.00
☐ Atlanta	1918	Elliott-Burke	Bell-Wellborn	53.00	110.00	405.00	1900.00
☐ Chicago	1915	Teehee-Burke	McLallen-McDougal	53.00	110.00	420.00	1750.00
☐ St. Louis	1918	Teehee-Burke	Attebery-Wells	57.00	115.00	600.00	4500.00
☐ Kan. City	1915	Teehee-Burke	Anderson-Miller	50.00	100.00	400.00	1725.00
☐ Kan. City	1915	Teehee-Burke	Cross-Miller	50.00	100.00	400.00	1725.00
☐ Dallas	1915	Teehee-Burke	Hoopes-VanZandt	53.00	110.00	420.00	3450.00
☐ Dallas	1915	Teehee-Burke	Gilbert-VanZandt	55.00	120.00	470.00	1750.00
☐ Dallas	1915	Teehee-Burke	Talley-VanZandt	55.00	120.00	470.00	1750.00

TWENTY DOLLAR NOTES (1929) FEDERAL RESERVE BANK NOTES

(Small Size)
NOTE NO. 103A

Face Design: Portrait of President Jackson center, name of bank left, brown seal right. Brown serial number, district letter in black. Signatures of Jones-Woods.

Back Design: The White House.

BANK	A.B.P.	V.FINE	UNC.	BANK	A.B.P.	V.FINE	UNC.
☐ Boston	20.75	23.50	80.00	☐ Chicago	20.75	23.50	67.00
☐ New York	20.75	23.50	67.00	☐ St. Louis	20.75	23.50	80.00
☐ Philadelphia	20.75	23.50	67.00	☐ Minneapolis	20.75	23.50	75.00
☐ Cleveland	20.75	23.50	67.00	☐ Kansas City	20.75	23.50	90.00
☐ Richmond	20.75	23.50	67.00	☐ Dallas	24.00	38.00	400.00
☐ Atlanta	20.75	23.50	75.00	☐ San Francisco	22.00	28.00	150.00

FIFTY DOLLAR NOTES

ORDER OF ISSUE

	FIRST ISSUE	LAST ISSUE	PAGE
1. UNITED STATES NOTES	1862	1880	140
2. NATIONAL BANK NOTES	1863	1929	143
3. SILVER CERTIFICATES	1878	1891	148
4. GOLD CERTIFICATES	1882	1928	150
5. TREASURY OR COIN NOTES	1890	1891	152
6. FEDERAL RESERVE NOTES	1914	present	153
7. FEDERAL RESERVE BANK NOTES	1918	1929	156

140 / FIFTY DOLLAR NOTES

FIFTY DOLLAR NOTES (1862-1863) UNITED STATES NOTES
(ALSO KNOWN AS LEGAL TENDER NOTES)
(Large Size)
NOTE NO. 104

Face Design: Portrait of Hamilton to left.

Back Design

SERIES	SIGNATURES	SEAL	A.B.P.	GOOD	V. FINE	UNC.
☐1862	Chittenden-Spinner*	Red	340.00	685.00	4000.00	10500.00
☐1862	Chittenden-Spinner**	Red	340.00	685.00	4000.00	10500.00
☐1863	Chittenden-Spinner**	Red	340.00	685.00	4000.00	10000.00

*First Obligation: Similar to Note No. 33
**Second Obligation: Shown above.

FIFTY DOLLAR NOTES / 141

FIFTY DOLLAR NOTES (1869) UNITED STATES NOTES
(ALSO KNOWN AS LEGAL TENDER NOTE)
(Large Size) **NOTE NO. 105**

Face Design: Portrait of Henry Clay to right.

Back Design

SERIES	SIGNATURES	SEAL	A.B.P.	GOOD	V. FINE	UNC.
☐1869	Allison-Spinner	Red	900.00	1800.00	7500.00	12500.00

NOTE: Only 24 pieces of this Note remain unredeemed.

142 / FIFTY DOLLAR NOTES

FIFTY DOLLAR NOTES (1874-1880) UNITED STATES NOTES
(Large Size)   **NOTE NO. 106**

Face Design: Franklin to left.

Back Design

SERIES	SIGNATURES	SEAL	A.B.P.	GOOD	V. FINE	UNC.
☐ 1874	Allison-Spinner	Sm. Red	235.00	475.00	1950.00	5200.00
☐ 1875	Allison-Wyman	Sm. Red	210.00	450.00	1850.00	5125.00
☐ 1878	Allison-Gilfillan	Sm. Red	200.00	425.00	1875.00	4350.00
☐ 1880	Bruce-Gilfillan	Lg. Brown	120.00	250.00	1000.00	2975.00
☐ 1880	Bruce-Wyman	Lg. Brown	120.00	250.00	1000.00	2975.00
☐ 1880	Rosecrans-Jordan	Lg. Red	120.00	250.00	800.00	2300.00
☐ 1880	Rosecrans-Hyatt	Lg. Red	120.00	250.00	800.00	2300.00
☐ 1880	Rosecrans-Hyatt	Lg. Red	120.00	250.00	800.00	2300.00
☐ 1880	Rosecrans-Huston	Lg. Red	120.00	250.00	800.00	2300.00
☐ 1880	Rosecrans-Huston	Lg. Brown	120.00	250.00	810.00	3150.00
☐ 1880	Tillman-Morgan	Sm. Red	100.00	210.00	715.00	2085.00
☐ 1880	Bruce-Roberts	Sm. Red	100.00	210.00	715.00	2085.00
☐ 1880	Lyons-Roberts	Sm. Red	100.00	210.00	715.00	2085.00

FIFTY DOLLAR NOTES / 143

FIFTY DOLLAR NOTES (1875) NATIONAL BANK NOTES
FIRST CHARTER PERIOD (Large Size)   NOTE NO. 107

Face Design: Washington crossing Delaware left, Washington at Valley Forge, right.

Back Design: Embarkation of the Pilgrims.

SERIES	SIGNATURES	SEAL	A.B.P.	V. FINE	UNC.
☐ Original	Chittenden-Spinner	Red/rays	685.00	3175.00	8750.00
☐ Original	Colby-Spinner	Red/rays	685.00	3175.00	8750.00
☐ Original	Allison-Spinner	Red/rays	685.00	3175.00	8750.00
☐ 1875	Allison-New	Red/Scals.	660.00	3000.00	8000.00
☐ 1875	Allison-Wyman	Red/Scals.	660.00	3000.00	8000.00
☐ 1875	Allison-Gilfillan	Red/Scals.	660.00	3000.00	8000.00
☐ 1875	Scofield-Gilfillan	Red/Scals.	660.00	3000.00	8000.00
☐ 1875	Bruce-Gilfillan	Red/Scals.	660.00	3000.00	8000.00
☐ 1875	Bruce-Wyman	Red/Scals.	660.00	3000.00	8000.00
☐ 1875	Rosecrans-Huston	Red/Scals.	660.00	3000.00	8000.00
☐ 1875	Rosecrans-Nebeker	Red/Scals.	660.00	3000.00	8000.00
☐ 1875	Tillman-Morgan	Red/Scals.	660.00	3000.00	8000.00

144 / FIFTY DOLLAR NOTES

FIFTY DOLLAR NOTES (1882) NATIONAL BANK NOTES
SECOND CHARTER PERIOD (Large Size) **NOTE NO. 108**

First Issue—brown seal and brown backs.

Back Design of Note No. 108
Face Design: Similar to Note No. 107

SERIES	SIGNATURES	SEAL	A.B.P.	GOOD	V. FINE	UNC.
☐1882	Bruce-Gilfillan	Brown	100.00	210.00	470.00	2200.00
☐1882	Bruce-Wyman	Brown	100.00	210.00	470.00	2200.00
☐1882	Bruce-Jordan	Brown	100.00	210.00	470.00	2200.00
☐1882	Rosecrans-Jordan	Brown	100.00	210.00	470.00	2200.00
☐1882	Rosecrans-Hyatt	Brown	100.00	210.00	470.00	2200.00
☐1882	Rosecrans-Huston	Brown	100.00	210.00	470.00	2200.00
☐1882	Rosecrans-Nebeker	Brown	100.00	210.00	470.00	2200.00
☐1882	Rosecrans-Morgan	Brown	240.00	520.00	1200.00	2800.00
☐1882	Tillman-Morgan	Brown	100.00	210.00	470.00	2200.00
☐1882	Tillman-Roberts	Brown	100.00	210.00	470.00	2200.00
☐1882	Bruce-Roberts	Brown	100.00	210.00	470.00	2200.00
☐1882	Lyons-Roberts	Brown	100.00	210.00	470.00	2200.00
☐1882	Vernon-Treat	Brown	240.00	520.00	1300.00	2800.00

FIFTY DOLLAR NOTES (1882) NATIONAL BANK NOTES
SECOND CHARTER PERIOD (Large Size)   **NOTE NO. 108A**

Second Issue—blue seal, green back with date 1902-1908

Face Design: Washington crossing Delaware left, Washington at Valley Forge, right.

Back Design

SERIES	SIGNATURES	SEAL	A.B.P.	GOOD	V. FINE	UNC.
☐ 1882	Rosecrans-Huston	Blue	140.00	275.00	950.00	2725.00
☐ 1882	Rosecrans-Nebeker	Blue	140.00	275.00	950.00	2725.00
☐ 1882	Tillman-Morgan	Blue	140.00	275.00	950.00	2725.00
☐ 1882	Tillman-Roberts	Blue	140.00	275.00	950.00	2725.00
☐ 1882	Bruce-Roberts	Blue	140.00	275.00	950.00	2725.00
☐ 1882	Lyons-Roberts	Blue	140.00	275.00	950.00	2725.00
☐ 1882	Vernon-Treat	Blue	140.00	275.00	950.00	2725.00
☐ 1882	Napier-McClung	Blue	155.00	310.00	1000.00	2850.00

146 / FIFTY DOLLAR NOTES

FIFTY DOLLAR NOTES (1902) NATIONAL BANK NOTES
THIRD CHARTER PERIOD (Large Size)   NOTE NO. 109

First Issues—red seal and numbers.

Face Design: Portrait of Sherman left. Name of Bank center. Treasury Seal and numbers.

SERIES	SIGNATURES	SEAL	A.B.P.	GOOD	V. FINE	UNC.
☐1902	Lyons-Roberts	Red	165.00	330.00	2375.00	5600.00
☐1902	Lyons-Treat	Red	165.00	330.00	2375.00	5600.00
☐1902	Vernon-Treat	Red	165.00	330.00	2375.00	5600.00

Second Issue—Treasury Seal and numbers remain blue, date 1902-1908 added on back.

☐1902	Lyons-Roberts	Blue	51.00	62.00	175.00	650.00
☐1902	Lyons-Treat	Blue	51.00	62.00	175.00	650.00
☐1902	Vernon-Treat	Blue	51.00	62.00	175.00	650.00
☐1902	Vernon-McClung	Blue	51.00	62.00	175.00	650.00
☐1902	Napier-McClung	Blue	51.00	62.00	175.00	650.00
☐1902	Napier-Thompson	Blue	52.00	62.00	210.00	800.00
☐1902	Napier-Burke	Blue	51.00	62.00	175.00	650.00
☐1902	Parker-Burke	Blue	51.00	62.00	175.00	650.00
☐1902	Teehee-Burke	Blue	55.00	80.00	250.00	650.00

Third Issue—Treasury Seal and numbers remain blue, date of 1902-1908 removed from back.

☐1902	Lyons-Roberts	Blue	53.00	65.00	125.00	585.00
☐1902	Lyons-Treat	Blue	53.00	65.00	125.00	585.00
☐1902	Vernon-Treat	Blue	53.00	65.00	125.00	585.00
☐1902	Vernon-McClung	Blue	53.00	65.00	125.00	585.00
☐1902	Napier-McClung	Blue	53.00	65.00	125.00	585.00
☐1902	Napier-Thompson	Blue	58.00	90.00	180.00	585.00
☐1902	Napier-Burke	Blue	54.00	70.00	135.00	585.00
☐1902	Parker-Burke	Blue	54.00	70.00	135.00	585.00
☐1902	Teehee-Burke	Blue	53.00	65.00	125.00	585.00
☐1902	Elliott-Burke	Blue	53.00	65.00	125.00	585.00
☐1902	Elliott-White	Blue	53.00	65.00	125.00	585.00
☐1902	Speelman-White	Blue	53.00	65.00	125.00	585.00
☐1902	Woods-White	Blue	53.00	65.00	125.00	585.00

FIFTY DOLLAR NOTES / 147
FIFTY DOLLAR NOTES (1929) NATIONAL BANK NOTES
(Small Size)
NOTE NO. 110

Face Design: Portrait of President Grant center. Bank left. Brown seal right. Brown serial numbers, black Charter numbers.

Back Design: The Capitol.

SERIES	SIGNATURES	SEAL	A.B.P.	V. FINE	UNC.
☐ 1929 TYPE I*	Jones-Wood	Brown	53.00	85.00	150.00
☐ 1929 TYPE II*	Jones-Wood	Brown	58.00	100.00	575.00

*See Page 63. TYPE I—Charter number in black.
TYPE II—Similar. Charter number added in brown.

148 / FIFTY DOLLAR NOTES

FIFTY DOLLAR NOTES (1878-1880) SILVER CERTIFICATES
(Large Size)
NOTE NO. 111

Face Design: Portrait of Edward Everett.

Back Design

SERIES	SIGNATURES	SEAL	A.B.P.	GOOD	V. FINE
☐ 1878	Varied	Red		VERY RARE	
☐ 1880	Scofield-Gilfillan	Brown	1075.00	2150.00	6500.00
☐ 1880	Bruce-Gilfillan	Brown	1075.00	2150.00	6500.00
☐ 1880	Bruce-Wyman	Brown	1075.00	2150.00	6500.00
☐ 1880	Rosecrans-Huston	Brown	1075.00	2150.00	6500.00
☐ 1880	Rosecrans-Nebeker	Red	1075.00	2150.00	6500.00

FIFTY DOLLAR NOTES (1891) SILVER CERTIFICATES
(Large Size) **NOTE NO. 111A**

Face Design: Portrait of Edward Everett.

Back Design

SERIES	SIGNATURES	SEAL	A.B.P.	GOOD	V. FINE	UNC.
☐ 1891	Rosecrans-Nebeker	Red	90.00	180.00	600.00	5500.00
☐ 1891	Tillman-Morgan	Red	90.00	180.00	600.00	5500.00
☐ 1891	Bruce-Roberts	Red	90.00	180.00	600.00	5500.00
☐ 1891	Lyons-Roberts	Red	90.00	180.00	600.00	5500.00
☐ 1891	Vernon-Treat	Red	90.00	180.00	600.00	5500.00
☐ 1891	Parker-Burke	Blue	90.00	180.00	600.00	5500.00

150 / FIFTY DOLLAR NOTES

FIFTY DOLLAR NOTES (1882) GOLD CERTIFICATES
(Large Size)   NOTE NO. 112

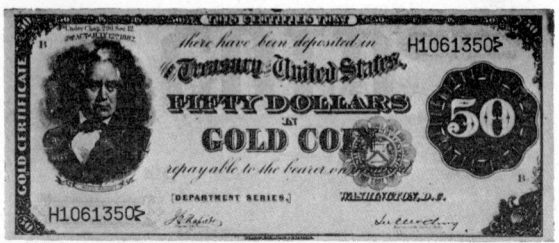

Face Design: Portrait of Silas Wright to left.

Back Design: Bright yellow color.

SERIES	SIGNATURES	SEAL	A.B.P.	GOOD	V. FINE	UNC.
☐ 1882	Bruce-Gilfillan	Brown	450.00	1175.00	3500.00	17500.00
☐ 1882	Bruce-Wyman	Brown	130.00	275.00	2375.00	11750.00
☐ 1882	Rosecrans-Hyatt	Red	130.00	275.00	2150.00	11750.00
☐ 1882	Rosecrans-Huston	Brown	130.00	275.00	2050.00	11750.00
☐ 1882	Lyons-Roberts	Red	118.00	235.00	975.00	4225.00
☐ 1882	Lyons-Treat	Red	118.00	235.00	975.00	4225.00
☐ 1882	Vernon-Treat	Red	118.00	235.00	975.00	4225.00
☐ 1882	Vernon-McClung	Red	118.00	235.00	975.00	4225.00
☐ 1882	Napier-McClung	Red	118.00	235.00	975.00	4225.00

FIFTY DOLLAR NOTES (1913) GOLD CERTIFICATES
(Large Size) NOTE NO. 113

Face Design: Portrait of President Grant.

Back Design: Bright yellow color.

SERIES	SIGNATURES	SEAL	A.B.P.	GOOD	V. FINE	UNC.
☐ 1913	Parker-Burke	Gold	80.00	150.00	510.00	3500.00
☐ 1913	Teehee-Burke	Gold	63.00	110.00	470.00	2500.00
☐ 1922	Speelman-White	Gold	56.00	90.00	350.00	1500.00

152 / FIFTY DOLLAR NOTES

FIFTY DOLLAR NOTES (1928) GOLD CERTIFICATES
(Small Size)   **NOTE NO. 114**

Back Design: Same as Note No. 110.

SERIES	SIGNATURES	SEAL	A.B.P.	GOOD	V. FINE	UNC.
☐1928	Woods-Mellon	Gold	52.00	60.00	110.00	585.00

FIFTY DOLLAR NOTES (1891) TREASURY NOTES
(Large Size)   **NOTE NO. 114A**

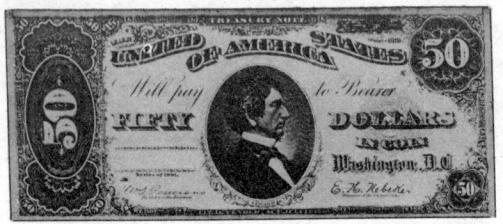

Face Design: Portrait of William H. Seward. Only 25 pieces remain unredeemed.

Back Design: Green.

SERIES	SIGNATURES	SEAL	A.B.P.	GOOD	V. FINE	UNC.
☐1891	Rosecrans-Nebeker	Red	1450.00	3200.00	11250.00	RARE

FIFTY DOLLAR NOTES / 153

FIFTY DOLLAR NOTES (1914) FEDERAL RESERVE NOTES
(Large Size)   NOTE NO. 115

SERIES OF 1914 — SIGNATURES OF BURKE-McADOO
RED SEAL AND RED SERIAL NUMBERS

CITY	A.B.P.	GOOD	V.FINE	UNC.	CITY	A.B.P.	GOOD	V.FINE	UNC.
☐Boston	53.00	80.00	285.00	1200.00	☐Chicago	53.00	80.00	285.00	1200.00
☐New York	53.00	80.00	285.00	1200.00	☐St. Louis	53.00	80.00	285.00	1200.00
☐Philadelphia	53.00	80.00	285.00	1200.00	☐Minneapolis	53.00	80.00	285.00	1200.00
☐Cleveland	53.00	80.00	285.00	1200.00	☐Kansas City	53.00	80.00	285.00	1200.00
☐Richmond	53.00	80.00	285.00	1200.00	☐Dallas	53.00	80.00	285.00	1200.00
☐Atlanta	53.00	80.00	285.00	1200.00	☐San Fran.	53.00	80.00	285.00	1200.00

SERIES OF 1914—DESIGN CONTINUES AS PREVIOUS NOTE.
THE SEAL AND SERIAL NUMBERS ARE NOW BLUE.
*(This Note was issued with various signatures for each Bank.)

BANK	A.B.P.	GOOD	V.FINE	UNC.	BANK	A.B.P.	GOOD	V.FINE	UNC.
☐Boston	52.00	65.00	115.00	500.00	☐Chicago	52.00	65.00	115.00	500.00
☐New York	52.00	65.00	115.00	500.00	☐St. Louis	52.00	65.00	115.00	500.00
☐Philadelphia	52.00	65.00	115.00	500.00	☐Minneapolis	52.00	65.00	115.00	500.00
☐Cleveland	52.00	65.00	115.00	500.00	☐Kansas City	52.00	65.00	115.00	500.00
☐Richmond	52.00	65.00	115.00	500.00	☐Dallas	52.00	65.00	115.00	500.00
☐Atlanta	52.00	65.00	115.00	500.00	☐San Fran.	52.00	65.00	115.00	500.00

*Signatures: Burke-McAdoo, Burke-Glass, Burke-Huston, White-Mellon.

154 / FIFTY DOLLAR NOTES

FIFTY DOLLAR (1928) FEDERAL RESERVE NOTES
(Small Size)　　　　　　　　　　　　　　　　　**NOTE NO. 116**

Face Design: Portrait of President Grant center. Black Federal Reserve Seal with number to left. Green Treasury Seal to right.

Back Design: Same as Note No. 110.

SERIES OF 1928 — SIGNATURES OF WOODS-MELLON, GREEN SEAL

	A.B.P.	V.FINE	UNC.
Issued for all Federal Reserve Banks (Small Size)	53.00	65.00	130.00

NOTE NO. 116A

SERIES OF 1928A — SIGNATURES OF WOODS-MELLON, GREEN SEAL
LETTER REPLACES NUMERAL IN FEDERAL RESERVE SEAL

	A.B.P.	V.FINE	UNC.
Issued for all Federal Reserve Banks. (Small Size)	52.00	60.00	110.00

NOTE NO. 116B

SERIES OF 1934 — SIGNATURES OF JULIAN-MORGENTHAU, GREEN SEAL

	A.B.P.	V.FINE	UNC.
Issued for all Federal Reserve Banks	——	58.00	89.00

SERIES OF 1934A — SIGNATURES OF JULIAN-MORGENTHAU, GREEN SEAL

	A.B.P.	V.FINE	UNC.
Issued for all Federal Reserve Banks except Philadelphia.	——	56.00	85.00

SERIES OF 1934B — SIGNATURES OF JULIAN-VINSON, GREEN SEAL

	A.B.P.	V.FINE	UNC.
Issued for all Federal Reserve Banks except Boston and New York.	52.00	59.00	105.00

SERIES OF 1934C — SIGNATURES OF JULIAN-SNYDER, GREEN SEAL

	A.B.P.	V.FINE	UNC.
Issued for all Federal Reserve Banks except San Francisco.	——	56.00	87.00

SERIES OF 1934D — SIGNATURES OF CLARK-SNYDER, GREEN SEAL

	A.B.P.	V.FINE	UNC.
Issued for Cleveland, St. Louis, Minneapolis, Kansas City, San Francisco.	——	55.00	80.00

FIFTY DOLLAR NOTES (1950) FEDERAL RESERVE NOTES
(Small Size)   **NOTE NO. 116C**

SERIES OF 1950 — SIGNATURES OF CLARK-SNYDER
FEDERAL RESERVE AND TREASURY SEALS ARE NOW SMALLER
                                                                                                         UNC.
Issued for all Federal Reserve Banks..75.00
SERIES OF 1950A — SIGNATURES OF PRIEST-HUMPHREY
Issued for all Federal Reserve Banks except Minneapolis............................73.00
SERIES OF 1950B — SIGNATURES OF PRIEST-ANDERSON
Issued for all Federal Reserve Banks except Atlanta and Minneapolis................70.00
SERIES OF 1950C — SIGNATURES OF SMITH-DILLON
Issued for all Federal Reserve Banks except Atlanta...............................72.00
SERIES OF 1950D — SIGNATURES OF GRANAHAN-DILLON
Issued for all Federal Reserve Banks..62.00
SERIES OF 1950E — SIGNATURES OF GRANAHAN-FOWLER
Issued only for New York, Chicago, San Francisco..................................61.00

FIFTY DOLLAR (1963) FEDERAL RESERVE NOTES
(Small Size) "IN GOD WE TRUST" ADDED ON BACK   **NOTE NO. 116D**
SERIES OF 1963, NO NOTES WERE PRINTED
SERIES OF 1963A — SIGNATURES OF GRANAHAN-FOWLER
Issued for all Federal Reserve Banks..61.00

FIFTY DOLLAR (1969) FEDERAL RESERVE NOTES
(WORDING IN GREEN SEAL CHANGED FROM LATIN TO ENGLISH)
                                                                                         NOTE NO. 116E
SERIES OF 1969 — SIGNATURES OF ELSTON-KENNEDY
Issued for all Federal Reserve Banks..57.00
SERIES OF 1969A — SIGNATURES OF KABIS-CONNALLY
Issued for all Federal Reserve Banks..57.00
SERIES OF 1969B — SIGNATURES OF BANUELOS-CONNALLY
Issued for Boston, New York, Philadelphia, Richmond,
Atlanta, Chicago, Dallas...57.00
SERIES OF 1969C — SIGNATURES OF BANUELOS-SHULTZ
Issued for all Federal Reserve Banks..57.00
SERIES OF 1974 — SIGNATURES OF NEFF-SIMON
Issued for all Federal Reserve Banks..57.00
SERIES OF 1977 — SIGNATURES OF MORTON-BLUMENTHAL
Issued for all Federal Reserve Banks..57.00
SERIES OF 1977A — SIGNATURES OF MORTON-MILLER
Issued for all Federal Reserve Banks..57.00
SERIES OF 1981 — SIGNATURES OF BUCHANAN-REGAN, GREEN SEAL
Issued for all Federal Reserve Banks..53.00
SERIES OF 1981A — SIGNATURES OF ORTEGA-REGAN, GREEN SEAL
Issued for all Federal Reserve Banks...CURRENT

156 / FIFTY DOLLAR NOTES

FIFTY DOLLAR NOTES (1918) FEDERAL RESERVE BANK NOTES
(Large Size)
NOTE NO. 117

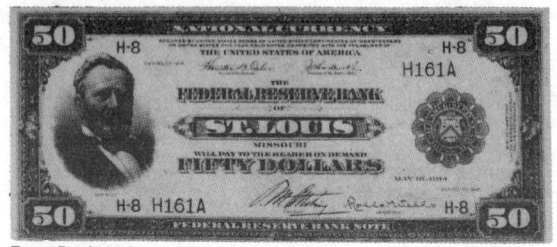

Face Design: Portrait of President Grant to left, Federal Reserve Bank in center, blue seal right.
Back Design: Female figure of Panama between merchant ship and battleship. Plates were made for all 12 Federal Reserve Districts. Only St. Louis bank was issued. Less than 30 notes are known today.

CITY	SERIES	GOVERNMENT SIGNATURES	BANK SIGNATURES	BANK A.B.P.	FINE	UNC.
☐St. Louis	1918	Teehee-Burke	Attebery-Wells	1325.00	3000.00	9750.00

FIFTY DOLLAR NOTES (1929) FEDERAL RESERVE BANK
(Small Size)
NOTE NO. 117A

Face Design: Portrait of Grant center, name of Bank left, brown serial numbers, black letter for Federal Reserve District.
Back Design: Same as Note No. 110.

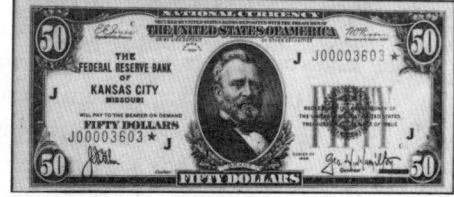

BANK	SERIES	SIGNATURES	SEAL	A.B.P.	V. FINE	UNC.
☐New York	1929	Jones-Woods	Brown	53.00	68.00	160.00
☐Cleveland	1929	Jones-Woods	Brown	53.00	68.00	160.00
☐Chicago	1929	Jones-Woods	Brown	53.00	70.00	180.00
☐Minneapolis	1929	Jones-Woods	Brown	53.00	82.00	235.00
☐Kansas City	1929	Jones-Woods	Brown	53.00	70.00	190.00
☐Dallas	1929	Jones-Woods	Brown	53.00	82.00	235.00
☐San Francisco	1929	Jones-Woods	Brown	53.00	70.00	185.00

ONE HUNDRED DOLLAR NOTES

ORDER OF ISSUE

	FIRST ISSUE	LAST ISSUE	PAGE
1. UNITED STATES NOTES	1862	1966	158
2. NATIONAL BANK NOTES	1863	1929	161
3. SILVER CERTIFICATES	1878	1891	164
4. GOLD CERTIFICATES	1882	1928	166
5. TREASURY OR COIN NOTES	1890	1891	167
6. FEDERAL RESERVE NOTES	1914	present	168
7. FEDERAL RESERVE BANK NOTES	1915	1929	171

158 / ONE HUNDRED DOLLAR NOTES

ONE HUNDRED DOLLAR NOTES (1862-1863) U.S. NOTES
(ALSO KNOWN AS LEGAL TENDER NOTE)
(Large Size) NOTE NO. 118

Face Design: Eagle with spread wings left, three discs with "100", red seal numbers.

Back Design: Green, two variations of the wording in obligation.

SERIES	SIGNATURES	SEAL	A.B.P.	GOOD	V. FINE	UNC.
☐1862	Chittenden-Spinner*	Red	650.00	1300.00	6000.00	13750.00
☐1862	Chittenden-Spinner**	Red	650.00	1300.00	6000.00	13750.00
☐1863	Chittenden-Spinner**	Red	650.00	1300.00	6000.00	13750.00

*First Obligation: Similar to Note No. 33   **Second Obligation: Shown above.

ONE HUNDRED DOLLAR NOTES / 159

ONE HUNDRED DOLLAR NOTES (1869-1880) U.S. NOTES
(Large Size) NOTE NO. 119

Face Design: Portrait of President Lincoln

Back Design: No. 119A.

Back Design: No. 119.

SERIES	SIGNATURES	SEAL	A.B.P.	GOOD	V. FINE	UNC.
☐ 1869	Allison-Spinner	Red	825.00	1675.00	7900.00	17500.00

THE FOLLOWING NOTES HAVE A MODIFIED BACK DESIGN
(Small Size) NOTE NO. 119A

☐ 1875	Allison-New	Sm. Red	525.00	1100.00	7000.00	12000.00
☐ 1875	Allison-Wyman	Sm. Red	425.00	775.00	6750.00	11500.00
☐ 1878	Allison-Gilfillan	Sm. Red	425.00	775.00	6750.00	11500.00
☐ 1880	Bruce-Gilfillan	Lg. Brown	425.00	775.00	2450.00	6000.00
☐ 1880	Bruce-Wyman	Lg. Brown	425.00	775.00	2450.00	6000.00
☐ 1880	Rosecrans-Jordan	Lg. Red	425.00	775.00	2450.00	6000.00
☐ 1880	Rosecrans-Hyatt	Lg. Red	425.00	775.00	2450.00	6000.00
☐ 1880	Rosecrans-Hyatt	Lg. Red	425.00	775.00	2450.00	6000.00
☐ 1880	Rosecrans-Huston	Lg. Red	400.00	775.00	2450.00	5875.00
☐ 1880	Rosecrans-Huston	Lg. Brown	400.00	775.00	2450.00	5875.00
☐ 1880	Tillman-Morgan	Sm. Red	400.00	775.00	2375.00	5380.00
☐ 1880	Bruce-Roberts	Sm. Red	400.00	775.00	2375.00	5380.00
☐ 1880	Lyons-Roberts	Sm. Red	400.00	775.00	2375.00	5380.00

160 / ONE HUNDRED DOLLAR NOTES

ONE HUNDRED DOLLAR NOTES (1966) U.S. NOTES
(ALSO KNOWN AS LEGAL TENDER NOTE)

(Small Size)   NOTE NO. 119B

Face Design: Portrait of Franklin red seal, red serial numbers.

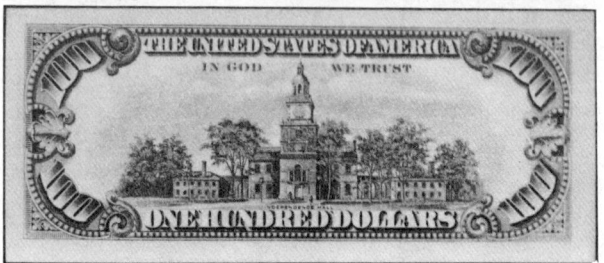

Back Design: Independence Hall.

SERIES	SIGNATURES	SEAL	V. FINE	UNC.
☐1966*	Granahan-Fowler	Red	125.00	170.00
☐1966A	Elston-Kennedy	Red	125.00	170.00

*This is the first Note to be issued with the new Treasury Seal with wording in English instead of Latin.

ONE HUNDRED DOLLAR NOTES (1875) NATIONAL BANK NOTES
(ALL HAVE RED SEAL)
FIRST CHARTER PERIOD (Large Size)   **NOTE NO. 120**

Face Design: Perry leaving the Lawrence, left.

Face Design: Border green, center black, Signing of the Declaration of Independence.

SERIES	SIGNATURES	SEAL	A.B.P.	GOOD	V. FINE
☐ Original	Chittenden-Spinner	Red	520.00	1050.00	3675.00
☐ Original	Colby-Spinner	Red	520.00	1050.00	3675.00
☐ Original	Allison-Spinner	Red	520.00	1050.00	3675.00
☐ 1875	Allison-New	Red	450.00	975.00	3550.00
☐ 1875	Allison-Wyman	Red	450.00	975.00	3550.00
☐ 1875	Allison-Gilfillan	Red	450.00	975.00	3550.00
☐ 1875	Scofield-Gilfillan	Red	450.00	975.00	3550.00
☐ 1875	Bruce-Gilfillan	Red	450.00	975.00	3550.00
☐ 1875	Bruce-Wyman	Red	450.00	975.00	3550.00
☐ 1875	Rosecrans-Huston	Red	450.00	975.00	3550.00
☐ 1875	Tillman-Morgan	Red	450.00	975.00	3550.00

ONE HUNDRED DOLLAR NOTES (1882) NATIONAL BANK NOTES
SECOND CHARTER PERIOD (Large Size)   NOTE NO. 120A
First Issue—brown seal and brown backs

Face Design: Similar to Note No. 120.
Back Design: Similar to Note No. 39.

SERIES	SIGNATURES	SEAL	A.B.P.	GOOD	V. FINE	UNC.
☐1882	Bruce-Gilfillan	Brown	145.00	280.00	650.00	2825.00
☐1882	Bruce-Wyman	Brown	145.00	280.00	650.00	2825.00
☐1882	Bruce-Jordan	Brown	145.00	280.00	650.00	2825.00
☐1882	Rosecrans-Jordan	Brown	145.00	280.00	650.00	2825.00
☐1882	Rosecrans-Hyatt	Brown	145.00	280.00	650.00	2825.00
☐1882	Rosecrans-Huston	Brown	145.00	280.00	650.00	2825.00
☐1882	Rosecrans-Nebeker	Brown	145.00	280.00	650.00	2825.00
☐1882	Rosecrans-Morgan	Brown	145.00	280.00	625.00	2825.00
☐1882	Tillman-Morgan	Brown	145.00	280.00	625.00	2825.00
☐1882	Tillman-Roberts	Brown	145.00	280.00	625.00	2825.00
☐1882	Bruce-Roberts	Brown	145.00	280.00	625.00	2825.00
☐1882	Lyons-Roberts	Brown	145.00	280.00	625.00	2825.00

SECOND CHARTER PERIOD (Large Size)   NOTE NO. 121
Second Issue—blue seal, green back with date 1902-1908

Face Design: Similar to Note No. 120.
Back Design: Green with date 1882-1908, center.

SERIES	SIGNATURES	SEAL	A.B.P.	V. FINE	UNC.
☐1882	Rosecrans-Huston	Blue	345.00	700.00	3375.00
☐1882	Rosecrans-Nebeker	Blue	345.00	700.00	3375.00
☐1882	Tillman-Morgan	Blue	345.00	700.00	3375.00
☐1882	Tillman-Roberts	Blue	345.00	700.00	3375.00
☐1882	Bruce-Roberts	Blue	345.00	700.00	3375.00
☐1882	Lyons-Roberts	Blue	345.00	700.00	3375.00
☐1882	Vernon-Treat	Blue	345.00	700.00	3375.00
☐1882	Napier-McClung	Blue	345.00	730.00	3450.00

This Note was also issued with (value) "ONE HUNDRED DOLLARS" on the back. Very Rare.

ONE HUNDRED DOLLAR NOTES / 163

ONE HUNDRED DOLLAR NOTES (1902) NATIONAL BANK NOTES
THIRD CHARTER PERIOD (Large Size)   **NOTE NO. 122**

Face Design: Portrait of John J. Knox, left.

Back Design: Male figures with shield and flags.

First Issue—red seal

SERIES	SIGNATURES	SEAL	A.B.P.	GOOD	V. FINE	UNC.
☐ 1902	Lyons-Roberts	Red	215.00	425.00	1100.00	6200.00
☐ 1902	Lyons-Treat	Red	215.00	425.00	1100.00	6200.00
☐ 1902	Vernon-Treat	Red	215.00	425.00	1100.00	6200.00

Second Issue—design is similar to previous Note. Seal and serial numbers are now blue, back of Note has date 1902-1908 added.

                         Blue   115.00   140.00   310.00   785.00

Third Issue—design continues as previous Notes. Seal and serial numbers remain blue, date 1902-1908 removed from back.

The Notes of the **SECOND AND THIRD ISSUE** appeared with various Signatures: LYONS-ROBERTS, LYONS-TREAT, VERNON-TREAT, VERNON-McCLUNG, NAPIER-McCLUNG, PARKER-BURKE, TEEHEE-BURKE, ELLIOTT-BURKE, ELLIOTT-WHITE, SPEELMAN-WHITE, WOODS-WHITE.

                         Blue   112.00   132.00   285.00   735.00

164 / ONE HUNDRED DOLLAR NOTES

ONE HUNDRED DOLLAR NOTES (1929) NATIONAL BANK NOTES
(Small Size)   **NOTE NO. 123**

Face Design: Portrait of Franklin, center. Name of Bank and City, left. Brown seal, right.

SERIES	SIGNATURES	SEAL	A.B.P.	V. FINE	UNC.
☐ 1929 TYPE I	Jones-Woods	Brown	108.00	160.00	195.00
☐ 1929 TYPE II	Jones-Woods	Brown	120.00	200.00	575.00

ONE HUNDRED DOLLAR NOTES (1878) SILVER CERTIFICATES

SERIES	SIGNATURES	SEAL	A.B.P.	GOOD	V.FINE	UNC.
☐ 1878	Scofield-Gilfillan-White	Red			UNIQUE	
☐ 1878	Scofield-Gilfillan-Hopper	Red		NO SPECIMENS KNOWN		
☐ 1878	Scofield-Gilfillan-Hillhouse	Red		NO SPECIMENS KNOWN		
☐ 1878	Scofield-Gilfillan-Anthony	Red			UNIQUE	
☐ 1878	Scofield-Gilfillan-Wyman	Red		NO SPECIMENS KNOWN		
☐ 1878	Scofield-Gilfillan-Wyman (printed signature of Wyman)	Red	2175.00	4250.00	15000.00	30000.00

SERIES	SIGNATURES	SEAL	A.B.P.	GOOD	V. FINE	UNC.
☐ 1880	Scofield-Gilfillan	Brown		EXTREMELY RARE		
☐ 1880	Bruce-Gilfillan	Brown	1175.00	2500.00	6500.00	16000.00
☐ 1880	Bruce-Wyman	Brown	1175.00	2500.00	6500.00	16000.00
☐ 1880	Rosecrans-Huston	Brown	950.00	2050.00	5275.00	15500.00
☐ 1880	Rosecrans-Nebeker	Red	950.00	2050.00	5275.00	15250.00

ONE HUNDRED DOLLAR NOTES / 165

ONE HUNDRED DOLLAR NOTES (1891) SILVER CERTIFICATES
(Large Size)   NOTE NO. 124

Face Design: Portrait of President Monroe.

SERIES	SIGNATURES	SEAL	A.B.P.	GOOD	V. FINE	UNC.
☐1891	Rosecrans-Nebeker	Red	525.00	1100.00	4125.00	11000.00
☐1891	Tillman-Morgan	Red	525.00	1100.00	4125.00	11000.00

This Note was also issued in the Series of 1878 and 1880. They are Very Rare.

ONE HUNDRED DOLLAR NOTES (1882-1922) GOLD CERTIFICATES
(Large Size)   NOTE NO. 125

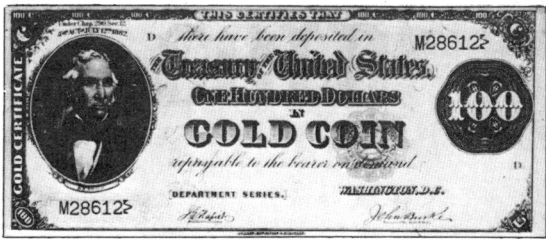

Face Design: Portrait of Thomas H. Benton.

166 / ONE HUNDRED DOLLAR NOTES

SERIES	SIGNATURES	SEAL	A.B.P.	GOOD	V. FINE	UNC.
☐ 1882	Bruce-Gilfillan	Lg. Brown	410.00	900.00	3500.00	12000.00
☐ 1882	Bruce-Wyman	Lg. Brown	360.00	800.00	3250.00	10750.00
☐ 1882	Rosecrans-Hyatt	Lg. Red	360.00	800.00	3250.00	10750.00
☐ 1882	Rosecrans-Huston	Lg. Brown	360.00	800.00	3250.00	10750.00
☐ 1882	Lyons-Roberts	Sm. Red	145.00	300.00	600.00	4875.00
☐ 1882	Lyons-Treat	Sm. Red	145.00	300.00	600.00	4875.00
☐ 1882	Vernon-Treat	Sm. Red	165.00	350.00	650.00	6000.00
☐ 1882	Vernon-McClung	Sm. Red	145.00	300.00	600.00	4750.00
☐ 1882	Napier-McClung	Sm. Red	145.00	300.00	600.00	4750.00
☐ 1882	Napier-Thompson	Sm. Red	145.00	300.00	600.00	4750.00
☐ 1882	Napier-Burke	Sm. Red	145.00	300.00	600.00	4750.00
☐ 1882	Parker-Burke	Sm. Red	145.00	300.00	600.00	4750.00
☐ 1882	Teehee-Burke	Sm. Red	145.00	300.00	600.00	4750.00
☐ 1922	Speelman-White	Sm. Red	145.00	300.00	600.00	4750.00

ONE HUNDRED DOLLAR NOTES (1928) GOLD CERTIFICATES
(Small Size)

NOTE NO. 126

Face Design: Portrait of Franklin, center. Yellow seal to left. Yellow numbers.

SERIES	SIGNATURES	SEAL	A.B.P.	GOOD	V. FINE	UNC.
☐ 1928	Woods-Mellon	Gold	102.00	112.00	180.00	690.00

ONE HUNDRED DOLLAR NOTES / 167

ONE HUNDRED DOLLAR (1890-1891) TREASURY NOTES
(Large Size)   **NOTE NO. 127**

Face Design: Portrait of Commodore Farragut to right.

Back Design: Large "100", called "Watermelon Note."

Back Design: "One Hundred" in scalloped medallion.

SERIES	SIGNATURES	SEAL	A.B.P.	GOOD	V. FINE	UNC.
☐ 1890	Rosecrans-Huston	Brown	2400.00	5250.00	15250.00	RARE
☐ 1891	Rosecrans-Nebeker	Red	2150.00	4675.00	14000.00	RARE

168 / ONE HUNDRED DOLLAR NOTES

ONE HUNDRED DOLLAR NOTES (1914) FEDERAL RESERVE
(Large Size)   **NOTE NO. 128**

Face Design: Portrait of Franklin in center.
Back Design: Group of five allegorical figures.
SERIES OF 1914 — SIGNATURES OF BURKE-McADOO
RED SEAL AND RED SERIAL NUMBERS

CITY	A.B.P.	GOOD	V.FINE	UNC.	CITY	A.B.P.	GOOD	V.FINE	UNC.
☐Boston	105.00	145.00	340.00	2200.00	☐Chicago	105.00	145.00	340.00	2200.00
☐New York	105.00	145.00	340.00	2200.00	☐St. Louis	105.00	145.00	340.00	2200.00
☐Phil.	105.00	145.00	340.00	2200.00	☐Minn.	105.00	145.00	340.00	2200.00
☐Cleveland	105.00	145.00	340.00	2200.00	☐Kan. Cy.	105.00	145.00	340.00	2200.00
☐Richmond	105.00	145.00	340.00	2200.00	☐Dallas	105.00	145.00	340.00	2200.00
☐Atlanta	105.00	145.00	340.00	2200.00	☐San Fran.	105.00	145.00	340.00	2200.00

SERIES OF 1914—DESIGN CONTINUES AS PREVIOUS NOTE.
THE SEAL AND SERIAL NUMBERS ARE NOW BLUE.
*(This Note was issued with various signatures for each Bank.)

BANK	A.B.P.	V.FINE	UNC.	BANK	A.B.P.	V.FINE	UNC.
☐Boston	103.00	165.00	620.00	☐Chicago	103.00	165.00	620.00
☐New York	103.00	165.00	620.00	☐St. Louis	103.00	165.00	620.00
☐Philadelphia	103.00	165.00	620.00	☐Minneapolis	103.00	165.00	620.00
☐Cleveland	103.00	165.00	620.00	☐Kansas City	103.00	165.00	620.00
☐Richmond	103.00	165.00	620.00	☐Dallas	103.00	165.00	620.00
☐Atlanta	103.00	165.00	620.00	☐San Francisco	103.00	165.00	620.00

*Signatures: Burke-McAdoo, Burke-Glass, Burke-Huston, White-Mellon.

ONE HUNDRED DOLLAR NOTES / 169

ONE HUNDRED DOLLAR NOTES (1928)
FEDERAL RESERVE NOTES

(Small Size) NOTE NO. 129

Face Design: Portrait of Franklin. Black Federal Reserve Seal left with number, green Treasury Seal right.

SERIES OF 1928 — SIGNATURES OF WOODS-MELLON, GREEN SEAL

CITY	A.B.P.	V.FINE	UNC.	CITY	A.B.P.	V.FINE	UNC.
☐ Boston	103.00	130.00	190.00	☐ Chicago	103.00	130.00	190.00
☐ New York	103.00	130.00	190.00	☐ St. Louis	103.00	130.00	190.00
☐ Philadelphia	103.00	130.00	190.00	☐ Minneapolis	103.00	130.00	190.00
☐ Cleveland	103.00	130.00	190.00	☐ Kansas City	103.00	130.00	190.00
☐ Richmond	103.00	130.00	190.00	☐ Dallas	103.00	130.00	190.00
☐ Atlanta	103.00	130.00	190.00	☐ San Francisco	103.00	130.00	190.00

SERIES OF 1928A — SIGNATURES OF WOODS-MELLON, GREEN SEAL
NUMBER IN BLACK, FEDERAL RESERVE SEAL IS CHANGED TO A LETTER

(Small Size) NOTE NO. 129A

CITY	A.B.P.	V.FINE	UNC.	CITY	A.B.P.	V.FINE	UNC.
☐ Boston	103.00	130.00	185.00	☐ Chicago	103.00	130.00	185.00
☐ New York	103.00	130.00	185.00	☐ St. Louis	103.00	130.00	185.00
☐ Philadelphia	103.00	130.00	185.00	☐ Minneapolis	103.00	130.00	185.00
☐ Cleveland	103.00	130.00	185.00	☐ Kansas City	103.00	130.00	185.00
☐ Richmond	103.00	130.00	185.00	☐ Dallas	103.00	130.00	185.00
☐ Atlanta	103.00	130.00	185.00	☐ San Francisco	103.00	130.00	185.00

SERIES OF 1934—SIGNATURES OF JULIAN-MORGENTHAU, GREEN SEAL
SERIES OF 1934A—SIGNATURES OF JULIAN-MORGENTHAU, GREEN SEAL
(The above two Notes were issued on all Federal Reserve Districts.)

SERIES OF 1934B* — SIGNATURES OF JULIAN-VINSON, GREEN SEAL
SERIES OF 1934C* — SIGNATURES OF JULIAN-SNYDER, GREEN SEAL
SERIES OF 1934D* — SIGNATURES OF CLARK-SNYDER, GREEN SEAL
(*Not all Districts issued in these series.)

	V.FINE	UNC.
AVERAGE PRICES ARE FOR ABOVE FIVE ISSUES	110.00	180.00

170 / ONE HUNDRED DOLLAR NOTES

ONE HUNDRED DOLLAR NOTES (1950) FEDERAL RESERVE
FEDERAL RESERVE NOTES, GREEN SEAL
(Small Size) **NOTE NO. 129C**

SERIES OF 1950 — SIGNATURES OF CLARK-SNYDER
Issued for all Federal Reserve Banks....................................148.00

SERIES OF 1950A — SIGNATURES OF PRIEST-HUMPHREY
Issued for all Federal Reserve Banks....................................135.00

SERIES OF 1950B — SIGNATURES OF PRIEST-ANDERSON
Issued for all Federal Reserve Banks....................................135.00

SERIES OF 1950C — SIGNATURES OF SMITH-DILLON
Issued for all Federal Reserve Banks....................................132.00

SERIES OF 1950D — SIGNATURES OF GRANAHAN-DILLON
Issued for all Federal Reserve Banks....................................130.00

SERIES OF 1950E — SIGNATURES OF GRANAHAN-FOWLER
Issued for New York, Chicago, San Francisco only....................................130.00

ONE HUNDRED DOLLAR NOTES (1963) FEDERAL RESERVE
NOTE NO. 129D

SERIES OF 1963 — NO NOTES WERE PRINTED FOR THIS SERIES

SERIES OF 1963A — "IN GOD WE TRUST" ADDED ON BACK

SERIES OF 1963A — SIGNATURES OF GRANAHAN-FOWLER
Issued for all Federal Reserve Banks....................................124.00

ONE HUNDRED DOLLAR NOTES (1969) FEDERAL RESERVE
NOTE NO. 129E

SERIES OF 1969 — ENGLISH WORDING IN TREASURY SEAL

SERIES OF 1969 — SIGNATURES OF ELSTON-KENNEDY
Issued for all Federal Reserve Banks....................................118.00

SERIES OF 1969A — SIGNATURES OF KABIS-CONNALLY
Issued for all Federal Reserve Banks....................................113.00

SERIES OF 1969B — NO NOTES WERE PRINTED

SERIES OF 1969C — SIGNATURES OF BANUELOS-SHULTZ
Issued for all Federal Reserve Banks....................................110.00

SERIES OF 1974 — SIGNATURES OF NEFF-SIMON
Issued for all Federal Reserve Banks....................................110.00

SERIES OF 1977 — SIGNATURES OF MORTON-BLUMENTHAL
Issued for all Federal Reserve Banks....................................110.00

SERIES OF 1977A — SIGNATURES OF MORTON-MILLER
Issued for all Federal Reserve Banks....................................108.00

SERIES OF 1981 — SIGNATURES OF BUCHANAN-REGAN, GREEN SEAL
Issued for all Federal Reserve Banks....................................105.00

SERIES OF 1981A — SIGNATURES OF ORTEGA-REGAN, GREEN SEAL
Issued for all Federal Reserve Banks....................................CURRENT

ONE HUNDRED DOLLAR NOTES / 171

ONE HUNDRED DOLLAR (1929)
FEDERAL RESERVE BANK NOTES
(ISSUED ONLY IN SERIES OF 1929)

(Small Size)

NOTE NO. 129F

Face Design: Portrait of Franklin, brown seal and numbers.

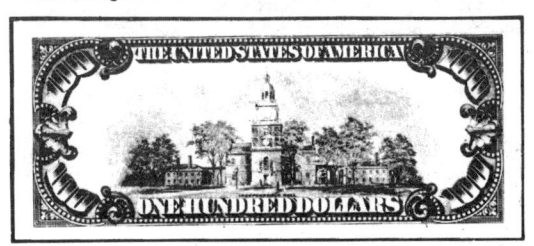

Back Design

BANK & CITY	SIGNATURES	SEAL	A.P.B.	V. FINE	UNC.
☐ New York	Jones-Woods	Brown	103.00	115.00	225.00
☐ Cleveland	Jones-Woods	Brown	103.00	115.00	250.00
☐ Richmond	Jones-Woods	Brown	103.00	115.00	275.00
☐ Chicago	Jones-Woods	Brown	103.00	115.00	225.00
☐ Minneapolis	Jones-Woods	Brown	103.00	115.00	225.00
☐ Kansas City	Jones-Woods	Brown	105.00	135.00	300.00
☐ Dallas	Jones-Woods	Brown	110.00	145.00	385.00

FIVE HUNDRED, ONE THOUSAND
FIVE THOUSAND and TEN THOUSAND DOLLAR NOTES
(Production of Notes in Denominations above One Hundred Dollars
were discontinued in 1969.)

MULES
(MIXED PLATE NUMBERS)

All United States Currency of every kind and denomination has a plate number on the face and back. These plate numbers are in the lower right corner somewhat close to the fine scroll design. They refer to the number of the engraved plate used to print the sheet of notes. Each plate can be used for about 100,000 impressions. It is then destroyed and a new plate with the next number in sequence is put into use.

During the term of Julian and Morgenthau the plate numbers were changed from almost microscopic to a larger size, more easy to read. Due to this improvement the series designation then in use was an advance on United States Notes, Silver Certificates and Federal Reserve Notes. The signatures remained Julian-Morgenthau. National Currency and Gold Certificates were not affected as these were discontinued earlier.

During the changeover period in printing, plates were sometimes mixed up producing a note with a large number on one side and a small number on the other side. Notes of this variety are called **Mules or Mule Notes.** This is from a term applied to coins struck with the obverse or reverse die of one year and the opposite side from a die of another year.

Many collectors are eager to add one or more of these mule notes to their collection. Some of the most common mule notes are:

$2.00 UNITED STATES NOTES	$1.00 SILVER CERTIFICATES
1928-C 1928-D	1935 1935-A

$5.00 UNITED STATES NOTES	$5.00 SILVER CERTIFICATES
1928-B 1928-C 1928-D 1928-E	1934 1934-A 1934-B 1934-C

$10.00 SILVER CERTIFICATES
1934   1934-A

Mules were also issued in the Federal Reserve Note series. However, these are not as popular with collectors as the United States Notes and Silver Certificates because of the higher denominations and the 12 districts involved.

Many collectors are eager to add one or more of these mule notes to their collection. Schedule below shows some of the most common mule notes and their values in new condition.

The combination of the Prefix and Suffix letters of the Serial Numbers on Notes is known as Blocks. For instance: A—A Block B—A Block etc.

			UNC.
$2.00 UNITED STATES NOTE	1928-D ...	B — A	325.00
		C — A	30.00
		* — A	45.00

MULES / 173

			UNC.
$5.00 UNITED STATES NOTE	1928-B . . .	E — A	85.00
		* — A	400.00
	1928-C . . .	E — A	45.00
		* — A	100.00
$1.00 SILVER CERTIFICATE	1935	N — A	
		Thru	115.00
		P — A	
	1935-A . . .	M — A	
		Thru	35.00
		V — A	
		C — B	65.00
$5.00 SILVER CERTIFICATE	1934-A . . .	D — A	
		Thru	35.00
		G — A	
		* — A	140.00
$10.00 SILVER CERTIFICATE	1934	A — A	50.00
		* — A	95.00
	1934-A . . .	A — A	135.00

Front   **SIZES DIFFERENT**   **Back**

INTRODUCTION TO
UNITED STATES FRACTIONAL CURRENCY

Events following the outbreak of the Civil War resulted in a shortage of circulating coinage. Trade was hampered as many merchants, especially in large cities, were unable to make change and only customers presenting the exact amount for a purchase could buy — but they were generally as short on coins as the shop proprietors. Various attempts were made to solve this problem, by issuing credit slips (which most customers didn't care for), tokens (which they also didn't care for), and using postage stamps as money. Finally in 1862 the government stepped in, recognizing that the economy was being seriously hurt, and issued a series of small paper notes in the equivalent of coinage denominations. They carried designs adapted from the current postage stamps of the day and were known as Postage Currency or Postal Currency. The more popular title is now Fractional Currency. There were five separate issues of fractional currency, three of which occurred during the Civil War and two thereafter, the final one as late as 1874. That a need existed for coin substitutes as late as the 1870's demonstrates the drain placed upon coinage during the war and the long period of recovery. A total of six denominations were issued, from 3¢ to 50¢, comprising 23 designs and more than 100 varieties. Because of its small size and lack of visual impact, fractional currency was long shunned by collectors. In recent years it has enjoyed an unprecedented surge of popularity, which, if continued, promises to drive prices beyond present levels. All told, more than $360,000,000 worth of fractional currency was circulated. It would be extremely plentiful today but for the fact that most notes were redeemed, leaving only about $2,000,000 outstanding. This is what collectors have to work with, and a good deal of **these** are in badly preserved condition.

FIRST ISSUE — Postage Currency August 21st, 1862
5 — 10 — 25 — 50

SECOND ISSUE — Fractional Currency October 10th, 1863
5 — 10 — 25 — 50

THIRD ISSUE — Fractional Currency December 5th, 1864
3 — 5 — 10 — 15 — 25 — 50

FOURTH ISSUE — Fractional Currency July 14th, 1869
10 — 15 — 25 — 50

FIFTH ISSUE — Fractional Currency February 26th, 1874
10 — 25 — 50

THE FRACTIONAL CURRENCY SHIELD

Fractional Currency Shields were sold by the Treasury Department in 1866. Specimen Notes printed only on one side were used. Very good condition Shields are valued at $1000 to $1500. Choice condition shields in contemporary frames can sell for $3000.00 Shields with pink, green or other colored backgrounds are more valuable.

UNITED STATES FRACTIONAL CURRENCY
These Notes may be collected by issue or by denomination.
We list them here by denomination for convenience.

NOTE: Since most of these notes were hastily cut from large sheets, the margin size can vary. Specimens with larger than normal margins command premium prices.

THREE-CENT NOTES

THIRD ISSUE NOTE NO. 142

Face Design: Portrait of President Washington.

Back Design: large "3", green.

	A.B.P.	GOOD	V.FINE	UNC.
☐ With Light Portrait	5.00	9.00	25.00	90.00
☐ With Dark Portrait	6.00	11.00	35.00	150.00

FIVE-CENT NOTES

FIRST ISSUE NOTE NO. 143

Face Design: Portrait of President Jefferson, brown

Back Design: "S" black

	A.B.P.	GOOD	V.FINE	UNC.
☐ Perforated edges. Monogram ABNCO on back	4.00	7.00	30.00	145.00
☐ Perforated edges. Without monogram on back	6.00	10.00	35.00	175.00
☐ Straight edges. Monogram ABNCO on back	3.50	6.00	15.00	85.00
☐ Straight edges. Without monogram on back	6.00	11.00	40.00	165.00

FIVE-CENT NOTES

SECOND ISSUE NOTE NO. 144

Face Design: Portrait of President Washington

Back Design: shield and "5'S", brown.

	A.B.P.	GOOD	V.FINE	UNC.
☐ Value only in bronze on back	3.00	5.50	15.00	85.00
☐ Surcharges 18-63 on back	3.00	5.50	15.00	85.00
☐ Surcharges S-18-63 on back	3.50	8.00	30.00	135.00
☐ Surcharges R-1-18-63 on back Fiber Paper	7.00	14.00	55.00	300.00

176 / FRACTIONAL CURRENCY

UNITED STATES FRACTIONAL CURRENCY
FIVE-CENT NOTES

THIRD ISSUE

NOTE NO. 145

Face Design:
Portrait of
Spencer M. Clark.

Back Design:
green or red

	A.B.P.	GOOD	V.FINE	UNC.
☐ Without letter "A" on face. Green back	5.00	10.00	17.00	110.00
☐ With letter "A" on face. Green back	6.00	11.00	22.00	115.00
☐ Without letter "A" on face. Red back	7.00	13.00	30.00	155.00
☐ With letter "A" on face. Red back	8.75	16.00	40.00	175.00

NOTE: This note was authorized to have the portraits of the explorers Lewis and Clark on the face. Mr. Spencer M. Clark, who was then head of the Bureau of Currency, flagrantly placed his own portrait on this Note. This caused Congress to pass legislation forbidding the likeness of any living person on U.S. currency.

TEN-CENT NOTES

FIRST ISSUE

NOTE NO. 146

Face Design:
Portrait of
President Washington.

Back Design:
"10", black

	A.B.P.	GOOD	V.FINE	UNC.
☐ Perforated edges. Monogram ABNCO on back	4.00	7.00	35.00	165.00
☐ Perforated edges. Without monogram on back	4.00	7.00	38.00	190.00
☐ Plain edges. Monogram ABNCO on back	3.00	4.50	20.00	105.00
☐ Plain edges. Without monogram on back	6.00	11.00	50.00	225.00

TEN-CENT NOTES

SECOND ISSUE

NOTE NO. 147

Face Design:
Portrait of
President Washington.

Back Design:
"10", green.

	A.B.P.	GOOD	V.FINE	UNC.
☐ Value only surcharge on back	3.00	6.00	18.00	90.00
☐ Surcharge 18-63 on back	3.50	6.50	23.00	100.00
☐ Surcharge S-18-63 on back	3.50	6.50	25.00	110.00
☐ Surcharge I-18-63 on back	8.00	14.00	60.00	245.00
☐ Surcharge O-63 on back	145.00	325.00	975.00	1800.00
☐ Surcharge T-I-18-63 on back—fiber paper	7.00	12.00	50.00	275.00

FRACTIONAL CURRENCY / 177

UNITED STATES FRACTIONAL CURRENCY
TEN-CENT NOTES

THIRD ISSUE NOTE NO. 148

Face Design:
Portrait of
President
Washington.

Back Design:
"10", green or
red.

	A.B.P.	GOOD	V.FINE	UNC.
☐ Printed signatures of Colby-Spinner. Green back	6.00	12.00	25.00	90.00
☐ As above. Figure "1" near left margin on face	5.50	11.00	22.00	95.00
☐ Printed signatures Colby-Spinner. Red back	7.00	13.00	25.00	150.00
☐ As above. Figure "1" near left margin. Red back	8.00	14.00	30.00	175.00
☐ Autographed signatures Colby-Spinner. Red back	12.00	22.00	65.00	225.00
☐ Autographed signatures Jeffries-Spinner. Red back	9.00	18.00	45.00	280.00

TEN-CENT NOTES

FOURTH ISSUE NOTE NO. 149

Face Design:
Bust
of Liberty.

Back Design:
Green with
"Ten" & "10".

	A.B.P.	GOOD	V.FINE	UNC.
☐ Large red seal. Watermarked paper	3.00	5.00	13.00	55.00
☐ Large red seal. Pink fibers in paper	3.00	5.00	14.00	55.00
☐ Large seal. Pink fibers in paper. Right end blue	3.50	6.00	21.00	60.00
☐ Large brown seal	14.00	27.00	115.00	500.00
☐ Small red seal. Pink fibers. Right end blue	3.25	5.50	18.00	57.50

TEN-CENT NOTES

FIFTH ISSUE NOTE NO. 150

Face Design:
William
Meredith.

Back Design:
Green.

	A.B.P.	GOOD	V.FINE	UNC.
☐ Green seal. Long narrow key	4.00	7.00	20.00	75.00
☐ Red seal. Long narrow key	2.50	5.00	10.00	52.00
☐ Red seal. Short stubby key	2.50	5.00	11.00	57.00

178 / FRACTIONAL CURRENCY

UNITED STATES FRACTIONAL CURRENCY
FIFTEEN-CENT NOTES
FACE AND BACKS PRINTED SEPARATELY

THIRD ISSUE

NOTE NO. 151

Face Design:
Sherman
and President
Grant.

Back Design:
Green
or red.

	NARROW MARGIN	WIDE MARGIN
☐ With printed signatures Colby-Spinner	200.00	325.00
☐ With autographed signatures Colby-Spinner	1200.00	4500.00
☐ With autographed signatures Jeffries-Spinner	250.00	375.00
☐ With autographed signatures Allison-Spinner	275.00	450.00
☐ Green back	165.00	195.00
☐ Red back	165.00	215.00

FIFTEEN-CENT NOTES

FOURTH ISSUE

NOTE NO. 152

Face Design:
Bust
of Columbia.

Back Design:
Green
with "15's".

	A.B.P.	GOOD	V.FINE	UNC.
☐ Large seal. Watermarked paper	5.00	10.00	25.00	150.00
☐ Large seal. Pink fibers in paper	6.00	13.00	45.00	190.00
☐ Large seal. Pink fibers in paper. Right end blue	5.50	11.00	30.00	185.00
☐ Large brown seal	23.00	40.00	200.00	1500.00
☐ Smaller red seal. Pink fibers. Right end blue	6.00	12.00	30.00	170.00

TWENTY-FIVE CENT NOTES

FIRST ISSUE

NOTE NO. 153

Face Design:
Five 5¢
Jefferson Stamps.

Back Design:
Black,
large "25".

	A.B.P.	GOOD	V.FINE	UNC.
☐ Perforated edges. Monogram ABNCO on back	6.50	13.00	50.00	210.00
☐ Perforated edges. Without monogram on back	7.00	14.00	65.00	285.00
☐ Straight edges. Monogram ABNCO on back	6.00	11.00	45.00	125.00
☐ Straight edges. Without monogram on back	9.00	19.00	110.00	330.00

A.B.P. — *Average Buying Price in better than good condition.*

UNITED STATES FRACTIONAL CURRENCY
TWENTY-FIVE-CENT NOTES

SECOND ISSUE **NOTE NO. 154**

(Time and climatic reaction have changed the purple color on the back of this note into many variations.)

Face Design:
Portrait of
President Washington.

Back Design:
Purple
with "25".

	A.B.P.	GOOD	V.FINE	UNC.
☐ Value only surcharge on back	4.00	7.00	24.00	135.00
☐ Surcharge 18-63 on back	6.00	12.00	28.00	160.00
☐ Surcharge A-18-63 on back	5.00	11.00	25.00	165.00
☐ Surcharge I-18-63 on back	27.00	55.00	135.00	500.00
☐ Surcharge 2-18-63 on back	7.00	13.00	30.00	150.00
☐ Surcharge S-18-63 on back	7.50	14.00	35.00	145.00
☐ Surcharge T-I-18-63 on back, fiber paper	9.00	17.00	50.00	300.00
☐ Surcharge T-2-18-63 on back, fiber paper	10.00	19.00	45.00	285.00
☐ Surcharge S-2-18-63, fiber paper		RARE		

TWENTY-FIVE-CENT NOTES

THIRD ISSUE **NOTE NO. 155**

(All Notes have printed signatures of COLBY-SPINNER.)

Face Design:
Portrait of
Fessenden.

Back Design:
Green or red
with "25 CENTS".

	A.B.P.	GOOD	V.FINE	UNC.
☐ Face—Bust of Fessenden between solid bronze surcharges. Fiber paper. Back — Green. Surcharge M-2-6-5 in corners	130.00	260.00	525.00	1450.00
☐ As above. With letter "A" in lower left corner of face	160.00	315.00	900.00	2175.00
☐ Face—Fessenden. Open scroll bronze surcharges. Fiber paper. Back — Green. Surcharges M-2-6-5 in corners	11.00	20.00	65.00	300.00
☐ As above with letter "A" in lower left corners of face	9.00	18.00	60.00	275.00
☐ Face—Fessenden. Open scroll surcharges. Plain paper. Back — Green. Value surcharges only	6.00	12.00	28.00	140.00
☐ As above. Letter "A" in lower left corner of face. Back — Green. Plain paper	13.00	23.00	80.00	160.00

180 / FRACTIONAL CURRENCY

UNITED STATES FRACTIONAL CURRENCY
TWENTY-FIVE-CENT NOTES

	A.B.P.	GOOD	V.FINE	UNC.
☐ Face — Fessenden. Red back. Value surcharge only	6.00	11.00	32.00	160.00
☐ As above. Letter "A" in lower left corner of face	8.00	15.00	39.00	195.00

FOURTH ISSUE — NOTE NO. 156

Face Design:
Portrait of
President Washington
and Treasury Seal.

Back Design:
Green.

	A.B.P.	GOOD	V.FINE	UNC.
☐ Large seal. Plain watermarked paper	3.50	7.00	19.00	90.00
☐ Large seal. Pink silk fiber in paper	3.00	6.00	18.00	95.00
☐ Large seal. Pink fibers in paper. Right end blue	3.50	7.00	23.00	135.00
☐ Large brown seal. Right end blue	35.00	70.00	350.00	1425.00
☐ Smaller red seal. Right end blue	3.50	7.00	17.00	85.00

TWENTY-FIVE-CENT NOTES

FIFTH ISSUE — NOTE NO. 157

Face Design:
Portrait of
Walker and red seal.

Back Design:
Black.

	A.B.P.	GOOD	V.FINE	UNC.
☐ With long narrow key in Treasury Seal	3.00	5.00	15.00	55.00
☐ With short stubby key in Treasury Seal	3.00	5.00	15.00	55.00

A.B.P. — *Average Buying Price in better than good condition.*

FIFTY-CENT NOTES

FIRST ISSUE — NOTE NO. 158

Face Design:
Five 10¢
Washington Stamps.

Back Design:
Green.

UNITED STATES FRACTIONAL CURRENCY

	A.B.P.	GOOD	V.FINE	UNC.
☐ Perforated edges. Monogram ABNCO on back	8.00	15.00	50.00	245.00
☐ Perforated edges. Without monogram on back	9.00	17.00	70.00	325.00
☐ Straight edges. Monogram ABNCO on back	7.00	13.00	40.00	130.00
☐ Straight edges. Without monogram	10.00	19.00	100.00	380.00

FIFTY-CENT NOTES

SECOND ISSUE　　　　　　　　　　　　　　　　　　　　NOTE NO. 159

Face Design:
Portrait of
President Washington

Back Design:
Red

	A.B.P.	GOOD	V.FINE	UNC.
☐ Value surcharge only in back	70.00	140.00	700.00	1875.00
☐ Surcharge 18-63 on back	9.00	16.00	50.00	325.00
☐ Surcharge A-18-63 on back	7.00	12.00	37.00	240.00
☐ Surcharge I-18-63	7.00	12.00	37.00	240.00
☐ Surcharge O-I-18-63. Fiber paper	9.00	16.00	45.00	300.00
☐ Surcharge R-2-18-63. Fiber paper	16.00	27.00	65.00	330.00
☐ Surcharge T-I-18-63. Fiber paper	8.00	11.00	40.00	250.00
☐ Surcharge T-18-63. Fiber paper	55.00	110.00	275.00	950.00

FIFTY-CENT NOTES

THIRD ISSUE　　　　　　　　　　　　　　　　　　　　　NOTE NO. 160
(NOTES WITH PRINTED SIGNATURES OF COLBY-SPINNER, GREEN BACKS)

Face Design:
Justice with
Sword,
Shield,
Scales.

Back Design:
Green
or red.

	A.B.P.	GOOD	V.FINE	UNC.
☐ Value surcharge and S-2-6-4 on back. Fiber paper		VERY RARE		
☐ Value surcharge and A-2-6-5 on back. Fiber paper	12.00	23.00	70.00	400.00
☐ As above with "1" and letter "A" on face. A-2-6-5 on back	28.00	55.00	375.00	1350.00
☐ As above with "1" only on face. A-2-6-5 on back	13.00	26.00	75.00	425.00
☐ As above with letter "A" only on face. A-2-6-5 on back	15.00	30.00	100.00	450.00

182 / FRACTIONAL CURRENCY

UNITED STATES FRACTIONAL CURRENCY

	A.B.P.	GOOD	V.FINE	UNC.
☐ A-2-6-5 on back, narrowly spaced. Plain paper	5.00	9.00	25.00	185.00
☐ As above. Numeral "1" and letter "A" on face	14.00	25.00	75.00	270.00
☐ As above. Numeral "1" only on face	5.00	8.00	28.00	150.00
☐ As above. Letter "A" only on face	10.00	17.00	35.00	190.00
☐ A-2-6-5 on back, widely spaced. Plain paper	5.50	11.00	40.00	190.00
☐ As above. Numeral "1" and letter "A" on face	12.00	25.00	125.00	600.00
☐ As above. Numeral "1" only on face	4.00	8.00	37.00	240.00
☐ As above. Letter "A" only on face	5.00	10.00	50.00	280.00
☐ Without position letters or back surcharges	5.00	9.00	30.00	115.00
☐ As above with numeral "1" and letter "A" on face	12.00	27.00	60.00	250.00
☐ As above with numeral "1" only on face	4.00	7.50	25.00	125.00
☐ As above with letter "A" only on face	5.00	10.00	35.00	150.00

(NOTES WITH PRINTED SIGNATURES OF COLBY-SPINNER, RED BACKS.)

	A.B.P.	GOOD	V.FINE	UNC.
☐ Value surcharge and S-2-6-4 on back. Fiber	65.00	175.00	425.00	975.00
☐ As above. Numeral "1" and letter "A"	150.00	375.00	800.00	RARE
☐ As above. Numeral "1" only on face	100.00	200.00	525.00	1900.00
☐ As above. Letter "A" only on face	125.00	250.00	575.00	1700.00
☐ Value surcharge and A-2-6-5 on back Plain	5.00	10.00	30.00	100.00
☐ As above. Numeral "1" and letter "A"	12.00	30.00	75.00	200.00
☐ As above. Numeral "1" only on face	8.00	14.00	35.00	145.00
☐ As above. Letter "A" only on face	8.00	15.00	40.00	180.00
☐ Value surcharge only on back. Plain paper	9.00	15.00	35.00	175.00
☐ As above. Numeral "1" and letter "A" on face	12.00	25.00	65.00	290.00
☐ As above. Numeral "1" only on face	8.00	17.00	40.00	200.00
☐ As above. Letter "A" only on face	8.00	20.00	60.00	235.00

(NOTES WITH AUTOGRAPHED SIGNATURES OF COLBY-SPINNER, RED BACKS.)

	A.B.P.	GOOD	V.FINE	UNC.
☐ Value surcharge and S-2-6-4 on back. Fiber	50.00	100.00	360.00	1100.00
☐ Value surcharge and A-2-6-5 on back. Fiber	13.00	25.00	120.00	450.00
☐ Value surcharge only on back. Plain paper	8.00	15.00	75.00	290.00

FIFTY-CENT NOTES

THIRD ISSUE

NOTE NO. 161

Face Design: Bust of Spinner with surcharges.

Back Design: Green or red.

(NOTES WITH PRINTED SIGNATURES OF COLBY-SPINNER, GREEN BACKS.)

UNITED STATES FRACTIONAL CURRENCY

	A.B.P.	GOOD	V.FINE	UNC.
☐ Value surcharge and A-2-6-5 on back	7.00	13.00	60.00	200.00
☐ As above. Numeral "1" and letter "A" on face	18.00	35.00	110.00	525.00
☐ As above. Numeral "1" only on face	5.00	10.00	35.00	200.00
☐ As above. Letter "A" only on face	6.00	12.00	45.00	220.00
☐ Value surcharge only on back	4.50	9.00	25.00	75.00
☐ As above. Numeral "1" and Letter "A" on face	10.00	20.00	40.00	150.00
☐ As above. Numeral "1" only on face	4.00	9.00	27.00	85.00
☐ As above. Letter "A" only on face	5.00	12.00	27.00	100.00

(TYPE II BACK DESIGN)

	A.B.P.	GOOD	V.FINE	UNC.
☐ Value surcharge only on back	4.00	8.00	20.00	75.00
☐ Numeral "1" and letter "A" on face	15.00	29.00	75.00	260.00
☐ Numeral "1" only on face	4.00	8.50	25.00	75.00
☐ Letter "A" only on face	5.00	8.50	25.00	90.00

(NOTES WITH PORTRAIT OF SPINNER. PRINTED SIGNATURES OF COLBY-SPINNER, RED BACKS, TYPE I)

	A.B.P.	GOOD	V.FINE	UNC.
☐ Value surcharge and A-2-6-5 on back	8.00	16.00	50.00	165.00
☐ As above with numeral "1" and letter "A"	18.00	38.00	185.00	450.00
☐ As above with numeral "1" only on face	8.00	16.00	55.00	175.00
☐ As above with letter "A" only on face	10.00	20.00	60.00	225.00

(NOTES WITH AUTOGRAPHED SIGNATURES, RED BACKS, TYPE I.)

	A.B.P.	GOOD	V.FINE	UNC.
☐ Autographed signatures COLBY-SPINNER Back surcharged Value and A-2-6-5	13.00	25.00	70.00	230.00
☐ Autographed signatures ALLISON-SPINNER Back surcharged Value and A-2-6-5	16.00	30.00	110.00	325.00
☐ Autographed signatures ALLISON-NEW Back surcharged Value and A-2-6-5	275.00	550.00	1500.00	3675.00

A.B.P. — *Average Buying Price in better than good condition.*

FIFTY-CENT NOTES

FOURTH ISSUE

NOTE NO. 162

Face Design: Bust of Lincoln.

Back Design: Green.

	A.B.P.	GOOD	V.FINE	UNC.
☐ Plain paper	11.00	20.00	55.00	275.00
☐ Paper with pink fibers	13.00	23.00	70.00	330.00

184 / FRACTIONAL CURRENCY

UNITED STATES FRACTIONAL CURRENCY
FIFTY-CENT NOTES

FOURTH ISSUE NOTE NO. 163

Face Design: Bust of Stanton.

Back Design: Green with "50".

	A.B.P.	GOOD	V.FINE	UNC.
☐ Red seal and signatures ALLISON-SPINNER. Paper with pink fibers. Blue ends	8.00	15.00	32.00	175.00

FIFTY-CENT NOTES

FOURTH ISSUE NOTE NO. 164

Face Design: Bust of Samuel Dexter.

Back Design: Green with "50".

	A.B.P.	GOOD	V.FINE	UNC.
☐ Green seal. Pink fibers. Blue ends	5.00	10.00	29.00	135.00

FIFTY-CENT NOTES

FIFTH ISSUE NOTE NO. 165

Face Design: Bust of Crawford.

Back Design: Green with "50".

	A.B.P.	GOOD	V.FINE	UNC.
☐ Signatures ALLISON-NEW. Paper with pink fibers. Blue ends	4.50	8.00	18.00	75.00

A.B.P. — *Average Buying Price in better than good condition.*

ERROR OR FREAK NOTES

Notes have been misprinted, from time to time, since the earliest days of currency. The frequency of misprintings and other abnormalities has increased in recent years, due to heavier production and highspeed machinery. This has provided a major sub-hobby for note collectors. Freaks and errors have come into great popularity, their appeal and prices showing upward movement each year.

On the following pages we have pictured and described most of the more familiar and collectible error notes. Pricing is approximate only because many notes bearing the same general type of error differ in severity of error from one specimen to another. As a general rule, the less glaring or obvious errors carry a smaller premium value. Very valuable error notes include double denominations, or bills having the face of one denomination and reverse side of another.

Error and freak notes do turn up in everyday change. Specimens are located either in that fashion or from bank packs. As far as circulated specimens are concerned, some error notes have passed through so many hands before being noticed that the condition is not up to collector standard. This, of course, results in a very low premium valuation.

Values given below are for the specimens pictured and described. Different premiums may be attached to other specimens with similar errors, or notes showing the same errors but of different denominations.

1. MISMATCHED SERIAL NUMBERS

On ordinary notes, the serial number in the lower left of the obverse matches that in the upper right. When it fails to, even by the difference of a single digit, this is known as a MISMATCHED SERIAL NUMBER. It occurs as the result of a cylinder or cylinders in the highspeed numbering machine becoming jammed. If more than one digit is mismatched, the value will be greater.

	V.FINE	UNC.
☐ $1 Federal Reserve Note, Series 1969, Signatures Elston-Kennedy	25.00	65.00

186 / ERROR OR FREAK NOTES

	V. FINE	UNC.
☐ $1 Silver Certificate, Series 1957B, Signatures Granahan-Dillon	32.00	80.00

	V. FINE	UNC.
☐ $1 Federal Reserve Note, Series 1977A, Signatures Morton-Miller	80.00	225.00

2. INVERTED THIRD PRINT

The inverted third print is also known as Inverted Overprint. The Treasury Seal, District Seal, Serial Numbers and District Number are inverted on the obverse side of the note, or printed upside-down. Caused by the sheet of notes — having already received the primary design on front and back — being fed upside-down into the press for this so-called "third print." (The back design is the "first print," the front is the "second print," and these various additions comprise the "third print." It is not possible to print these "third print" items at the same time as the obverse design, since they are not standard on every bill. At one time the signatures were included in the "third print" but these are now engraved directly into the plate and are part of the "second print.")

Though very spectacular, inverted third print errors are not particularly scarce and are especially plentiful in 1974 and 1976 series notes.

ERROR OR FREAK NOTES / 187

	V.FINE	UNC.
☐ $5 Federal Reserve Note, Series 1974, Signatures Neff-Simon....	75.00	135.00

	V. FINE	UNC.
☐ $2 Federal Reserve Note, Series 1976, Signatures Neff-Simon....	110.00	325.00

	V. FINE	UNC.
☐ $1 Federal Reserve Note, Series 1974. Signatures Neff-Simon....	75.00	180.00

188 / ERROR OR FREAK NOTES

	V. FINE	UNC.
☐ $50 Federal Reserve Note, Series 1977, Signatures Morton-Blumenthal	215.00	475.00

	V. FINE	UNC.
☐ $20 Federal Reserve Note, Series 1974, Signatures Neff-Simon	110.00	235.00

	V. FINE	UNC.
☐ $10 Federal Reserve Note, Series 1974, Signatures Neff-Simon	100.00	190.00

3. COMPLETE OFFSET TRANSFER

Offset transfers are not, as is often believed, caused by still-wet printed sheets coming into contact under pressure. Though very slight offsetting can occur in that manner, it would not create notes as spectacular as those pictured here, in which the offset impression is almost as strong as the primary printing. These happen as a result of the printing press being started up an instant or so before the paper is fed in. Instead of contacting the paper, the inked plate makes its impression upon the machine bed. When the paper is then fed through, it picks up this "ghost" impression from the bed, in addition to the primary impression it is supposed to receive. Each successive sheet going through the press will acquire the impression **until all ink is totally removed from the machine bed.** But, naturally, the first sheet will show the transfer strongest, and the others will be weaker and weaker. Obviously, the market value of such notes depends largely on the strength of the offset impression. The heavier and more noticeable it is, the more valuable the note will be — all other things being equal.

	V.FINE	UNC.
☐ $5 Federal Reserve note, Series 1977, Signatures Morton-Blumenthal. Offset of reverse side of face.		
☐ Dark	45.00	95.00
☐ Light	22.00	55.00

	V. FINE	UNC.
☐ $1 Federal Reserve note, Series 1974, Signatures Neff-Simon. Offset of reverse side of face.		
☐ Dark	70.00	150.00
☐ Light	32.00	65.00

190 / ERROR OR FREAK NOTES

4. PARTIAL OFFSET TRANSFER

The most logical explanation for this error is that a sheet of paper fed into the press incorrectly, became mangled or torn, and part of the inked plate contacted the printing press bed. Therefore wet ink was left on those portions of the press bed not covered by paper. When the next sheet was fed through, it received the correct impression plus it acquired a **partial offset transfer** by contacting this wet area of the press bed. Just as with #3 the first sheet going through the press following an accident of this kind will receive the strongest transfer, and it will become gradually less noticeable on succeeding sheets.

	V. FINE	UNC.
☐ $1 Federal Reserve Note, Series 1969D, Signatures Banuelos-Schultz. Offset of a portion of reverse side on face.		
☐ Dark	12.00	28.00
☐ Light	9.00	21.00

5. PRINTED FOLD

Notes showing printed folds occur as the result of folds in the paper before printing, which probably happen most often when the sheet is being fed into the press. If the sheet is folded in such a manner that a portion of the reverse side is facing upward, as shown here, it will receive a part of the impression intended for its obverse. Naturally the positioning of these misplaced portions of printing is very random, depending on the nature and size of the fold.

	V. FINE	UNC.
☐ $20 Federal Reserve Note, Series 1977, Signatures Morton-Blumenthal. Federal Reserve district seal and district number printed on reverse	75.00	110.00

6. THIRD PRINT ON REVERSE

The cause of this error is obvious, the sheet having been fed through the press on the wrong side (back instead of front) for the third impression or "third print." In the so-called "third print", the note receives the Treasury and Federal Reserve District seals, district numbers and serial numbers.

	V. FINE	UNC.
☐ $1 Federal Reserve Note. Third print on reverse	100.00	225.00

7. BOARD BREAKS

The terminology of this error is misleading. It suggests that the fern-like unprinted areas were caused by a broken printing plate. Actually they must have resulted from something, probably linty matter, sticking to the printing ink. The assumption reached by the public, when it encounters such a note, is that the blank streaks were caused by the paper being folded in printing. This, however, is not possible, as that would yield an error of a much different kind (see PRINTED FOLD).

It should be pointed out that Board Breaks are easily created by counterfeiters by erasing portions of the printed surface, and that the collector ought to examine such specimens closely.

	V. FINE	UNC.
☐ $20 Federal Reserve Note. Board breaks on reverse	35.00	65.00

8. MISSING SECOND PRINT

The "second print" is the front, face or obverse of the note — the "first" print being the reverse or back. A note with Missing Second Print has not received the primary impression on its obverse, though the back is normal and the front carries the standard "third print" matter (Treasury seal, serial numbers, etc.). These errors, while they probably occur pretty frequently, are so easily spotted by B.E.P. checkers that such notes are very scarce on the market.

	V.FINE	UNC.
☐ $10 Federal Reserve Note. Missing second print	200.00	500.00

9. PRINTED FOLD

This note was folded nearly in half before receiving the "third print," which fell across the waste margin on the reverse side. Had the note not been folded, this waste margin would have been removed in the cutting process. This note, when unfolded, is grotesque in shape.

	V. FINE	UNC.
☐ $1 Federal Reserve Note. Printed fold with Federal Reserve District seal, district numbers, and serial numbers on reverse. (Naturally, this note lacks the "third print" matter, such as the Treasury seal, that was supposed to appear on the righthand side of the obverse.)	150.00	285.00

ERROR OR FREAK NOTES / 193

	V. FINE	UNC.
☐ $5 Federal Reserve Note. Printed fold with entire Federal Reserve District seal, portion of another Federal Reserve District seal, and portion of two **different** serial numbers on the reverse. It may be hard to imagine how a freak of this nature occurs. This note was folded diagonally along a line bisecting the Lincoln Memorial building slightly to the right of center. The lefthand portion of the reverse side was thereby drawn down across the lefthand side of the **obverse**, extending well below the bottom of the note. It reached far enough down to catch the district seal intended for the note beneath it, as well as a bit of the serial number. This is why the two serial numbers are different; they were supposed to go on two different notes. Obviously, when something this dramatic happens in printing, not only one error note is created but several — at least — at the same time. Not all necessarily reach circulation, however	150.00	325.00

10. THIRD PRINT BLACK INK MISSING OR LIGHT

Though the machinery used is ultra-modern, U.S. currency notes are printed by the same basic technique used when printing was first invented more than 500 years ago. Ink is spread on the metal plates and these are pressed on the sheets as they go through the press. Because the inking is manually fed (as is the paper), an even flow is usually achieved. When an under-inked note is found, it is generally merely "light," giving a faded appearance. But sometimes the plate will be very improperly inked, due to mechanical misfunction or some other cause, resulting in whole areas being unprinted or so lightly printed that they cannot be seen without close inspection. These are not especially valuable notes but **counterfeit specimens are made.**

194 / ERROR OR FREAK NOTES

	V. FINE	UNC.
☐ $1 Federal Reserve Note, Series 1977. Signatures of Morton-Blumenthal. Federal Reserve district seal and district numbers missing from lefthand side, remainder of "third print" material light but distinct. If the lefthand serial number was strong, there might be suspicion of this being a counterfeit	15.00	35.00

11. THIRD PRINT GREEN INK MISSING OR LIGHT

In this case, the green rather than the black ink was too lightly applied to the printing plate.

	V. FINE	UNC.
☐ $5 Federal Reserve Note, Series 1977, Signatures of Morton-Blumenthal..................................	15.00	35.00

12. NOTE FOLDED DURING OVERPRINT

This note was folded as it was being overprinted and failed to receive the district seal and district numbers at the left side of its obverse. This kind of error, like all involving missing portions of printing, has been extensively counterfeited.

ERROR OR FREAK NOTES / 195

	V. FINE	UNC.
☐ $2 Federal Reserve note, Series 1976, Signatures of Neff Simon .	23.50	55.00

13. FAULTY ALIGNMENT

Notes of this kind used to be automatically called "miscut," and sometimes still are. "Faulty alignment" is a more inclusive term which encompasses not only bad cutting but accidents in printing. If the sheet shifts around in the press, it will not receive the printed impressions exactly where they should be. Even if the cutting is normal, the resulting note will be misaligned; the cutting machine cannot correct botched printing. It is **very easy** to determine where the fault lies. If one side of the note has its design higher than the opposite side, this is a printing error. If the misalignment occurs equally on both sides, the problem was in cutting. Since the two sides are not printed in the same operation, it would be a 1-in-a-million chance for them to become equally misaligned.

The value of such notes depends upon the degree of misalignment. Collectors are especially fond of specimens showing a portion — even if very slight, as with the one pictured of an adjoining note.

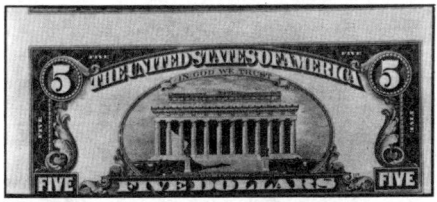

	V.FINE	UNC.
☐ $5 Federal Reserve Note. Bottom left of reverse shaved (or "bled"), corresponding portion of adjoining note just visible at top. This ranks as a "dramatic" specimen.		
☐ Slight	14.00	35.00
☐ Dramatic	28.00	80.00

196 / ERROR OR FREAK NOTES

14. INSUFFICIENT PRESSURE

Underinking of the printing plate is not the only cause of weak or partially missing impressions. If the press is not operating correctly and the inked plate meets the sheet with insufficient pressure, the result is similar to underinking. This probably happens as a result of a sheet going through just as the press is being turned off for the day, or at other intervals. Supposedly all action ceases at the instant of turn-off, but considering the rapidity of this operation, it is likely that a random sheet could pass through and be insufficiently impressed. The note pictured here received normal "third prints," as is generally the case with notes whose first or second print is made with insufficient pressure.

	V. FINE	UNC.
☐ $20 Federal Reserve Note, Series 1977, Signatures of Morton-Blumenthal	55.00	130.00

15. PRINTED FOLD

This note, along with a large portion of the adjoining note, became folded after the second print. When it passed through the press to receive the third print or overprints (seals, serial numbers, etc.), these naturally failed to appear on the folded area.

	V. FINE	UNC.
☐ $1 Federal Reserve Note. Printed fold with overprints partialy missing.		
Small	23.50	50.00
☐ Large	75.00	200.00

16. DOUBLE IMPRESSION

Double impressions have traditionally been blamed on the sheet of notes passing through the press twice, which would be the logical explanation. However, in considering the method by which currency is printed, it would seem more likely that double impression notes have **not** made two trips through the press. They probably result, in most instances, from the automatic paper feed jamming. The sheet just printed fails to be ejected, and the printing plate falls upon it a second time instead of falling on a fresh sheet. This does **not** merely create a strong impression, but a twin or ghost impression, since the sheet is not positioned exactly the same for the second strike. Though the paper feed may not be operating properly, there will still be some slight movement — enough to prevent the second impression from falling directly atop the first.

	V. FINE	UNC.
☐ $1 Federal Reserve Note, Series 1977A, Signatures of Morton-Miller. Double "second print" impression.		
☐ Partial	110.00	250.00
☐ Complete	325.00	950.00

17. DOUBLE IMPRESSION OF OVERPRINTS ("DOUBLE THIRD PRINT")

This note is normal as far as the primary obverse and reverse printings are concerned. It received twin impressions of the overprints or "third print." This was not caused by jamming of the paper feed as discussed above. Naturally, the serial numbers are different, as the automatic numbering machine turns with every rise and fall of the press.

198 / ERROR OR FREAK NOTES

	V. FINE	UNC.
☐ $20 Federal Reserve Note, Series 1950. Signatures of Priest-Humphrey. Double impression of overprints.		
☐ Partial	115.00	325.00
☐ Complete	250.00	700.00

18. THIRD PRINT (OR OVERPRINTS) SHIFTED

Whenever the overprints (serial number, seals, etc.) are out of position, vertically or horizontally, this is known as "third print shifted" or "overprints shifted." In the example pictured, shifting is extreme. This is a premium value specimen which would command the higher of the two sums quoted. Normally, the overprinting on a "shifted" note fails to touch the portrait, or touches it only slightly. The cause of this kind of error is a sheet feeding incorrectly into the press for the overprinting operation. As striking and desirable as these notes are to collectors, they are often unnoticed by the public.

	V. FINE	UNC.
☐ $100 Federal Reserve Note, Series 1969C, Signatures of Banuelos-Schultz. Third print shifted.		
☐ Slight	115.00	170.00
☐ Dramatic	150.00	250.00

ERROR OR FREAK NOTES / 199

19. INK SMEAR

Ink smearing is one of the more common abnormalities of currency notes. Generally it can be attributed to malfunction of the automatic inking device which inks the printing plate. When performing properly, ink is applied at a steady controlled pace to the printing plate. A very minor disorder in the machine can dispense enough extra ink to yield very spectacular "smeared notes," such as the one illustrated. The value of ink smear notes depends upon the area and intensity of the smear. They are quite easily faked, so the buyer should be cautious.

	V. FINE	UNC.
☐ $1 Federal Reserve Note. Ink smear.		
☐ Small	7.00	15.00
☐ Large	20.00	45.00

20. PRINTING FOLD

This note was crumpled along the right side prior to the third printing or application of overprints. Hence the "third print" matter on the lefthand side is normal, but portions of the overprint on the right appear on the note's reverse side.

	V. FINE	UNC.
☐ $20 Federal Reverse Note, Series 1977, Signatures Morton-Blumenthal	60.00	135.00

200 / ERROR OR FREAK NOTES

21. BLANK CREASE

It occasionally happens that a note becomes creased prior to the reverse or obverse printing, in such a way that a small fold is created. During the printing procedure this fold hides a portion of the note's surface, which therefore fails to receive the impression. These notes are actually double errors, in a way — the cutting machine cuts them without knowledge of the fold, and when the fold is opened out the bill is then of larger than normal size. Since "crease errors" are difficult to spot in the B.E.P.'s checking, they find their way into circulation in rather sizable numbers. It is difficult to place standard values on them because the price depends on the exact nature of the specimen. The wider the crease, the more valuable the note will be. Premium values are attached to notes with multiple creases that cause the blank unprinted area to fall across the portrait.

	V. FINE	UNC.
☐ Blank crease Note, any denomination. Value stated is collector premium over and above face value (if note has additional value because of series, signatures, etc., this too must be added).		
☐ Single crease	4.00	12.00
☐ Multiple crease	17.00	35.00

22. MIXED DENOMINATION

These two notes are normal in themselves, and if they were not owned together as a set no premium value would be attached to them. The error (which may be dubious to term as such) lies with their serial numbers. The $5 note has a serial number one digit higher than the $1, suggesting that it was fed into the printing machine intended to print overprints (or "third prints") on $1 bills. Even when this does happen, which is probably infrequent, it is very difficult to obtain "matching" notes of the kind illustrated, in which the serial numbers are only a single digit apart. Even if you had a $5 note and $1 note (or other combination of denominations) from sheets that were fed one after the other, the odds on getting one-digit-apart serial numbers are extremely small.

The value is given for an Uncirculated set only, as there would be no possibility of finding such matched notes except in a bank pack. Once released into circulation, they can never again be mated.

	UNC.
☐ Mixed denomination pair from bank pack, $5 Federal Reserve Note within pack of $1 Federal Reserve notes	600.00

23. BLANK REVERSE

U.S. currency has its reverse printed before the obverse — in other words, back before front. The only logical explanation for blank reverse notes is that blank paper found its way into the batch of sheets on which reverses had already been printed. They were then fed — without detection — into the press for application of the obverse. They continued to escape notice during printing of the overprints, and very miraculously got into circulation.

	V.FINE	UNC.
☐ $100 Federal Reserve Note. Blank reverse	200.00	500.00

	V. FINE	UNC.
☐ $20 Federal Reserve Note, Series 1977, Signatures of Morton-Blumenthal. Blank reverse	100.00	250.00

202 / ERROR OR FREAK NOTES

	V. FINE	UNC.
☐ $10 Federal Reserve Note, Series 1974, Signatures of Neff-Simon. Blank reverse	80.00	195.00

	V. FINE	UNC.
☐ $1 Federal Reserve Note, Series 1977, Signatures of Morton-Blumenthal. Blank reverse	70.00	150.00

24. DOUBLE DENOMINATION COUNTERFEIT

This is a COUNTERFEIT or faked error. We include it simply to show the kind of work done by counterfeiters, and how such items can be made to resemble genuine errors. This happens to be a counterfeit of an error note **that cannot exist** in genuine state. Thus, there can be no hesitancy in proclaiming it a fake. Anyone who is even slightly familiar with the way currency is printed should instantly recognize this item as a fraud. Nevertheless, fakers succeed in selling (often at high prices) specimens of this kind, probably because some collectors want the impossible for their albums. **Genuine** double or twin denomination notes have the **obverse** of one denomination and the **reverse** of a different denomination. They do not consist of two obverses or two reverses, such as the one pictured. The note illustrated carries four serial numbers. For it to be genuine, it would have had to pass through the "third print" (overprinting) process twice. Obviously it was made by gluing a $1 and $5 note together. Much more deceptive paste-ups, with the notes correctly paired so that obverse of one and reverse of the other shows, are made. Beware!

ERROR OR FREAK NOTES / 203

25. INVERTED OBVERSE

U.S. currency is printed reverse first. Therefore, when the back and front do not face in the same vertical direction (as they should), the note is known as an INVERTED OBVERSE. The term "inverted reverse" is never used. This, of course, results from the sheet being fed through upside-down for the obverse or second print. Though these specimens are scarce in uncirculated condition, they often pass through many hands in circulation before being spotted. The uninformed public is not even aware that a note with faces in opposite directions is an error and has premium value.

	V. FINE	UNC.
☐ $2 Federal Reverse Note, Series 1976, Signatures of Neff-Simon. Inverted obverse.	120.00	275.00

26. MISSING THIRD PRINT

Also known as **missing overprint.** Note released into circulation without having gone through the "third print" operation.

204 / ERROR OR FREAK NOTES

	V. FINE	UNC.
☐ $1 Federal Reserve Note, Series 1977, Signatures Morton-Blumenthal. Missing third print	85.00	200.00

27. FOREIGN MATTER ON OBVERSE

Sometimes foreign matter, usually paper scraps of one kind or another, gets between the printing plate and the sheet. This naturally results in the area covered by such matter being blank on the note. Because of the extreme pressure exerted in printing, the foreign matter is occasionally "glued" to the note and travels with it into circulation. If the appendage is paper, it will normally be found to be of the same stock from which the note is made — apparently a shred from one of the sheet margins that worked its way into a batch of sheets awaiting printing. **The value of such notes varies successfully,** depending on the size of the foreign matter and its placement. It's **rare** to find notes in which foreign matter became attached before the first or second print. Nearly always, they found their way to the note after the second print and before the third.

	V. FINE	UNC.
☐ $1 Federal Reserve Note, Series 1974, Signatures Neff-Simon. Foreign matter on obverse	60.00	110.00

	V. FINE	UNC.
☐ $1 Silver Certificate, Series 1935E. Signatures of Priest-Humphrey. Foreign matter on obverse. More valuable than the preceding because of the note's age and the foreign matter being larger	250.00	550.00

28. MISSING PORTION OF REVERSE DESIGN (DUE TO ADHERENCE OF SCRAP PAPER)

In this instance, the foreign matter got in the way of the first print, or reverse printing. It prevented the covered area from being printed, but it **later became dislodged** and is no longer present. What appears on the illustration to be a strip of paper on the note is really the blank unprinted area once covered by the strip. Obviously a note that merely had a random strip of paper attached, over a normally printed design, would have no collector interest.

	V.FINE	UNC.
☐ $1 Federal Reserve Note. Missing portion of reverse design due to adherence of scrap paper	50.00	100.00

29. OVERPRINT PARTIALLY MISSING

The overprint or third print on this note is normal on the righthand side and missing entirely on the left. This was caused by the note being folded (more or less in half, vertically) immediately before overprinting. Had the lefthand side been folded **over the face,** this would have interfered with the

206 / ERROR OR FREAK NOTES

overprints on the righthand side. Instead, this specimen was folded **over the reverse side,** or downward, with the result that the missing portion of overprint did not strike the note at all — it simply hit the printing press bed. The reverse side of this note is normal.

	V. FINE	UNC.
$1 Federal Reserve Note, Series 1963A. Overprint partially missing	30.00	65.00

30. THIRD PRINT OFFSET ON REVERSE

This note is normal on the obverse but carries an "offset" of the third print or overprints on its reverse. It would appear that the overprints are showing through to the reverse, as if the note were printed on very thin paper. Actually, this "mirror image" is caused by a malfunction in the printing or paper-feeding machinery. The inked plate for printing the overprints contacted the machine bed without a sheet of paper being in place. Therefore, as the next sheet came through it received the normal overprint on its face and picked up the offset impression on its reverse from the machine bed. Each successive sheet going through the press also received an offset, but it natually became fainter and fainter as the ink was absorbed. The value of a note of this kind depends on the intensity of impression.

	V. FINE	UNC.
☐$5 Federal Reserve Note. Offset impression of overprints on reverse	125.00	285.00

CONFEDERATE MONEY

The Civil War Centennial of 1961-65 has generally been credited with sparking a rise of interest in the collecting and study of Confederate or C.S.A. notes. This, however, is not totally borne out by facts, as C.S.A. currency had advanced steadily in value since the 1940's. It rides a crest of popularity today well surpassing the early 1960's. This is due in part to the exhaustive research carried out since that time and numerous books and articles published. Even today, some C.S.A. notes would still appear to be undervalued based on their availability vs. regular U.S. issues.

History. It became apparent upon the outbreak of the Civil War that both sides would experience extreme coinage shortages and each took to the printing of notes that could be exchanged in lieu of bullion or "real money" (which, we must understand, always meant coined money until the 1860's). The South suffered more serious difficulties than the North, as it did not have as many skilled printers or engravers at its command. Also, with the war being fought on its territory rather than the North's, there was an ever-present danger of sabotage to plants printing money or engaging in related activities. The Confederacy tried by all available means to satisfy the currency demand, and succeeded in distributing quite a large quantity of notes. Its shortage was taken up by notes issued by private banks, individual states, counties, railroads, and private merchants. Merchant tokens, to take the place of rapidly disappearing small change, poured forth in abundance during this period. All told, the Confederate Congress authorized the printing of about one and a half billion dollars worth of paper currency. It is impossible to determine the total actually produced but it would appear that this figure was far surpassed. At the war's conclusion, these notes were worthless as the C.S.A. no longer existed and the federal government refused to redeem them. Many were undoubtedly discarded as scrap but a surprising number were held faithfully by their owners, who believed "the South will rise again." The South did indeed rise, industrially and economically, and those old C.S.A. notes rose too. They still aren't spendable but many are worth sums in excess of face value as collectors' pieces. Until about 1900, however, practically no value was placed on Confederate currency — even by collectors.

Designs. Some surprising designs will be observed, including mythological gods and goddesses that seem to relate very little to the South's artistic or cultural climate of the 1860's. Many scholarly efforts have been made to explain away the use of such motifs but the simple fact is that they appeared not so much by choice as necessity. Southern printers, not having the facilities of their Northern counterparts, were compelled to make do with whatever engravings or "stock cuts" were already on hand, as inappropriate as they might have proved. However, a number of original designs were created reflecting unmistakably regional themes and at times picturing heros or leaders of the Confederacy. Slaves at labor, used as a symbol of the South's economic strength and its supposed advantage over the North, where labor was hired, was a frequent motif.

Sailors were also depicted, as well as railroad trains and anything else that appeared symbolic of Southern industry. Probably the most notable single design, not intended to carry the satirical overtones it now possesses, is "General Francis Marion's Sweet Potato Breakfast" on the $10 1861. In general, the C.S.A. notes are not so badly designed a group as might be anticipated in light of conditions. The designing, was in fact, several leagues improved over the printing, which often left much to be desired. George Washington is depicted — not for being the first U.S. President but as a native son of Virginia. Jefferson Davis, President of the C.S.A., is among the more common portraits. He became even more disliked in the North than he otherwise might have been, because of his picture turning up on currency. But after the war he took a moderate stand and erased the old ill feelings; he even had words of praise for Lincoln. Other individuals whose portraits (not necessarily very faithful) will be encountered are:

John C. Calhoun, U.S. Senator who led the battle for slavery and Southern Rights (later called "states rights").

Alexander H. Stephen, Davis' Vice-President of the C.S.A.

Judah P. Benjamin, holder of various official titles in the Southern government.

C. G. Memminger, Secretary of the Treasury and Secretary of War.

Lucy Pickens, wife of South Carolina's governor and the only woman (aside from mythological types) shown on C.S.A. currency.

John E. Ward.

R. M. T. Hunter.

Printers. The study of printers of C.S.A. notes is complex, made no less so by the fact that some contractors produced only plates, others did only printing (from plates procured elsewhere), while some did both. The principal Southern printer was the lithography firm of Hoyer & Ludwig of Richmond, Virginia. Also located at Richmond were Keatinge & Ball, which did commendable if not exactly inspired work, and B. Duncan, who also worked at Columbia, South Carolina. Another firm involved in quite a bit of note printing was J. T. Paterson of Columbia. The so-called "Southern Bank Note Company" was a fictitious name used to disguise the origin of notes prepared in the North. Some early notes were marked "National Bank Note Co., New York," but it was subsequently decided to remove correct identification from the notes of this printer, undoubtedly on the latter's request (fearing prosecution for aiding the enemy).

Cancellations. Two varieties of cancels are commonly found on C.S.A. notes. First is the cut cancel (CC), in which a knife or similar instrument has been used to make piercings in a design or pattern. Unless roughly executed, such cuts do not materially reduce a specimen's value. In the case of some notes, examples without cancellation are almost impossible to find. The COC or Cut Out Cancel is more objectionable because, instead of merely leaving slits, a portion of the paper was removed. The reduction of value for a Cut Out Cancel averages around 25 percent. These are considered "space fillers" if the issue is fairly common, but a rare note with a COC may be very desirable. Pen Cancellations (PC) are far less frequently encountered. These show the word "Canceled" written out by hand across the note's face, in ink. Unless the ink is heavy or blotchy, a pen cancel will not have too much bearing on value. As the note is not physically injured, it would seem to be the least offensive of the three varieties. Whenever a note is being sold, presence of a cancel, or whatever type, should be plainly spelled out. Some collectors are not interested in canceled specimens. In time, as the scarce issues become even scarcer, they will probably have to be accepted as a fact of life.

Signatures. There are so many signature combinations on C.S.A. notes that utter confusion would await anyone attempting to collect them on this basis. The names are unknown and in most instances difficult to trace, representing not government officials but employees authorized to sign for the Treasurer and Registrar of the Treasury. Only the first six notes bear the actual signatures of these officials.

Condition Grades. While condition standards are basically the same for Confederate currency as other notes of their age, some allowance must be made for paper quality and deficiencies in printing and cutting. These matters have nothing to do with the **preservation** or wear and can be observed just as frequently in uncirculated specimens as those in average condition. Without a source of good paper, printers were obliged to use whatever was most easily and quickly obtainable. Often the paper was thin, or stiff, or contained networks of minute wrinkles which interfered somewhat with printing. Cutting was generally not done by machine, as in the North, but by hand with a pair of scissors — workers actually took the sheets and cut apart notes individually. When paper-cutting devices were employed, they were apparently not of the best quality. In any case, regular edges on C.S.A. notes are uncommon and their absence does not constitute grounds for classifying an otherwise perfect specimen in a condition grade below Uncirculated. When the occasional gem is located — a well-printed, well-preserved note on good paper, decently cut — its value is sure to be higher than those listed. The collecter is not advised to confine himself to such specimens, as his activities would become seriously limited.

UNCIRCULATED - UNC. An uncirculated note shows no evidence of handling and is as close to "new condition," as possible. An uncirculated specimen may, however, have pinholes or a finger smudge, which should be mentioned in a sales offering. If these are readily noticeable, the note deserves to be classified as "almost uncirculated." Crispness is hardly a criterion of uncirculation as this quality is expected in notes graded as low as Very Fine.

ALMOST UNCIRCULATED - A.U. Similar to the above grade but not quite as good as an uncirculated specimen. The note bears no indication of having actually circulated but has minor flaws resulting from accident or mishandling, such as counting crinkles.

EXTREMELY FINE - X.F. An X.F. note is on the borderline between uncirculated and circulated. It has not been heavily handled but may reveal several imperfections: a pinhole, finger smudge, counting crinkles, or a light wallet fold. The fold is not so heavy as to be termed a crease.

VERY FINE - V.F. Has been in circulation but is not worn or seriously creased. It must still be clean and crisp, without stains or tears. Fine to Very Fine condition is considered the equivalent of "average circulated" but not "average condition" (which is another term for **poor**).

FINE - F. A note that has been in circulation and shows it, but has no physical injuries or just slight ones.

VERY GOOD - V.G. A well-circulated note bearing evidence of numerous folding. It may possibly have creased corners and wrinkles as well as light staining, smudging, or pinholes, but major defects (such as a missing corner) would place it into an even lower category.

GOOD - G. Heavily circulated, worn, possibly stained or scribbled on, edges could be frayed or "dog-eared." There may be holes larger than pinpunctures, but not on the central portion of design. This is the lowest grade of condition acceptable to a collector, and only when nothing better is available. Unless very rare, such specimens are considered space-fillers only.

A.B.P. - AVERAGE BUYING PRICES. The average buying prices given here are the approximate sums paid by retail dealers for specimens in good condition. As selling prices vary, so do buying prices, and in fact they usually vary a bit more. A dealer overstocked on a certain note is sure to offer less than one who has no specimens on hand. The dealer's location, size of operation and other circumstances will also influence the buying price. We present these figures merely as rough guides.

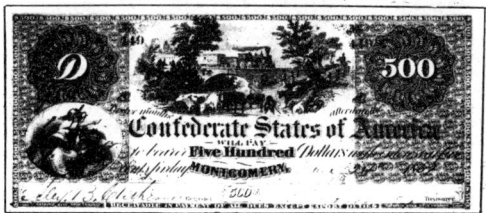

CONFEDERATE STATES OF AMERICA — 1861 ISSUE
MONTGOMERY, ALABAMA
$1,000,000 Authorized by Act of "March 9th". Written Dates "1861".

"NATIONAL BANK NOTE CO., NY."

T1

Face Design: Green and black, bears "Interest Ten Cents Per Day", 607 issued. John C. Calhoun left, Andrew Jackson right.

CRISWELL #	NOTE	A.B.P.	GOOD	UNC.
☐1	$1000	1800.00	2500.00	9000.00

"NATIONAL BANK NOTE CO., NY."

T2

Face Design: Green and black, bears "Interest Five Cents Per Day", 607 issued. Cattle crossing a brook.

CRISWELL #	NOTE	A.B.P.	GOOD	UNC.
☐2	$500	1750.00	2500.00	9000.00

212 / CONFEDERATE MONEY

CONFEDERATE STATES OF AMERICA—1861 ISSUE

"NATIONAL BANK NOTE CO., NY."

T3

Face Design: Green and black, bears "Interest One Cent Per Day". Railway train, Minerva left.

CRISWELL #	NOTE	A.B.P.	GOOD	UNC.
☐ 3	$100	750.00	1400.00	2600.00

"NATIONAL BANK NOTE CO., NY."

T4

Face Design: Green and black, bears "Interest Half A Cent Per Day". Negroes hoeing cotton.

CRISWELL #	NOTE	A.B.P.	GOOD	UNC.
☐ 4	$50	600.00	1250.00	2000.00

CONFEDERATE MONEY / 213

CONFEDERATE STATES OF AMERICA—1861 ISSUE

AMERICAN BANK NOTE CO., NY."
(Though ostensibly by the "SOUTHERN BANK NOTE CO.")

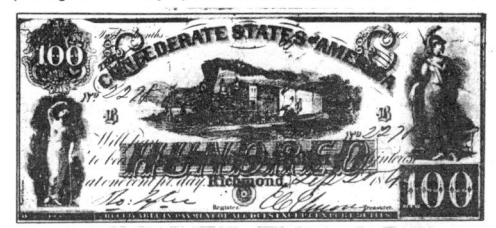

T5

Face Design: Green and black, red fibre paper, bears "Interest One Cent Per Day". Railway train, Justice left and Minerva right.

CRISWELL #	NOTE	A.B.P.	GOOD	UNC.
☐ 5	$100	75.00	175.00	450.00

T6

Face Design: Green and black, red fibre paper, bears "Interest Half A Cent Per Day". Pallas and Ceres seated on bale of cotton, Washington at right.

CRISWELL #	NOTE	A.B.P.	GOOD	UNC.
☐ 6	$50	65.00	125.00	375.00

214 / CONFEDERATE MONEY

CONFEDERATE STATES OF AMERICA—1861 ISSUE

$20,000,000 Authorized by Act of "May 16th, 1861"

"HOYER & LUDWIG, RICHMOND, VA."
(All Lithographic Date "July 25th, 1861")

T7

Face Design: Ceres and Proserpina flying, Washington left.

CRISWELL #	NOTE	A.B.P.	GOOD	UNC.
☐ 7-13	$100	75.00	150.00	450.00

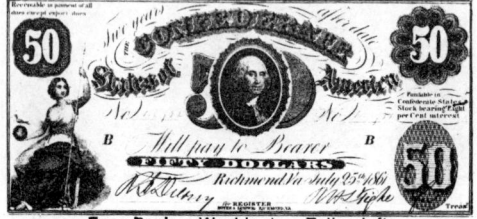

T8

Face Design: Washington, Tellus left.

CRISWELL #	NOTE	A.B.P.	GOOD	UNC.
☐ 14-22	$50	9.00	22.00	40.00

CONFEDERATE MONEY / 215

CONFEDERATE STATES OF AMERICA—1861 ISSUE

Face Design: Exists in a variety of colors with plain and printed fancy reverses.

☐21 $20 .... $18.00   30.00   65.00

NOTE: The above type notes were bogus. For years it was thought they were a regular Confederate issue, and evidence exists that they were circulated as such. No collection of Confederate notes is complete without one. There is no evidence as to who the printer was, but the authors have reason to believe he was located somewhere in Ohio. It is not a product of S. C. Upham, of Philadelphia, the well-known counterfeiter of Confederate notes.

T9

Face Design: Large sailing vessel, "20" at left.

CRISWELL #	NOTE	A.B.P.	GOOD	UNC.
☐23-33	$20	6.00	12.00	45.00

216 / CONFEDERATE MONEY

CONFEDERATE STATES OF AMERICA—1861 ISSUE

T10

Face Design: Liberty seated by Eagle, with shield with flag.

NOTE: There are at least 42 minor varieties of this note, including a supposed 10 or 11 stars on shield. Usually the stars are so indistinct that a note may show from six to 15 stars. The other differences are in minute changes in the size of the "10" in the upper corners. We list only the major type.

CRISWELL #	NOTE	A.B.P.	GOOD	UNC.
☐34-40	$10	10.00	18.00	400.00

T11

Face Design: Liberty seated by Eagle, sailor left.

CRISWELL #	NOTE	A.B.P.	GOOD	UNC.
☐42-44	$5	100.00	225.00	8000.00

CONFEDERATE STATES OF AMERICA—1861 ISSUE

"J. MANOUVRIER, NEW ORLEANS"
(Written Date "July 25th, 1861")

T12

Face Design: "Confederate States of America" in blue on blue reverse.

CRISWELL #	NOTE	A.B.P.	GOOD	UNC.
☐ 46-49	$5	125.00	350.00	4000.00

$100,000,000 authorized by Act of "Aug. 19th, 1861".
$50,000,000 authorized by Act of "Dec. 24th, 1861".

"HOYER & LUDWIG, RICHMOND, VA."
(Lithographic Date, "September 2nd, 2d, & s, 1861".)

T13

Face Design: Negros loading cotton, sailor left.

CRISWELL #	NOTE	A.B.P.	GOOD	UNC.
☐ 50-58	$100	6.50	12.00	35.00

218 / CONFEDERATE MONEY

CONFEDERATE STATES OF AMERICA—1861 ISSUE

T14

Face Design: Moneta seated by treasure chests, sailor left.

CRISWELL #	NOTE	A.B.P.	GOOD	UNC.
☐ 59-78	$50	6.00	9.00	25.00

"SOUTHERN BANK NOTE CO., NEW ORLEANS"

T15

Face Design: Black and red on red fibre paper. Railway train, Justice right, Hope with anchor left.

CRISWELL #	NOTE	A.B.P.	GOOD	UNC.
☐ 79	$50	200.00	400.00	3000.00

CONFEDERATE STATES OF AMERICA—1861 ISSUE

"KEATINGE & BALL, RICHMOND, VA."

T16

Face Design: Black and green, red fibre paper. Portrait of Jefferson Davis.

CRISWELL #	NOTE	A.B.P.	GOOD	UNC.
☐80-94	$50	9.00	15.00	125.00

"HOYER & LUDWIG, RICHMOND, VA."

T17

Face Design: Black with green ornamentation, plain paper. Ceres seated between Commerce and Navigation, Liberty left.

CRISWELL #	NOTE	A.B.P.	GOOD	UNC.
☐99-100	$20	40.00	75.00	350.00

220 / CONFEDERATE MONEY

CONFEDERATE STATES OF AMERICA—1861 ISSUE

"HOYER & LUDWIG, RICHMOND, VA."

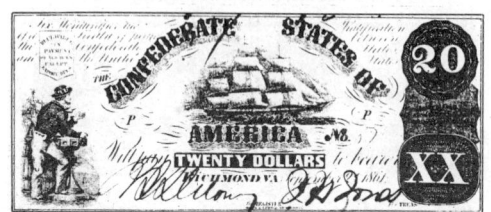

T18

Face Design: Large sailing vessel, sailor at capstan left.

CRISWELL #	NOTE	A.B.P.	GOOD	UNC.
☐ 101-136	$20	2.00	4.00	20.00

"SOUTHERN BANK NOTE CO., NEW ORLEANS"

T19

Face Design: Black and red on red fibre paper. Navigation seated by charts, Minerva left, blacksmith right.

CRISWELL #	NOTE	A.B.P.	GOOD	UNC.
☐ 137	$20	110.00	200.00	2000.00

CONFEDERATE MONEY / 221

CONFEDERATE STATES OF AMERICA—1861 ISSUE

T20

Face Design: Industry seated between cupid and beehive, bust of A. H. Stevens left.

PRINTED BY "B. DUNCAN, COLUMBIA, SC."

CRISWELL #	NOTE	A.B.P.	GOOD	UNC.
☐139-140	$20	3.50	8.00	35.00

PRINTED BY "B. DUNCAN, RICHMOND, VA."

| ☐141-143 | $20 | 3.00 | 5.00 | 30.00 |

"KEATINGE & BALL, COLUMBIA, SC."

T21

Face Design: Portrait of Alexander H. Stephens.

YELLOW GREEN ORNAMENTATION

CRISWELL #	NOTE	A.B.P.	GOOD	UNC.
☐144	$20	9.00	16.00	180.00

DARK GREEN ORNAMENTATION

| ☐145-149 | $20 | 10.00 | 15.00 | 175.00 |

222 / CONFEDERATE MONEY

CONFEDERATE STATES OF AMERICA—1861 ISSUE

"SOUTHERN BANK NOTE CO., NEW ORLEANS"

T22

Face Design: Black and red, red fibre paper. Group of indians, Thetis left, maiden with "X" at right.

CRISWELL #	NOTE	A.B.P.	GOOD	UNC.
☐ 150-152	$10	40.00	80.00	275.00

"LEGGETT, KEATINGE & BALL, RICHMOND, VA."

T23

Face Design: Black and orange red. Wagonload of cotton, harvesting sugar cane right. John E. Ward left.

CRISWELL #	NOTE	A.B.P.	GOOD	UNC.
☐ 153-155	$10	80.00	150.00	800.00

CONFEDERATE STATES OF AMERICA—1861 ISSUE

"LEGGETT, KEATINGE & BALL, RICHMOND, VA."

T24

Face Design: Black and orange red. R. M. T. Hunter left, vignette of child right.

CRISWELL #	NOTE	A.B.P.	GOOD	UNC.
☐ 156-160	$10	10.00	30.00	150.00

"KEATINGE & BALL, RICHMOND, VA."

| ☐ 161-167 | $10 | 9.75 | 25.00 | 140.00 |

"KEATINGE & BALL, RICHMOND, VA."

T25

Face Design: Hope with anchor, R. M. T. Hunter left, C. G. Memminger, right.

CRISWELL #	NOTE	A.B.P.	GOOD	UNC.
☐ 168-171	$10	9.00	15.00	125.00

224 / CONFEDERATE MONEY

CONFEDERATE STATES OF AMERICA—1861 ISSUE

"KEATINGE & BALL, RICHMOND, VA."

T26

Face Design: Hope with anchor, R. M. T. Hunter left, C. G. Memminger, right.

NOTE: There are three types of red "X" and "X" overprint. That section of the note on which the overprints appear is illustrated in double size.

Face Design: Solid red "X" and "X" overprint.

CRISWELL #	NOTE	A.B.P.	GOOD	UNC.
☐ 173-188	$10	12.00	20.00	125.00

Face Design: Coarse lace "X" and "X" red overprint.

CRISWELL #	NOTE	A.B.P.	GOOD	UNC.
☐ 189-210	$10	11.00	20.00	135.00

CONFEDERATE STATES OF AMERICA—1861 ISSUE

Face Design: Fine lace "X" and "X" red overprint.

CRISWELL #	NOTE	A.B.P.	GOOD	UNC.
☐211-220	$10	10.00	18.00	120.00

"HOYER & LUDWIG, RICHMOND, VA."

T27

Face Design: Liberty seated by shield and eagle.

CRISWELL #	NOTE	A.B.P.	GOOD	UNC.
☐221-229	$10	600.00	800.00	V.RARE

226 / CONFEDERATE MONEY

CONFEDERATE STATES OF AMERICA—1861 ISSUE

"HOYER & LUDWIG, RICHMOND, VA."

T28

Face Design: Ceres and Commerce with an urn.

CRISWELL #	NOTE	A.B.P.	GOOD	UNC.
☐ 230-234	$10	2.00	3.50	45.00

"J. T. PATERSON, COLUMBIA, SC."

CRISWELL #	NOTE	A.B.P.	GOOD	UNC.
☐ 235-236	$10	2.50	4.75	50.00

"B. DUNCAN, RICHMOND, VA."

T29

Face Design: Negro picking cotton.

CRISWELL #	NOTE	A.B.P.	GOOD	UNC.
☐ 237	$10	12.00	20.00	125.00

CONFEDERATE STATES OF AMERICA—1861 ISSUE

"B. DUNCAN, COLUMBIA, SC."

T30

Face Design: Gen. Francis Marion's "Sweet Potato Dinner." R. M. T. Hunter left, Minerva right.

CRISWELL #	NOTE	A.B.P.	GOOD	UNC.
☐238	$10	4.00	8.00	40.00

NO ENGRAVER'S NAME

CRISWELL #	NOTE	A.B.P.	GOOD	UNC.
☐239-241	$10	5.00	9.00	40.00

"SOUTHERN BANK NOTE CO., NEW ORLEANS"

T31

Face Design: Black and red on red fibre paper. Minerva left, Agriculture, Commerce, Industry, Justice and Liberty seated at center, statue of Washington right.

CRISWELL #	NOTE	A.B.P.	GOOD	UNC.
☐243-245	$5	35.00	65.00	275.00

228 / CONFEDERATE MONEY

CONFEDERATE STATES OF AMERICA—1861 ISSUE

"LEGGETT, KEATINGE & BALL, RICHMOND, VA."

T32

Face Design: Black and orange red. Machinist with hammer, boy in oval left.

CRISWELL #	NOTE	A.B.P.	GOOD	UNC.
☐246-249	$5	60.00	125.00	650.00

"LEGGETT, KEATINGE & BALL, RICHMOND, VA."

T33

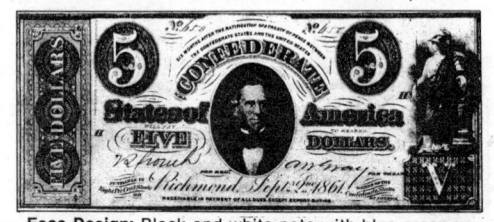

Face Design: Black and white note with blue green ornamentation. C. G. Memminger, Minerva right.

CRISWELL -	NOTE	A.B.P.	GOOD	UNC.
☐250-253	$5	6.00	8.00	100.00

"KEATINGE & BALL, RICHMOND, VA."

| ☐254-257 | $5 | 7.50 | 20.00 | 125.00 |

NO ENGRAVER'S NAME

| ☐258-261 | $5 | 8.00 | 10.00 | 120.00 |

CONFEDERATE MONEY / 229

CONFEDERATE STATES OF AMERICA—1861 ISSUE

"KEATINGE & BALL, RICHMOND, VA."

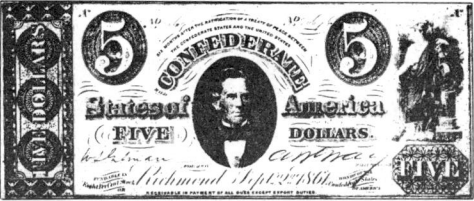

T34

Face Design: C. G. Memminger, Minerva right.

CRISWELL #	NOTE	A.B.P.	GOOD	UNC.
☐262-270	$5	8.00	18.00	100.00

"PRINTED BY HOYER & LUDWIG, RICHMOND, VA."

T35

Face Design: Loading cotton left, "Indian Princess" right.

CRISWELL #	NOTE	A.B.P.	GOOD	UNC.
☐271	$5	450.00	1250.00	V.RARE

230 / CONFEDERATE MONEY

CONFEDERATE STATES OF AMERICA—1861 ISSUE

"HOYER & LUDWIG, RICHMOND, VA."

T36

Face Design: Ceres seated on bale of cotton, sailor left.

CRISWELL #	NOTE	A.B.P.	GOOD	UNC.
☐272	$5	4.00	6.00	32.50

"J. T. PATERSON & CO., COLUMBIA, SC."

☐274	$5	4.00	5.00	30.00

"J. T. PATERSON & CO., COLUMBIA, SC."

☐276-282	$5	4.00	5.50	30.00

CONFEDERATE STATES OF AMERICA—1861 ISSUE

"B. DUNCAN, RICHMOND, VA."

T37

Face Design: Sailor seated beside bales of cotton, C. G. Memminger left, Justice and Ceres right.

CRISWELL #	NOTE	A.B.P.	GOOD	UNC.
☐284	$5	7.00	17.00	50.00

"B. DUNCAN, COLUMBIA, SC."

| ☐285 | $5 | 5.00 | 9.00 | 45.00 |

"B. DUNCAN, COLUMBIA, SC."

T38

Face Design: Personification of South striking down Union, J. P. Benjamin left.

NOTE: Dated "September 2, 1861," through an error. No Confederate note less than $5 was authorized in 1861.

CRISWELL #	NOTE	A.B.P.	GOOD	UNC.
☐286	$2	50.00	150.00	V. RARE

Col. Grover C. Criswell

Known as the *"Richest Man in the World in Confederate Money"*, has been a Collector-Dealer for 35 years.

He has authored numerous books and articles on Confederate Currency, lectured extensively on the subject, had articles published and illustrated in *Parade Magazine, Life Magazine, People Magazine* and many hobby publications. He has appeared on such National T.V. Shows as *"What's My Line"*, *"To Tell The Truth"* and *"The Today Program"*.

A Life Member of the American Numismatic Association, he has served seven terms as a member of the Board of Governors, and President.

He is a member of over 100 Numismatic, Philatelic and Historical Societies, 60 of which are life memberships and served on the Florida Civil War Centennial Commission and as an advisor to the National Civil War Centennial Commission.

Other Books on Currency:

Confederate and Southern States Currency
This 291 page hard-cover book lists and prices ALL varieties of notes issued by the Confederate Central Government, and the Southern States, from 1821 to 1895. **$25.00**

Confederate and Southern States Bonds
This 374 page hard-cover book lists and prices ALL bonds issued by the Confederate and Southern States from 1861 to 1882. **$24.95**

A Banking History of Louisiana
A complete historical background of banking in the South from 1818 to 1930.
$10.00

Available from: Criswell's Publications
Ft. McCoy, FL. 32637

Criswell's Maintains an
"EXPERTIZING SERVICE" FOR PAPER MONEY AND BONDS

The Certificates are recognized throughout the world by Insurance Companies, Banks, Administrators, Dealers and Individuals.

One Certificate per item is furnished on currency, bonds, stocks, fiscal papers, etc. The fee is $1.00 per item or 10% of its value, but will not exceed $10.00 per item.

Criswell's also specialized in appraisals on collections or large lots. Arrangements should be made in advance before shipping very large lots. When writing please state the number and general type of items to be appraised and an estimate of the fee can be given.

DISCRIPTION	DATE PURCHASED	COST	DATE SOLD	PRICE	CONDITION

There is only one...
THE OFFICIAL® PRICE GUIDE

THE <u>MULTIPURPOSE</u> REFERENCE GUIDE!

THE OFFICIAL PRICE GUIDE SERIES has gained the reputation as the <u>standard barometer of values</u> on collectors' items. When you need to check the market price of a collectible, turn first to the OFFICIAL PRICE GUIDES ... for impartial, unbiased, current information that is presented in an easy-to-follow format.

- **CURRENT VALUES FOR BUYING AND SELLING.** ACTUAL SALES that have occurred in all parts of the country are CAREFULLY EVALUATED and COMPUTERIZED to arrive at the most ACCURATE PRICES AVAILABLE.

- **CONCISE REFERENCES.** Each OFFICIAL PRICE GUIDE is designed primarily as a *guide to current market values.* They also include a useful summary of the information most readers are seeking: a history of the item; how it's manufactured; how to begin and maintain a collection; how and where to sell; and addresses of periodicals and clubs.

- **ALPHABETICAL FORMAT.** The novice as well as the seasoned collector will appreciate the alphabetical format which provides easy access to information and prices.

- **FULLY ILLUSTRATED.** All the OFFICIAL PRICE GUIDES are profusely illustrated. Many feature COLOR SECTIONS as well as black-and-white photographs.

Over 21 years of experience has made
THE HOUSE OF COLLECTIBLES
the most respected price guide authority!

TRADE PRICE GUIDE SERIES

American Silver & Silver Plate — Over **16,000 current market values** for all types of American antique and modern silverware and holloware. • A pattern reference guide. • Silversmiths' marks. • Advice on building a collection. • ILLUSTRATED.
3rd Edition, 608 pgs., 5⅜" x 8", Paperback, ISBN: 0-87637-402-X, $9.95.

Anheuser Busch Collectibles — The official guide endorsed by Anheuser Busch • Thousands of values are given for every known product of this prestigious brewery. • Complete listings of steins, glasses, T-shirts, pool cues, trays and more. • ILLUSTRATED.
1st Edition, 576 pgs., 5⅜" x 8", Paperback, ISBN: 0-87637-417-8, $9.95.

Antique Clocks — Acclaimed by clock enthusiasts as the most **comprehensive** guide to antique American clocks in print today! • Over **10,000 current market values**. • List of museums, periodicals, and books. • Advice on display and storage. • ILLUSTRATED.
2nd Edition, 576 pgs., 5⅜" x 8", Paperback, ISBN: 0-87637-420-8, $9.95.

Antique & Modern Dolls — More than 6,500 current retail prices for Antique dolls in wax, carved wood, china, and bisque. • Modern dolls in celluloid, chalk, plastic, composition, and cloth. • Shirley Temples, Barbie, G.I. Joe and more. • ILLUSTRATED.
2nd Edition, 576 pgs., 5⅜" x 8", Paperback, ISBN: 0-87637-445-0, $9.95.

Antique & Modern Firearms — Serious gun enthusiasts have long recognized this work to be the **official definitive source** for pricing collector firearms. • Over **20,500 current market values** for pistols, rifles, and shotguns. • ILLUSTRATED.
4th Edition, 576 pgs., 5⅜" x 8", Paperback, ISBN: 0-87637-421-6, $9.95.

Antiques and Other Collectibles — Over **100,000 current values** and **detailed listings** for more than **300 categories** of antiques and collectibles. • Learn expert tactics for successful collecting • Fully Indexed. • ILLUSTRATED.
5th Edition, 960 pgs., 5⅜" x 8", Paperback, ISBN: 0-87637-444-5, $9.95.

Antique Jewelry — The **most respected** and **extensive guide** to antique and collectible jewelry **ever published**. • Over **8,300 current prices**, organized by category and cross-referenced in a complete index. • A history lesson in jewelry design. • ILLUSTRATED.
3rd Edition, 672 pgs., 5⅜" x 8", Paperback, ISBN: 0-87637-401-1, $9.95.

Bottles Old & New — Long recognized by the experts as the **most comprehensive and reliable value guide** in the antique and collectible bottle field! • Over **22,000 current collector values** for antique, figural and current production collectible bottles. • ILLUSTRATED.
7th Edition, 672 pgs., 5⅜" x 8", Paperback, ISBN: 0-87637-399-6, $9.95.

Collectible Cameras — **Astonishing prices** are being paid for many **antique, classic,** and even secondhand cameras. • More than **5,000 selling prices** for all types of popular collector cameras. • A step-by-step guide through the hobby. • ILLUSTRATED.
1st Edition, 320 pgs., 5⅜" x 8", Paperback, ISBN: 0-87637-383-X, $9.95.

Collectibles of the Third Reich — This extensive guide includes thousands of prices for firearms, badges, insignia, flags, standards, banners, uniforms, bayonets, daggers, swords, and much more. • ILLUSTRATED.
1st Edition, 320 pgs., 5⅜" x 8", Paperback, ISBN: 0-87637-422-4, $9.95.

Collectible Toys — The book no toy collector can afford to be without. Over **25,500 current values** for trains, windups, autos, soldiers, boats, banks, guns, musical toys, Disneyana, comic characters, Star Trek, Star Wars, and more. • ILLUSTRATED.
2nd Edition, 576 pgs., 5⅜" x 8", Paperback, ISBN: 0-87637-454-2, $9.95.

Collector Cars — Over **37,000 current collector prices** for **4,100 models** of U.S. and foreign antique and classic automobiles. • United States production figures — 1897 to date. • A list of reference publications, museums and clubs. • ILLUSTRATED.
5th Edition, 576 pgs., 5⅜" x 8", Paperback, ISBN: 0-87637-408-9, $9.95.

Collector Handguns — More than **5,000 current retail prices** for handguns of all styles and all calibers. • Every gun identified by manufacturer, model name, action, caliber, date, serial number and more. • Extensive ammo section. • ILLUSTRATED.
1st Edition, 544 pgs., 5⅜" x 8", Paperback, ISBN: 0-87637-367-8, $9.95.

For your convenience use the handy order form.

TRADE PRICE GUIDE SERIES

Collector Knives — *Over 14,000 current collector values.* • *1,250 worldwide knife manufacturers.* • *Special section for Case, Ka-Bar, and limited edition knives.* • *Valuable collector information.* • *Knife organizations and trade publications listed.* • *ILLUSTRATED.*
6th Edition, 736 pgs., 5⅜" x 8", Paperback, ISBN: 0-87637-389-9, $9.95.

Collector Plates — *The plate collector's bible!* Contains the **most complete listing** of all U.S. and foreign plate manufacturers and distributors **in print!** • *Over 18,000 current collector values.* • *Includes plates from 1895 to date.* • *ILLUSTRATED.*
2nd Edition, 672 pgs., 5⅜" x 8", Paperback, ISBN: 0-87637-393-7, $9.95.

Collector Prints — *Over 14,750 listings of collector prints for more than 400 of the world's leading artists.* • *A list of galleries, agents and publishers.* • *A glossary of printmaking and print collecting terminology.* • *ILLUSTRATED.*
5th Edition, 576 pgs., 5⅜" x 8", Paperback, ISBN: 0-87637-395-3, $9.95.

Comic Books and Collectibles — *Over 50,000 current values.* • *Exclusive sections on Big Little Books, Comic Character Memorabilia, Original Art, and Newspaper Comic Art.* • *Advice on buying, selling and investing.* • *ILLUSTRATED.*
7th Edition, 736 pgs., 5⅜" x 8", Paperback, ISBN: 0-87637-411-9, $9.95.

Depression Glass — *The largest price guide devoted exclusively to depression glass in print today! Thousands of items listed, every known pattern and manufacturer included.* • *Valuable collector tips on fakes, reproductions and more.* • *ILLUSTRATED.*
1st Edition, 416 pgs., 5⅜" x 8", Paperback, ISBN: 0-87637-433-X, $9.95.

Glassware — *Over 60,000 current market values for all types of collectible glass including Art, Carnival, Cut, Depression, and Pattern.* • *Includes museums, clubs, and manufacturers' marks.* • *Informative background histories.* • *ILLUSTRATED.*
1st Edition, 672 pgs., 5⅜" x 8", Paperback, ISBN: 0-87637-125-X, $9.95.

Hummel Figurines & Plates — *Over 18,000 current market values for every known Hummel.* • *Complete guide to trademarks and variations.* • *Information on clubs, exhibits, and publications.* • *Detailed history of Berta Hummel.* • *ILLUSTRATED.*
4th Edition, 448 pgs., 5⅜" x 8", Paperback, ISBN: 0-87637-390-2, $9.95.

Kitchen Collectibles — *The only value guide devoted* **exclusively** *to collectible kitchenware.* • *More than 28,000 current selling prices.* • *China, glassware, silver, copper, iron, and wood.* • *Comprehensive descriptions of every item.* • *ILLUSTRATED.*
1st Edition, 544 pgs., 5⅜" x 8", Paperback, ISBN: 0-87637-371-6, $9.95.

Military Collectibles — *The definitive guide to war memorabilia.* • *Over 12,000 totally revised prices for military objects from all over the world, 15th century to date: armor, weapons, uniforms, bayonets, rare, and unusual objects.* • *ILLUSTRATED.*
3rd Edition, 608 pgs., 5⅜" x 8", Paperback, ISBN: 0-87637-398-8, $9.95.

Music Collectibles — *Over 11,500 current market values.* • *Detailed descriptions, historical backgrounds, and values for all types of American and foreign made music machines from the 15th century to date.* • *Expert advice on condition and restoration.* • *ILLUSTRATED.*
4th Edition, 576 pgs., 5⅜" x 8", Paperback, ISBN: 0-87637-467-4, $10.95.

Old Books & Autographs — *Over 11,000 current market values for children's books, the old West, novels, detective fiction, book sets, Bibles, and collectible autographs.* • *Glossary of collector terminology.* • *Care and repair of old books.* • *ILLUSTRATED.*
5th Edition, 576 pgs., 5⅜" x 8", Paperback, ISBN: 0-87637-410-0, $9.95.

Oriental Collectibles — *Unravel the mystique of the Orient.* • *Over 10,000 current market values.* • *Listings for Chinese, Japanese, and Asian collectors' items including pottery, weapons, jade carvings, ivories, netsuke, rugs and more.* • *ILLUSTRATED.*
1st Edition, 512 pgs., 5⅜" x 8", Paperback, ISBN: 0-87637-375-9, $9.95.

Paper Collectibles — *Over 27,000 prices for paper items of every description dating from medieval times to the present including books, posters, checks, documents, photographs, newspapers, celebrity autographs, and much more!* • *ILLUSTRATED.*
3rd Edition, 576 pgs., 5⅜" x 8", Paperback, ISBN: 0-87637-394-5, $9.95.

For your convenience use the handy order form.

TRADE PRICE GUIDE SERIES

Pottery & Porcelain — This comprehensive guide has over **12,500 current market values** *for American pottery and porcelain from the 18th to the 20th century!* • Trademark reference guide. • Includes Rookwood, Roseville, Weller, Hull and more. • ILLUSTRATED.
4th Edition, 576 pgs., 5⅜" x 8", Paperback, ISBN: 0-87637-475-5, $10.95.

Radio, TV, and Movie Memorabilia — Includes thousands of actual selling prices on autographs, books, buttons, rings, costumes, fanzines, figurines, games, magazines, posters, press kits, stills, radio premiums and more. • ILLUSTRATED.
1st Edition, 576 pgs., 5⅜" x 8", Paperback, ISBN: 0-87637-416-X, $9.95.

Records — Discover if your "golden oldies" are worth a small fortune. • More than **32,000 current collector prices** *for all categories of old, rare, and modern records from 1953 to date!* • Exclusive photos and biographies of nearly 200 recording stars. • ILLUSTRATED.
5th Edition, 576 pgs., 5⅜" x 8", Paperback, ISBN: 0-87637-409-7, $9.95.

Royal Doulton — Acclaimed by critics as the **definitive value guide** to the delightful world of **Royal Doulton figurines.** • Over **5,500 current collector market values.** • Features market trends. • Includes the latest editions. • ILLUSTRATED.
3rd Edition, 576 pgs., 5⅜" x 8", Paperback, ISBN: 0-87637-407-0, $9.95.

Science Fiction and Fantasy Collectibles — Thousands of values given for "sci-fi" autographs, original art, posters, paperbacks, novels, Big Little Books, games, fanzines, lobby cards, comics, toys, and much more. • ILLUSTRATED.
1st Edition, 576 pgs., 5⅜" x 8", Paperback, ISBN: 0-87637-418-6, $9.95.

Wicker — All types of American made wicker furniture and accessories from the Victorian, Turn of the Century, and Art Deco eras. • Over 600 photos • Detailed descriptions. • Current collector values. • Professional repair methods. • ILLUSTRATED.
2nd Edition, 416 pgs., 5⅜" x 8", Paperback, ISBN: 0-87637-380-5, $9.95.

MINI PRICE GUIDE SERIES

Antiques & Flea Markets — Take along this **compact guide** to more than **15,000 collectors' items!** • Spot the bargains... avoid the fakes... make the best deals. • **Current market values** *for thousands of collectors' items in all categories.* • ILLUSTRATED.
2nd Edition, 320 pgs., 4" x 5½", Paperback, ISBN: 0-87637-392-5, $3.95.

Antique Jewelry — An indispensable guide to valuable yet affordable jewelry. • Over 2,500 current values *for jewelry from 1750 to 1930.* • Complete descriptions of styles, patterns, and identifying features. • **Grading information** *for diamonds, gold, and silver.* • ILLUSTRATED.
2nd Edition, 288 pgs., 4" x 5½", Paperback, ISBN: 0-87637-442-9, $3.95.

Baseball Cards — For thousands of fans, baseball card collecting is **a year round hobby.** This newly revised edition is the collector's standard reference. • Over **110,000 current market values.** • ILLUSTRATED.
4th Edition, 384 pgs., 4" x 5½", Paperback, ISBN: 0-87637-438-0, $3.95.

Beer Cans — Over 6,000 actual selling prices *for old, modern, rare, and common beer cans.* • **All brands** and all types of cans. Includes all label design variations. • **History of brewing.** • Tips on how to buy, sell, and trade • ILLUSTRATED.
2nd Edition, 288 pgs., 4" x 5½", Paperback, ISBN: 0-87637-440-2, $3.95.

Bottles — The **most convenient** guide to collectible **bottles** in print! Thousands of values given for all types of old and new bottles. • Includes buying, selling and condition tips, background histories, clubs, shapes, trademarks, and investment advice. • ILLUSTRATED.
1st Edition, 288 pgs., 4" x 5½", Paperback, ISBN: 0-87637-431-3, $3.95.

Cars and Trucks — Over 10,000 current auction and dealer prices *for all popular U.S. and foreign made antique, classic, and collector cars.* • Listings include: *the model name, engine specs and body style.* • Discover the profesional way to evaluate condition. • ILLUSTRATED.
1st Edition, 240 pgs., 4" x 5½", Paperback, ISBN: 0-87637-391-0, $2.95.

For your convenience use the handy order form.

MINI PRICE GUIDE SERIES

Collectible Records — One of the most enjoyable and profitable hobbies today. • Over 11,500 current market prices for Rock and Country recordings. A listing of discs from 1953 to date. • Listed by their original label and issue number. • ILLUSTRATED.
2nd Edition, 288 pgs., 4" x 5½", Paperback, ISBN: 0-87637-463-1, $3.95.

Collector Guns — This handy pocket guide contains over 9,000 dealer prices for handguns, rifles, and shotguns. Covers American and foreign manufacturers. • ILLUSTRATED.
1st Edition, 240 pgs., 4" x 5½", Paperback, ISBN: 0-87637-396-1, $2.95.

Comic Books — One of the fastest growing hobbies. • Current market values for over 5,000 old and new comics. • Learn how to start a comic collection and watch it grow into a profitable investment. • Tips on buying and selling. • ILLUSTRATED.
2nd Edition, 288 pgs., 4" x 5½", Paperback, ISBN: 0-87637-382-1, $3.95.

Dolls — Over 3,000 current market prices for dolls of all types and all manufacturers. • Positive identification by maker, name of doll, markings, hair color, eye color, date of manufacture, and size. • Extensive glossary of dollmaking terms. • ILLUSTRATED.
2nd Edition, 288 pgs., 4" x 5½", Paperback, ISBN: 0-87637-434-8, $3.95.

Football Cards — This revised edition features all the latest cards and price changes. • Over 51,000 current market values for collectible football cards. • Exclusive checklist system. • Valuable collector information on buying and selling. • ILLUSTRATED.
4th Edition, 288 pgs., 4" x 5½", Paperback, ISBN: 0-87637-462-3, $3.95.

Glassware — Contains thousands of values for the five major types of collectible glass — art, carnival, cut, depression, and pattern. • Includes history of each period, manufacturer's marks, pattern and motif identification guide, glossary and more. • ILLUSTRATED.
1st Edition, 288 pgs., 4" x 5½", Paperback, ISBN: 0-87637-432-1, $3.95.

Hummels — Handy pocket guide with over 2,000 current collector prices for the most common and most popular Hummels. All the latest releases are included. • A Hummel encyclopedia overviewing Berta Hummel's life and the growth of the Goebel firm. • ILLUSTRATED.
2nd Edition, 256 pgs., 4" x 5½", Paperback, ISBN: 0-87637-435-6, $3.95.

Military Collectibles — The indispensable guide to the fascinating world of war souvenirs. • Over 4,500 current prices for military objects from all over the world — 19th century to World War II. • Thorough descriptions given for all items. • ILLUSTRATED.
2nd Edition, 288 pgs., 4" x 5½", Paperback, ISBN: 0-87637-441-0, $3.95.

Paperbacks & Magazines — Over 10,000 values are given on paperbacks and magazines dating from the 1800s through the 1980s compiled from actual sales between dealers and collectors. • ILLUSTRATED.
2nd Edition, 288 pgs., 4" x 5½", Paperback, ISBN: 0-87637-405-4, $3.95.

Pocket Knives — A complete price listing of all Case and Kabar pocket knives plus thousands of current values for all popular collector knives. • Complete identification of every knife. • Includes terminology, blade patterns, organizations and more. • ILLUSTRATED.
2nd Edition, 288 pgs., 4" x 5½", Paperback, ISBN: 0-87637-443-7, $3.95.

Scouting Collectibles — Attention, Scouts! Here's your "field guide" to the profitable hobby of scouting memorabilia. • Price listings for thousands of scouting items in all categories. • Includes tools, badges, medals, books and more. • ILLUSTRATED.
2nd Edition, 288 pgs., 4" x 5½", Paperback, ISBN: 0-87637-397-X, $3.95.

Sports Collectibles — All the popular collectibles of baseball, football, basketball, hockey, boxing, hunting, fishing and horse racing. • Over 12,000 current prices that collectors are actually paying for sports memorabilia. • ILLUSTRATED.
2nd Edition, 288 pgs., 4" x 5½", Paperback, ISBN: 0-87637-439-9, $3.95.

Star Trek/Star Wars Collectibles — The popularity of these space age collectibles continues to skyrocket! • Over 6,000 current values for every category of Star Trek and Star Wars collector's items. • Complete calendar of conventions.
2nd Edition, 256 pgs., 4" x 5½", Paperback, ISBN: 0-87637-437-2, $3.95.

Toys — Whether eight to eighty, you are never too old to seriously enjoy toy collections. • Over 8,000 current values for every category of toys from animal-drawn vehicles to spaceships. • Valuable collector information on buying, selling and condition. • ILLUSTRATED.
2nd Edition, 288 pgs., 4" x 5½", Paperback, ISBN: 0-87637-436-4, $3.95.

For your convenience use the handy order form.

OFFICIAL IDENTIFICATION GUIDE SERIES

Collector's Journal — *This is the most **valuable** book any collector could own! Use it to record dealers, collectors, clubs, museums, and reference materials.* • Special inventory forms. • Value development chart. • Vital information on appraisal, insurance and taxes.
1st Edition, 256 pgs., 5¼" x 7¾", Paperback, ISBN: 0-87637-445-3, $4.95.

Encyclopedia of Antiques — *A total of more than **10,000 definitions, explanations, concise factual summeries** of names, dates, histories, confusing **terminology** for every popular field of collecting.* • An exclusive appendix includes many trademark and pattern marks as well as a categorized list of museums and reference publications.
1st Edition, 704 pgs., 5¾" x 8" Paperback, ISBN: 0-87637-365-1, $9.95.

Buying and Selling Guide to Antiques — *Covers every phase of collecting from beginning a collection to its ultimate sale. • Examines in detail the collecting potential of over **200 different categories of items in all price ranges**.* • Special features include a dealer directory, a condition grading report, list of museums and reference publications, plus a discussion of buying and selling techniques. • *ILLUSTRATED*.
1st Edition, 608 pgs., 5¾" x 8", Paperback, ISBN: 0-87637-369-4, $9.95.

Identification Guide to Early American Furniture — **A comprehensive guide to identifying antique American furniture** dating from 1603 to the 1840s. • Features the famous cabinetmakers Adam, Hepplewhite, Sheraton and more. • *ILLUSTRATED*.
1st Edition, 352 pgs., 4" x 8", Paperback, ISBN: 0-87637-414-3, $9.95.

Identification Guide to Glassware — *Over 100 types of glass are completely described.* • Hundreds of illustrated marks and line drawings. • Carnival, Custard, Cut, Depression, Pressed, Milk, Burmese, Amberina, Blown and dozens more. • *ILLUSTRATED*.
1st Edition, 352 pgs., 4" x 8", Paperback, ISBN: 0-87637-413-5, $9.95.

Identification Guide to Gunmarks — *Over 1,500 of the most commonly encountered trademarks on modern and antique guns.* • Learn which marks are valuable and how to spot fakes and forgeries. • *ILLUSTRATED*.
1st Edition, 256 pgs., 5¾" x 8", Paperback, ISBN: 0-87637-346-5, $6.95.

Identification Guide to Pottery and Porcelain — **Absolutely the most comprehensive guide to identifying pottery and porcelain in print today!** • Complete descriptions of characteristics and all known marks. • *ILLUSTRATED*.
1st Edition, 416 pgs., 4" x 8", Paperback, ISBN: 0-87637-412-7, $9.95.

Identification Guide to Victorian Furniture — *There is a **tremendous surge of interest** in the ornate furniture of the **Victorian Period**. • Complete descriptions of every piece.* • Extensive furniture glossary. • *ILLUSTRATED*.
1st Edition, 352 pgs., 4" x 8", Paperback, ISBN: 0-87637-415-1, $9.95.

NUMISMATIC SERIES

1985 Blackbook Price Guide of United States Coins — *A coin collector's guide to current market values for all U.S. coins from 1616 to date — over **16,500 prices**. THE OFFICIAL BLACKBOOK OF COINS has gained the reputation as the most reliable, up-to-date guide to U.S. Coin values.* This new edition features an exclusive gold and silver identification guide. Learn how to test, weigh and calculate the value of any item made of gold or silver. Proven professional techniques revealed for the first time. Detecting altered coins section. Take advantage of the current "BUYERS' MARKET" in gold and silver. *ILLUSTRATED*.
$3.95-23rd Edition, 336 pgs., 4" x 5½", Paperback, Order #: 456-9

1985 Blackbook Price Guide of United States Paper Money — *Over **9,000 buying and selling prices** covering U.S. currency from 1861 to date. Every note issued by the U.S. government is listed and priced including many Confederate States notes.* Error Notes are described and priced, and there are detailed articles on many phases of the hobby for beginner and advanced collector alike. Comprehensive grading section. *ILLUSTRATED*.
$3.95-17th Edition, 240 pgs., 4" x 5½", Paperback, Order #: 457-7

1985 Blackbook Price Guide of United States Postage Stamps — *Featuring all U.S. stamps from 1847 to date pictured in full color. Over **19,000 current selling prices**. General issues, airmails and special delivery.* United Nations, first day covers, and more. New listings for the most current commemorative and regular issue stamps, a feature not offered in any other price guide, at any price! Numerous developments in the fast moving stamp market during the past year are included in this ***NEW REVISED EDITION***. *ILLUSTRATED*.
$3.95-7th Edition, 240 pgs., 4" x 5½", Paperback, Order #: 458-5

— *For your convenience use the handy order form.* —

FOR IMMEDIATE DELIVERY
VISA & MASTER CARD CUSTOMERS
ORDER TOLL FREE!
1-800-327-1384

This number is for orders only, it is not tied into the customer service or business office. Customers not using charge cards must use mail for ordering since payment is required with the order — sorry no C.O.D.'s. Florida residents call (305) 857-9095 — ask for order department.

OR SEND ORDERS TO

THE HOUSE OF COLLECTIBLES, *ORLANDO CENTRAL PARK*
1904 PREMIER ROW, ORLANDO, FL 32809 (305) 857-9095

☐ Please send me the following price guides—
☐ I would like the most current edition of the books listed below.

☐ 402-X @ 9.95	☐ 393-7 @ 9.95	☐ 409-7 @ 9.95	☐ 462-3 @ 3.95	☐ 413-5 @ 9.95
☐ 417-8 @ 9.95	☐ 395-3 @ 9.95	☐ 407-0 @ 9.95	☐ 432-1 @ 3.95	☐ 448-8 @ 9.95
☐ 420-8 @ 9.95	☐ 411-9 @ 9.95	☐ 418-6 @ 9.95	☐ 435-6 @ 3.95	☐ 412-7 @ 9.95
☐ 445-0 @ 9.95	☐ 433-X @ 9.95	☐ 380-5 @ 9.95	☐ 441-0 @ 3.95	☐ 415-1 @ 9.95
☐ 421-6 @ 9.95	☐ 125-X @ 9.95	☐ 392-9 @ 3.95	☐ 405-4 @ 3.95	☐ 456-9 @ 3.95
☐ 444-5 @ 9.95	☐ 390-2 @ 9.95	☐ 442-9 @ 3.95	☐ 443-7 @ 3.95	☐ 457-7 @ 3.95
☐ 401-1 @ 9.95	☐ 371-6 @ 9.95	☐ 438-0 @ 3.95	☐ 397-X @ 3.95	☐ 458-5 @ 3.95
☐ 399-6 @ 9.95	☐ 398-8 @ 9.95	☐ 440-2 @ 3.95	☐ 439-9 @ 3.95	
☐ 383-X @ 9.95	☐ 467-4 @ 10.95	☐ 431-3 @ 3.95	☐ 437-2 @ 3.95	
☐ 422-4 @ 9.95	☐ 410-0 @ 9.95	☐ 391-0 @ 2.95	☐ 436-4 @ 3.95	
☐ 454-2 @ 9.95	☐ 375-9 @ 9.95	☐ 454-2 @ 3.95	☐ 445-3 @ 4.95	
☐ 408-9 @ 9.95	☐ 394-5 @ 9.95	☐ 396-1 @ 2.95	☐ 365-1 @ 9.95	
☐ 367-8 @ 9.95	☐ 475-5 @ 10.95	☐ 382-1 @ 9.95	☐ 369-4 @ 9.95	
☐ 389-9 @ 9.95	☐ 416-X @ 9.95	☐ 434-8 @ 3.95	☐ 414-3 @ 9.95	

POSTAGE & HANDLING RATE CHART

TOTAL ORDER/POSTAGE	TOTAL ORDER/POSTAGE	
0 to $10.00 - **$1.25**	$20.01 to $30.00 - **$2.00**	$50.01 & Over -
$10.01 to $20.00 - **$1.60**	$30.01 to $40.00 - **$2.75**	**Add 10% of your total order**
	$40.01 to $50.00 - **$3.50**	(Ex. $75.00 x .10 = $7.50)

☐ Check or money order enclosed $_____ (include postage and handling)

☐ Please charge $_____ to my: ☐ MASTERCARD ☐ VISA

Charge Card Customers Not Using Our Toll Free Number Please Fill Out The Information Below.

Account No. (All Digits)_____ Expiration Date_____

Signature_____

NAME (please print)_____ PHONE_____

ADDRESS_____ APT. #_____

CITY_____ STATE_____ ZIP_____